The Boeing 247

THE BOEING 247
The First Modern Airliner

F. Robert van der Linden

Illustrations by Victor J. Seely

Published for the

National Air and Space Museum

by the

University of Washington Press

Seattle and London

Library of Congress Cataloging–in–Publication Data

Van der Linden, F. Robert.
  The Boeing 247, the first modern airliner / F. Robert van der Linden ; illustrations by Victor J. Seely.
    p.   cm.
    Includes bibliographical references (p.   ) and index.
    ISBN 0–295–97094–4
    1. Boeing 247 (Transport plane)—History.   I. Title.
TL686.B65V36   1991
629.133'340423—dc20   90-2476

The paper used in this publication meets the minimum requirements of the American National Standard for Information Sciences—Permanence of Paper for Printed Library Materials, ANSI Z39.48–1984.   ∞

For Sue

Contents

CONTENTS

Acknowledgements

As the production and operation of the 247 was the result of the combined efforts of numerous invaluable people, so was the creation of this book. By far the greatest debt is owed to Victor Seely of the Museum of Flight in Seattle, Washington. His thorough knowledge of the 247 and his willingness to share his research, as well as his thorough review of the manuscript are greatly appreciated. He has shown unequalled generosity in allowing the reprinting of the drawings and the service histories he originally produced for his article in the *American Aviation Historical Society Journal*. I am also indebted to Robert E. Williams, the managing editor of the American Aviation Historical Society, who granted me official permission to use this material from the journal. The noted aviation historian and expert on Boeing aircraft, Peter Bowers, provided valuable assistance by correcting and improving the original manuscript, as did Jay P. Spenser, a well-respected writer who was formerly with the Museum of Flight and the National Air and Space Museum.

The majority of the primary sources on which this book is based were found in the collection of the Boeing Company Historical Services. Through the considerate guidance of Marilyn Phipps at Boeing, I unearthed countless unpublished documents and have been able to tell the complete story of the intricacies of the birth and development of the 247. Harvey Lippincott of United Technologies Archival and Historical Resource Center was most helpful in providing information on the engines and propellers of the 247 as well as details on the company's 247-A and the minutes of the corporation's Technical Advisory Committee Meetings.

In the quest for primary material I followed the footsteps of Dr. Richard Smith, who gave me invaluable advice on the aircraft and industry during the course of many enlightening conversations we had during his year as Verville Fellow at the National Air and Space Museum. It was he who first uncovered the original concept and design of the 247 as a high-speed mailplane replacement for the Boeing 40, not for the Boeing 80 transport, as is commonly believed.

Without the patience of Dr. Howard S. Wolko, NASM's Special Advisor for Technology in the Aeronautics Department, I would not have been able to fathom the intricacies of the technological aspects of aircraft design. His uncanny ability to convey clearly the most complex technological detail to this writer made chapters 2 and 3 possible. I am forever indebted to his kindness and constant willingness to listen and answer my incessant questions on structures and aerodynamics.

As my friend and former supervisor, R. E. G. Davies has lent his unwavering support and advice to me over the past four years. His generosity in turning this project over to me is deeply appreciated, as is his patience in allowing this book precedence over my other museum responsibilities. The wisdom of his indispensable works on the history of air transport were crucial to my understanding of commercial aviation and remain clearly the best works available of this important topic.

Through the kindness of Charles Baptie I was able to meet and interview several former Pennsylvania Central pilots and flight attendants whose insights into the 247 provided me with an appreciation of the aircraft and of the people who flew it. I am especially indebted to William C. "Tex" Guthrie, who invited me to his home to share his experiences and scrapbooks he collected while flying for PCA and United, as well as to Edward and Marion O'Donnell, and Ralph and Mary Jane Read, who gave freely of their time to assist me in my undertaking.

I am also grateful for the generosity of the retired pilots associations of United Airlines and Western Airlines for responding wholeheartedly to my request for correspondence and to those individuals who freely shared their knowledge with me. In particular, I wish to thank E. L. Anderson, Helen Huntley Brumley, Theodore J. Cochran, Henry Dreyer, Carlos Dufriche, Ralph J. Gibbons, Ernest Heiss, John McCullough Hodgson, J. D. Hutchinson, Alfred C. Kubitz, Alvar H. Lunn, Angie Riddell MacKenzie, C. L. "Jim" Newman, O. H. Schaller, Zay Smith, and Dick Wood.

To my colleagues at the National Air and Space Museum, past and present, I wish to express my appreciation for their assistance. Former Aeronautics Chairman E. T. Wooldridge, Jr. gave me the opportunity to write this, my first book. Dr. Von D. Hardesty provided me with the requisite financial and organizational support as well as encouragement for this undertaking. Furthermore, I wish to thank Mark Avino, Donna Corbett, Sybil Descheemaeker, Debbie Douglas, Anita Mason, Robert C. Mikesh, Dom Pisano, Glen Sweeting, and Larry Wilson. I am also indebted to Louis R. Eltscher of the Rochester Institute of Technology and former Verville Fellow for our many conversations concerning the aircraft industry and to Dr. Wesley P. Newton of Auburn University whose comments on the manuscript were especially valuable.

Most importantly, I wish to thank Sue, who patiently tolerated my obsession and many trials with this book, first as girlfriend, later as fiancee, and now as wife.

Introduction

The epitome of air travel in the late 1920s and early 1930s, was a large, ungainly-looking aircraft, covered by corrugated aluminum and equipped with two engines slung ungracefully on struts under the wings, and one implanted awkwardly in the nose directly in front of the cockpit. The engine arrangement was inefficient but was based on the best aeronautical knowledge available at the time. The number was dictated by the prevailing opinion that only a minimum of three powerplants provided a sufficient margin of safety in case of engine failure. The reasoning was well-intentioned and sound. The Ford Tri-Motor, like other similar designs, was a most reliable and sturdy aircraft.

Despite its strengths, the Ford was also slow, noisy, and uncomfortable. Long-distance air travel in the early 1930s was not an experience for the faint of heart. Before takeoff, a small package, wrapped in waxed paper, was distributed to every one of the ten passengers on board the Tri-Motor. Inside the carefully sealed wrapping was found a small piece of chewing gum and a wad of sterilized cotton. The contents were not peculiar souvenirs: they were items essential to the traveler if he or she were to withstand over 24 hours of the numbing noise and vibration of transcontinental air travel.

Flying at only 100 miles per hour, passengers sat on thinly padded seats of wicker or metal and needed the chewing gum to help sooth stomachs distressed by the continual bouncing of an all-day flight. With one engine in the nose, the vibration and sound echoing throughout the thinly insulated cabin was often unbearable without the cotton wadding for the ears deadening the deafening roar.

For years the Ford and other similar designs were the best and most up-to-date transports available. Suddenly, in the spring of 1933, all of this changed with the arrival of a new aircraft—the Boeing 247—and with it, a new generation of airliners which contributed directly to the tremendous expansion of air transportation across the globe.

The design and construction of the Boeing 247, embodying concepts which are in use today, established it as the first truly modern airliner and provided a revolutionary break with the past. The Boeing incorporated the latest discoveries in aerodynamics and employed a comprehensive array of new technology in aeronautics which gave the 247 a performance far superior to its competition. Compared to the Ford, the new Boeing was an astonishing 50 percent faster, even though it had one less engine, was much quieter and more comfortable, and, perhaps most important, looked right for its time. The Boeing defined the meaning of streamlining with contours smoothly blended into an efficient form. In an age when aeronautical technology captured the public imagination, the 247 symbolized the beginning of a new era, not just in aviation.

Although the arrival of the Boeing 247 heralded a new period in transportation that would eventually make flying a fast, safe, and efficient means of mass travel, in 1933, the average person was far more concerned with finding a way to survive one more day than with the future of aviation. Granted, the airplane was a glittering symbol of the wonders of science and the age of technology and served in no small way as a beacon for a more hopeful future. But in 1933, that prosperous and happy future, regardless of Roosevelt's positive rhetoric, was not just around the corner.

For millions of Americans fighting for survival, aviation fired the imagination but was little practical use. Few really cared that this latest technological masterpiece could carry its passengers in heated comfort much faster than ever before. Few really cared that transcontinental travel time was now cut to a remarkable 19 3/4 hours—little more than the record time flown by famed race pilot Frank Hawks just four years earlier. In fact, few flew.

Commercial aviation was for the affluent minority. The price of air fare was too high. Instead, the average person either drove, took the bus, or rode the train, if there was enough money to travel. For all of the publicity touting the advantages of flight, when Americans of virtually every economic strata traveled, they did not go to the airport. In 1934, after the 247 had been flying for over a year and the even better Douglas DC-2 was entering service, 462,000 flew over the commercial air routes.

Despite the Depression, air travel grew significantly from its beginnings in the mid-1920s. All other forms of transportation suffered losses in ridership and profits. Regardless of the apparent trend towards aviation, while fewer than half a million people flew, 372 million rode the bus between cities and 187.1 million traveled by train. What is more revealing when these three figures are added is the fact that this represents only 15 percent of the traveling public. With the impressive growth of highway construction in the United States in the 1920s and 1930s, the remaining 85 percent of Americans chose to drive between cities.

The account that follows does not attempt to provide only a technical "nuts and bolts" history of this important transport. Though included, these facts are incidental to the important story and are emphasized only when relevant to the greater whole. Instead, the reasons behind the creation of the 247 and the actions of those individuals whose contributions led to its construction are examined in detail.

This is a story about people. The 247, as with all machines, was an instrument designed and built by people to aid others as well as themselves. It was the product of the inventive genius of scores of individuals and was built to satisfy the needs of the traveling public and of the industry created to serve that need.

This is also a story about business and government. The rapid growth of the U.S. aviation industry was sponsored to a great extent by an enlightened government policy of establishing a new and rational transportation system. This development fostered the creation of an entire industry dedicated to fulfilling new requirements and taking advantage of the lucrative economic opportunities that this policy offered.

For all of its advanced performance and capabilities, the Boeing 247, as with all of aviation, was only one small, though important, part of the overall story of the development of air transportation and the aviation industry. This book attempts to explain the significance of the Boeing 247 seen against this greater picture.

1

Boeing and the Birth
of the U.S. Aviation Industry

Seattle was buzzing with excitement. The Boeing Airplane Company had promised the city the first public showing of the airliner which was capturing the imagination of the aviation community. When the gates opened at noon on Sunday, 2 April 1933, the first Boeing 247 was revealed to an enthusiastic crowd of more than 15,000 onlookers. Amidst the free, gala six-hour air show, complete with stunt flying and a bombing display, some 5500 citizens elbowed their way into the United Air Lines hangar on the eastern edge of Boeing Field, eager to get a closer look at this silver-gray transport they had heard so much about. They were not disappointed.[1]

Before them rested a graceful all-metal, twin-engined, low-winged monoplane—a stark contrast to the slow, bulky, fabric-covered or corrugated metal airliners to which the public had grown accustomed. With internally braced cantilevered wings and tail surfaces, there were no ugly, drag-producing wires or struts to disturb the flowing lines of the new transport. A compact, supercharged Pratt & Whitney Wasp engine was integrated into each wing, the protruding lines of the cylinder heads smoothed by a close-fitting ring. Below, the novel landing gear could retract into the lower wing, to permit greater speed by decreasing drag.

Speed was the hallmark of this craft. It could cruise at 150 miles per hour, the crowd was told, fifty percent faster than the competition, and possessed the remarkable top speed of 182 miles per hour. The airliner could carry ten passengers up to 485 miles before refueling, drastically cutting transcontinental travel time. More important, it could do so with unprecedented comfort and safety. Flown by a pilot and copilot in an enclosed cockpit which was blended into the nose of the airplane, the 247 also carried a flight attendant to care for the passengers while providing a luxurious, thermostatically-controlled, air-conditioned and soundproofed cabin, with individual reading lights and vents. A lavatory catered to the

1

Interested Seattle citizens examined the sleek new Boeing 247 during its public debut on 2 April 1933. (*Boeing 6259B*)

traveler's needs. The latest navigation and communications equipment, particularly the autopilot and Boeing-developed two-way radio, enabled the machine to fly safely at night and through inclement weather.

All these features, though commonplace by the latter 1930s, were innovative, almost revolutionary, in 1933. Furthermore, the 247 coincided with a new political, economic, and social revolution that was sweeping the nation in the wake of the inauguration of President Franklin Delano Roosevelt and the coming of the New Deal. American air transportation would never again be the same.

The design of the 247 established a significant aeronautical precedent, yet its moment in the limelight would be brief. Almost as quickly as the Boeing 247 appeared, it was superseded by the very designs it inspired and was soon relegated to secondary roles. Its limited success was also caused in no small part by the consequences of corporate monopoly, which arbitrarily restricted sales in a potential growth market.

As the first airliner to embody the technological attributes associated with modern aircraft—cantilever wing design, all-metal construction and streamlined aerodynamics—the 247 was the product of a synthesis of ideas originating from many sources. This revolutionary aircraft resulted from the complex interplay of engineering advances, economic trends, and political forces which occurred during the latter half of the 1920s and into the early 1930s. Despite its technical brilliance, however, the 247 was the offspring of compromise which would eventually prove to be the aircraft's undoing.

During the 1920s and 1930s, the aviation industry grew with unprecedented vigor. From virtually nothing, the manufacturers blossomed as the government sponsored the development of an intricate network of air routes. With the financial backing of Wall Street and other sources of large capital, the air transportation industry grew with unprecedented speed in the years immediately following Lindbergh's dramatic conquest of the Atlantic. Continuous technical innovation sparked the creation of increasingly capable aircraft to satisfy the difficult needs of transcontinental commercial service.

The Boeing 247 was foremost a machine built by a corporation and designed to be an economic as well as a technical success. The difficult decisions which led to its production were always made with the interests of the company in mind. The technical advantages of a new design were of no use to the corporation unless sufficient profits could be made from the sales of the aircraft, which in turn depended on its ability to generate revenues for airlines.

To understand the reasons behind the creation of the 247, it is necessary to examine the many forces which led to its birth. As an airliner, it was built expressly to carry passengers, mail, and cargo for an air transport company over designated routes across the United States with the greatest dispatch and reliability.

The Boeing Airplane Company had built impressive aircraft since its founding in 1916. The son of a wealthy, German-born, lumber magnate, the tall, bespectacled William E. Boeing followed his father into the family business after attending Yale. He established his own company in Seattle, Washington, to exploit the magnificent forests of the Pacific Northwest. Boeing was introduced to aviation in 1914 when he flew as a passenger in an early Curtiss flying boat off nearby Lake Washington. In 1916, he pooled his resources with U.S. Navy Commander G. Conrad Westervedt to produce the B & W floatplane, patterned after the Martin TA aircraft that Boeing had purchased earlier. The B & W aircraft performed well enough for Boeing to incorporate this new business as the Pacific Aero Products Company. In the age of wooden airframe construction, the establishment of an aircraft company in the lumber-rich Northwest was a logi-

3

William E. Boeing (1881–1956). *Courtesy Smithsonian Institution.* (*SI 87–11937*)

cal step. In short order, as the country entered the World War, the U.S. Navy awarded the new firm a contract to manufacture trainers and Curtiss HS-2L flying boats under license. The firm was renamed the Boeing Airplane Company in 1917 and soon moved from its first site on Lake Union to a larger facility on the Duwamish River, south of the city center.[2]

Military and naval contracts dried up briefly for the Boeing Airplane Company after the armistice, temporarily forcing the company, with its force of skilled woodworkers, into the manufacture of furniture and boats. In search of new uses for aircraft and alternative sources of money, Bill Boeing first entered the field of air transport with an improved version of his Type C floatplane, which he had built for the navy, and named the Model CL-4S. With this aircraft, Boeing and pilot Edward (Eddie) Hubbard flew sixty letters from Vancouver, British Columbia, to Seattle on 3 March 1919. Inspired by this flight, Hubbard flew a second route in October 1920, from Victoria, British Columbia to Seattle, using a B-1 flying boat purchased from Boeing. With this flight, Hubbard Air Transport, later known as the Seattle-Victoria Air Mail Line, became the first

4

company to exercise a U.S. Post Office Foreign Air Mail contract. Hubbard Air Transport cut one day off the delivery time of U.S.-bound letters arriving in Victoria on steamships crossing the Pacific and made the same improvement on the outbound journeys. This small independent enterprise continued flying until 1937. In the meantime, Eddie Hubbard soon became a major figure in Boeing's plans for future air transport.[3]

Despite this initial step, it was too early for a substantial and successful venture into commercial aviation. For Boeing, government orders were the primary source of company profits. The first major postwar aircraft contract for Boeing was awarded by the Army Air Service in 1921 for the construction of 200 Thomas Morse MB-3A wooden biplane fighters. During the early 1920s, Boeing also undertook the modification of almost 300 American-made de Havilland DH-4 light bombers for the army. Boeing and its competitors had previously received three captured Fokker D.VII fighters from the army in order to examine German construction techniques. These revolutionary fighters introduced the structural and performance advantages of welded steel-tube fuselages to the U.S. aviation industry. Although it was known for woodworking, Boeing remanufactured 177 DH-4s in 1923 by replacing the wooden fuselage structure with one made of steel tubing. The structure of the modified DH-4s was arc-welded using techniques pioneered by company engineers. Thus began Boeing's interest in metal aircraft.[4]

Following the successful MB-3A and DH-4 contracts, Boeing used its own funds to develop what would become a famous series of biplane fighters for the army and navy. Employing the advanced designs of the Fokker D.VII as a guide, the company produced the Model 15, known as the PW-9 for the army and the FB for the navy.[5] More important, the mixed metal fuselage and wooden wing construction were the mainstay of most of Boeing's designs throughout the rest of the decade.

While Boeing was increasing its expertise in aircraft construction, an unexpected party took steps to provide the nation with a coherent and integrated network of commercial air transport. Despite a long tradition of noninterference in commercial affairs dating back to the birth of the United States, the federal government, through the Post Office, sought the means to exploit the potential of aviation for the benefit of the public. As early as 1916, the Post Office was aware of the considerable time savings that the aerial delivery of mail could provide. Accordingly, on 15 May 1918, using aircraft and pilots borrowed from the army, the Post Office opened service between Washington, D.C. and New York City.[6] After overcoming initial teething troubles, the U.S. Aerial Mail Service soon settled into a modestly successful routine along the East Coast. However, the Post Office had a much more ambitious plan in the works.

Using specially modified American-made DH-4s powered by Liberty engines, the Post Office quickly brought a transcontinental airmail scheme to fruition. By September 1920, the last link in the chain across the country was completed when the route through the Rocky Mountains was opened. The coast-to-coast line stretched in segments from New York to Cleveland, Chicago, Omaha, across Wyoming, on to Salt Lake City, and beyond to San Francisco. The route shortened the surface delivery time by twenty-two hours. Anxious to cut times ever further, the Post Office flew an experimental transcontinental delivery through the night, highlighted by Jack Knight's dramatic crossing of the Midwest guided by bonfires.[7] Night flying was essential if the Post Office were to compete effectively with the railroads.

The incoming Harding administration, with Colonel Paul Henderson as postmaster general, established a network of rotating beacons, known as the Lighted Airway, along the transcontinental route. In the summer of 1924, night mail service was under way along selected segments. By late 1925, the system was in full operation.

A series of events in 1925 radically altered the shape of American aviation. Spurred by the controversy surrounding the court martial of General William (Billy) Mitchell and the revelations of the inadequacies of military and civilian aviation, Congress belatedly passed much-needed reform and regulatory legislation. The first act, ironically, was backed by the railroad lobby, anxious to stop the Post Office's involvement which was cutting into their profits. By removing the government from business, the railroads could negotiate profitable cooperative agreements with the airmail carriers and even enter the business themselves. Sponsor Clyde Kelly, a representative from Pennsylvania, advocated the use of civilian contract carriers to deliver the airmail for a four year period. Routes would be awarded through competitive bidding. On 2 February 1925, the Contract Air Mail Act, known widely as the Kelly Act, became law.[8]

Convened at the request of President Calvin Coolidge to examine the state of American aviation, the Morrow Board, headed by financier Dwight Morrow, recommended a greatly increased role for the government in aviation affairs. The Air Commerce Act of 1926 resulted directly from the recommendations of the Board. Signed by the president on 20 May, the act authorized the Commerce Department to designate national airways, license pilots and aircraft, investigate accidents, and promote research and development in aerial navigation aids. Further, an amendment to the Kelly Act was passed on 3 June to provide for mail payments by weight of load carried.[9] With this new organizational structure in place and the solid foundation already provided by the U.S. Aerial Mail Service, the United States was ready to embark on a massive expansion of its commercial aviation.

Suddenly a host of carriers burst upon the scene, tantalized by the promise of lucrative contracts. In the West, former army pilot Walter T. Varney astutely bid for the route from Elko, Nevada to Pasco, Washington, by way of Boise, Idaho. The unlikely route connected the primary transcontinental line with the Pacific Northwest. By the summer of 1926, Varney Air Lines was in full operation. Cleverly, Varney soon shifted his terminus from Elko to Salt Lake City in order to take advantage of the mail deliveries arriving from southern California by Harris Hanshue's Western Air Express. After considerable economic trials, Varney Air Lines fought its way to profitability.[10]

Along the Pacific coast, another enterprising individual bid successfully for airmail contracts. Vern C. Gorst, a farsighted Oregon bus operator, sought to avert competition with his line by acquiring the mail contract linking Los Angeles with Seattle.[11] After months of careful preparations and detailed surveys of the hazardous route, Pacific Air Transport (P.A.T.) began service on 15 September 1926. Although a very successful promoter, Gorst lacked essential knowledge about financial management.[12] While seeking advice from the Wells Fargo Bank in San Francisco, Gorst became acquainted with a young bank officer who would figure prominently in the immediate future of air transportation, William A. Patterson. Pat Patterson's advice concerning aircraft purchases and investment as well as loans greatly aided the success of P.A.T.[13]

The final major link in the commercial air network of the Northwest was forged by William Boeing himself. He had already shown some interest in the possibilities of air transport when he flew with Eddie Hubbard from Canada in 1919 and had remained close to Hubbard during the ensuing years. Hubbard had served as a Boeing Airplane Company test pilot while still running his airmail operation. In 1926, Hubbard approached his friend with another idea. To seize the opportunity offered by the Post Office for the lucrative routes between San Francisco and Chicago, Hubbard suggested that the Boeing company enter into the airmail business.

First, Hubbard approached Clairmont (Claire) L. Egtvedt with the idea. Egtvedt, the designer-in charge, was a young, round-faced, soft-spoken man of Scandinavian background originally from Stoughton, Wisconsin. He had come to Boeing straight from the University of Washington in

7

Clairemont L. Egtvedt, vice-president and general manager of the Boeing Airplane Company. (*Boeing 2926-B*)

Philip G. Johnson, president of the Boeing Airplane Company and president of United Air Lines. (*Boeing 2814*)

1917 when William Boeing had asked the university for young engineers. Earlier, the company had wisely donated funds to assist the university's aeronautics studies and produce new talent. Egtvedt was to lead the company for decades and would eventually become chairman of the Boeing Aircraft Company. Another Washington undergraduate, Philip G. Johnson, also joined Boeing at this time and was to figure prominently in the future of the company. Hubbard and Egtvedt discussed the details at length; Hubbard examined the operational aspects of the proposal while Egtvedt worked on producing an aircraft suitable for airmail service. When they had jointly concluded that such a plan was feasible, they presented their case to Bill Boeing. At first, Boeing appeared cool to the idea despite the fact that such a system would produce an obvious market for his aircraft. After wrestling with the question of whether to enter the risky air transport business, Boeing recognized the potential of the project and agreed to finance the new airline.[14]

Hubbard was promptly assigned the task of creating Boeing Air Transport, with Philip Johnson as the first president. Hubbard immediately hired Duard B. Colyer, an ex-army pilot and formerly second assistant postmaster general, as superintendent of operations. Colyer in turn hired many veteran airmail pilots he had known while with the Post Office and thus rapidly established a reliable system with experienced personnel.[15]

On 29 January 1927, Boeing Air Transport (B.A.T.) won the airmail contract from an incredulous Western Air Express. Western, well established as an airline presence in the region, felt it had a lock on the bidding. Its sturdy, water-cooled, Liberty-engined, Douglas M-2/4 mailplanes had pioneered the air route from Los Angeles to Salt Lake City. Based on its substantial experience, Western bid a reasonable $2.24 per pound for the first 1000 miles and 24 cents per pound for each additional 100 miles. B.A.T.'s astoundingly low bid of $1.50 per pound for the first 1000 miles and 15 cents per pound for each additional 100 miles seemed ridiculously low. Nevertheless, B.A.T. commenced service as agreed on 1 July.[16]

Boeing Air Transport's success was based on Egtvedt's trump card, the Model 40-A. This remarkably efficient mailplane was the logical outgrowth of Boeing's experience in building sturdy metal-fuselage, wooden-winged biplane fighters and was the key to the subsequent designs which led directly to the 247. The first Model 40 was designed in 1925 in response to a Post Office request for new aircraft to replace its aging DH-4s. This version was powered by a single 400-horsepower V-12 water-cooled Liberty engine of World War I vintage, as required by the Post Office, and incorporated a fuselage of mixed wood and metal construction. Despite the sound-

The efficiency of the Boeing 40-A, with its Pratt & Whitney Wasp engine, enabled Boeing Air Transport to win the airmail contract for the Chicago-San Francisco route. *Courtesy Smithsonian Institution.* (SI 75–7029)

ness of its design, only one Model 40 was purchased.[17] In 1927, Egtvedt incorporated several significant improvements in the model 40.

First, he redesigned the fuselage with an all-welded steel-tube frame, which improved the aircraft's strength. Of greatest importance to B.A.T's future success as a commercial carrier, Egtvedt designed the 40-A to carry two passengers as well as 1200 pounds payload of mail. While the pilot sat exposed to the elements in an open cockpit well behind the trailing edge of the wings, the two passengers could ride in reasonable comfort in an enclosed cabin immediately behind the engine. This arrangement, although not ideal, was certainly an improvement over competing designs which paid little if any attention to the needs of the few courageous early passengers. This adequate extra space for passengers ensured B.A.T. a source of additional income. Finally, the incorporation of a major technological breakthrough in powerplant design, the air-cooled radial engine, made the 40-A an outstanding success.[18] The use of a 420-horsepower Pratt & Whitney Wasp was a result of Boeing's close relationship with the navy while building fighters, as well as William Boeing's friendship with Pratt & Whitney founder Frederick B. Rentschler.

A determined man of stern appearance and disposition, Rentschler learned metalworking first hand at his family's foundry in Hamilton, Ohio.

Frederick B. Rentschler, founder of Pratt & Whitney Aircraft and president of United Aircraft and Transport. *Courtesy Smithsonian Institution. (SI 75–12140)*

He was a formal man of German descent, who guarded his privacy and whose modesty and shyness could often be interpreted as coldness towards others. The six-feet two-inch, broad-shouldered Rentschler became obsessed with engines while working with his father's abortive experiments in automobile manufacturing. Educated at Princeton, the young Rentschler took these lessons with him when he entered the army as a captain in World War I. Assigned to the New York district, he was given the task of supervising the production of aircraft engines. After the war ended Rentschler joined the Wright Aeronautical Corporation where he could actively pursue his new interest in aircraft powerplants.[19]

During the early 1920s, the U.S. Navy became increasingly interested in the air-cooled engines produced by the tiny Lawrance Aero-Engine Corporation of New York City. In the immediate postwar years, the only engines producing enough horsepower for high performance aircraft were bulky water-cooled types. With the rise of the aircraft carrier as an important weapon, the navy had to find an engine that could produce sufficient power without the weight and maintenance problems of the water-cooled motors. The Lawrance J series of engines seemed ideal for the task as they had no troublesome and heavy radiator, water pumps or vulnerable cooling lines.

Wishing to find a large company with enough resources to produce and develop this engine, the navy threatened and cajoled Fred Rentschler, then president of the Wright Aeronautical Company, into purchasing the Lawrance company in 1923. By 1924, the Wright J-3 and J-4 engines, better known as the Whirlwind engines, were in service. Incorporating Englishman Samuel D. Heron's revolutionary sodium-cooled valves, which virtually eliminated the chronic problem of burned exhaust valves, the improved J-5 series was the first to offer power and great dependability.[20] This powerplant, the world's first truly reliable aero-engine, made possible Charles Lindbergh's non-stop flight from New York to Paris in 33½ hours with no problems. With such proof of its technical experience, Wright was producing vast numbers of Whirlwinds for the navy and civilian markets.

In 1924, frustrated with banker-dominated management, Rentschler left Wright after a dispute over the future development of the air-cooled engine, disagreeing with the director, whom he felt did not appreciate the engineering problems of aircraft engine production. Rentschler took with him two of his colleagues, Chief Designer George Mead and Assistant Engineer in Charge of Design, A. V. D. Willgoos. After securing the necessary financial backing, they formed the Pratt & Whitney Company in 1925, assuming the name of an idle tool factory in Hartford, Connecticut.[21]

The trio immediately began the development of a new, higher horsepower engine. Incorporating a two-piece crankshaft, a solid master rod, and enclosed valves, their new Wasp engine could generate 400 horsepower from nine cylinders at 1900 rpm, a vast improvement over the latest engines from Wright. By May 1925, the Wasp was undergoing flight tests. The navy was so enthusiastic over the results that 200 engines were soon ordered for its new series of combat aircraft.[22]

From Seattle, William Boeing followed these developments closely. He had worked with Rentschler before and had formed a close working relationship. Boeing realized that, with the Wasp engine, the extraneous weight of water and the cooling system could be exchanged for payload. Unfortunately, he was frustrated in his efforts to acquire the engine be-

George Mead designed the Wasp engine and was the champion of large transports. *Courtesy Smithsonian Institution.* (SI 75–12128)

cause all of the production Wasps for 1927 were earmarked for the navy. Keenly aware that the fate of his new commercial enterprise hung in the balance, Boeing approached his old acquaintance Rentschler, to see if any of the batch of 200 Wasps could be allocated to B.A.T. Rentschler, acting on his friend's request, persuaded the navy to delay acceptance of some of the Wasps, allowing Boeing to receive a sufficient number, on the assurance that Pratt & Whitney could step up production sufficiently to complete the navy contract on time.[23] Once in service, the twenty-five Wasp-powered Boeing 40-As fulfilled their potential and guaranteed B.A.T. a position as an important carrier almost overnight.

Towards the end of 1927, Vern Gorst's Pacific Air Transport was encountering stiff competition from Maddux Air Lines and West Coast Air Transport. Harris Hanshue, president of Western Air Express, had even offered to buy out P.A.T. Acting on the advice of his banker William Patterson, Gorst offered his airline to Boeing if the latter could compensate P.A.T. stockholders fairly. Agreeing to the terms of $200 per share and the hiring of all P.A.T.'s employees, Boeing assumed control on 1 January 1928. This astute move gave Boeing Air Transport a direct link from its headquarters

William "Pat" Patterson moved from the Wells Fargo Bank to Boeing Air Transport and eventually rose to the chairmanship of United Air Lines. *Courtesy United Air Lines.* (*UAL A-69859*)

in Seattle to San Francisco and B.A.T.'s mainline route while providing another market for Boeing aircraft.[24] Shortly thereafter, William Patterson accepted an invitation from Philip Johnson, now president of Boeing Airplane and Boeing Air Transport, to leave Wells Fargo and join B.A.T. He readily accepted the post of vice-president and soon was essentially running the airline while Johnson pursued his many other interests. Patterson's responsibilities increased again after the untimely death of Eddie Hubbard in 1929.[25]

Later in 1928, William Boeing reorganized his holdings to improve the management of his companies. As a result, on 30 October, the Boeing Airplane and Transport Company was formed as a holding company for the Boeing Airplane Company, Boeing Air Transport, and Pacific Air Transport. On 17 December, P.A.T. was completely absorbed, operating afterwards as a separate division of Boeing Air Transport.[26]

One of P.A.T.'s difficulties was the widespread introduction of the large trimotored Fokkers and Fords in the late 1920s. Offering the added safety of three engines and much greater comfort for up to ten passengers, these

14

aircraft represented a significant threat to B.A.T. and other companies which were not so equipped. In response, Bill Boeing turned to Claire Egtvedt and asked him to design a new trimotor aircraft using the Wasp engine. Known as the Model 80, this new large aircraft would provide Boeing Air Transport with a machine that could carry 12 people (18 in later versions) in much greater comfort than the smaller 40-A.

Work began early in 1928. By August, the first Model 80 was flying. The aircraft was conventional by Boeing standards, using the proven fabric-covered, steel tube fuselage construction with aluminum alloy tubing employed aft of the passenger cabin. Boeing went a step further in metal working by using a Duralumin tubed truss in the wing spar and Duralumin tubes for the ribs. Unlike the Fokker and Ford trimotors, however, the Boeing 80 retained the biplane wing. This apparent anachronism was not a symptom of conservative engineering but of the company's concern that the new aircraft have sufficient lift to fly over the treacherous stretch of the Rocky Mountains between Salt Lake City and Cheyenne, Wyoming. One Wasp was mounted in the nose with one suspended between the wings on each side of the aircraft. The transport had conventional fixed landing gear, and the pilot sat within an enclosed cockpit ahead of the passenger compartment.[27] Only four Model 80s were built before the appearance of another remarkable engine promised to enhance the aircraft's performance.

Acting on the navy's request for more powerful air-cooled engines to replace the water-cooled Packards then in service, Pratt & Whitney enlarged and modified the Wasp by increasing the displacement from 1344 cubic inches to 1690 cubic inches. Provisions were also made for a geared propeller that could maintain a steady propeller speed while absorbing the extra horsepower more efficiently. The Hornet, as the new engine was named, became available on the civilian market later in 1928, and could produce 525 horsepower, 115 more than its smaller brother.[28] With this new powerplant, Boeing re-engined the Model 80 with three Hornets. Redesignated the Model 80-A, the aircraft's capacity was increased from 12 to 18 passengers. Top speed increased from 128 to 138 miles per hour while the cruise speed was raised from 115 to 125 miles per hour.[29]

Two novel features gave the 80-A a significant advantage over the competition. Early aircraft were cramped, drafty, and incredibly noisy. Because these transports could not fly above the weather, flights were usually bumpy, often tossing the frequently airsick passengers unceremoniously about the cabin. Boeing sought to ease the travelers' discomfort by providing, for the first time, a well-trained female flight attendant and,

The Boeing 80 was designed by Claire Egtvedt to match the performance of the Ford Tri-Motor. *Courtesy Smithsonian Institution.* (*SI 76–16777*)

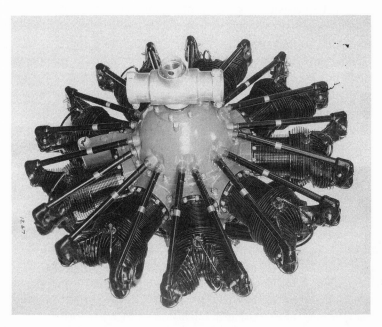

The Pratt & Whitney Hornet was an enlarged and more powerful development of the successful Wasp. *Courtesy Smithsonian Institution.* (*SI 87–11925*)

16

more important for obvious reasons, a lavatory. The first attendants in the United States, led by Ellen Church, were women nurses who were trained to sooth frazzled nerves and to see to the care and feeding of the paying customers. Brainchild of Steven A. Stimpson, the B.A.T. district manager in San Francisco, the idea was a complete success, relieving the over-worked pilots and copilots of many extra duties.[30] Equipped with the 80-A, Boeing Air Transport stood poised to expand its profitable network east-ward into unfriendly territory.

The aviation business was booming in the late 1920s. Coinciding with the government's increased influence in aviation matters and its direct sponsorship of the airmail system, Charles Lindbergh's daring solo flight across the Atlantic in 1927 and his subsequent triumphal tour of the United States highlighted for the public what was already known by an alert core of investors, that the business of aviation held the prospect of great wealth. Almost overnight, the general public became air-minded and was more willing to accept the airplane as a tool for transportation. With this wave of enthusiasm came an outpouring of money from smaller investors seeking to purchase a part of this new, growing industry. Many sought to take advantage of the craze by investing quickly, hoping thereby to generate vast sums of money through the rapid growth of questionable stocks—a national addiction which led millions of small investors to risk their savings on shaky business propositions, not only in aviation but in other enterprises as well.

Among these seeking to exploit the situation was Frederick Rentschler of Pratt & Whitney. Seizing upon his personal and professional relation-ship with William Boeing and the Boeing Airplane Company, Rentschler suggested an intriguing proposition to his friend in Seattle. In the age of mergers and consolidations, Rentschler broached the idea of forming a massive holding company composed of his and Boeing's interests. Bill Boeing readily agreed. Such a company could call upon vast resources to expand much farther and faster than possible individually. The terms of the agreement were swiftly completed. A third party, Mr. Chance Milton Vought, a producer of a famous line of naval aircraft, also participated. As arranged, Boeing first purchased Chance Vought. Rentschler and Boeing then turned over all of the stock in their companies in exchange for equal shares in the new United Aircraft and Transport Corporation. Rentschler became president and Boeing chairman of the board. Chance Vought and Philip Johnson both became vice-presidents, retaining operational control over their respective organizations.[31]

To solidify its position as an important aviation holding company,

United Aircraft sought to expand and integrate its product line. Rentschler's initial move was to acquire the Hamilton Propeller Company and the Standard Steel Propeller Company and combine them under the name of Hamilton Standard. Furthermore, Stearman Aircraft, a builder of robust general-purpose biplanes, was purchased as well as the Avion Corporation of John K. (Jack) Northrop. Significantly, the integration of Northrop's revolutionary ideas concerning metal aircraft and monocoque construction would prove to be a windfall for United Aircraft. Complementing this unique product line was the acquisition of the Sikorsky Aviation Corporation, manufacturer of large aircraft and flying boats. Altogether, United Aircraft's total capital grew to $146 million.[32]

With such a solid base, Boeing Air Transport actively sought to expand its route system as far as the corporate headquarters in New York City. In doing so in this age of massive financial empires, United Aircraft collided head-on with the powerful North American Aviation group, an even larger holding company under the control of Clement M. Keys.

In 1925 Keys, a former financial editor of the Wall Street Journal and head of his own investment banking house, was among the first to realize the business potential of aviation and the airmail. Keys became involved in aircraft manufacturing during World War I when he rose to the post of vice-president of the Curtiss Aeroplane and Motor Company. At the end of the war, he bought controlling interest in the firm and sought to create a vast intercontinental network of aviation-related industries. By May 1925, Keys had formed National Air Transport (N.A.T.) to pursue these goals and had raised sufficient capital—an unheard of sum of $10 million—to form an airline to carry mail between Chicago, Detroit, and New York.[33]

When the Post Office offered airmail contracts in 1927, Keys barely managed to win Contract Air Mail Route 17 for the Chicago-New York section. After a difficult start, particularly handling the "Hell Stretch" over the Alleghenies, N.A.T.'s Curtiss Carrier Pigeons and Douglas mailplanes opened service. Unlike B.A.T., National Air Transport was reluctant to carry passengers because the additional weight of the radiator and associated plumbing of the water-cooled engines in its aircraft drastically restricted payload. If there was space available, a traveler could squeeze on board. The chances were good, however, that the poor soul would be left stranded if additional sacks of mail were picked up en route.[34]

N.A.T. also had designs on the Chicago to San Francisco route and hoped to forge a cooperative arrangement with Harris Hanshue of Western Air Express to place a bid and open transcontinental airmail service. Confident in his ability to win the contract on his own and distrustful of eastern businessmen, Hanshue declined.[35] Had he accepted, Boeing Air Transport might never have been born.

United Aircraft and Boeing Air Transport hoped to counter Keys's persistent efforts to push westward, especially after North American Aviation purchased an interest in Varney and its routes to Seattle—Boeing's home. Keys had already established Transcontinental Air Transport (TAT) in May 1928 to provide New York to Los Angeles service along a southern route. Unlike National Air Transport, TAT operated the popular Ford Tri-Motor, which was far more comfortable than the single-engined aircraft operated by National. With Charles Lindbergh as technical advisor, TAT opened a combination air-rail service from coast to coast. Keys was therefore a major threat, especially when it was learned that he was about to introduce the new Curtiss Condor sleeper transport to his line. United Aircraft attempted to undermine his operation by seizing control of N.A.T.

Early in 1930, Rentschler proposed a merger between United Aircraft and National Air Transport to N.A.T.'s Board of Directors. Keys brusquely refused. By the end of March, however, Rentschler had managed to outmaneuver Keys and acquire one-third interest in N.A.T. stock. When he attempted to gain control of 70,000 shares by proxy, Rentschler was thwarted by Keys, who changed N.A.T.'s corporate bylaws at the last minute. Taken aback, Rentschler turned to the courts and had Keys's maneuver declared illegal; United Aircraft's financial agents worked feverishly to buy N.A.T. stock, and with 57 percent control, Rentschler called a special stockholder's meeting on 22 April. Keys was outflanked and defeated. After a brief reorganization, United Aircraft absorbed N.A.T. and gained clear control of the first transcontinental mainline air route.[36]

With this victory firmly in hand, United Aircraft consolidated its gains by snapping up Stout Air Service with its fleet of Fords and by purchasing outright away from Keys Varney Air Lines in the West. More important, Rentschler realized that a reorganization of United Aircraft's transport operations was necessary if he was to exploit fully the new opportunities offered by the recent events. Consequently, the headquarters of the B.A.T. was moved from Seattle to Chicago, a more centrally located point along the new "mainline" route. Underscoring the importance of the change, B.A.T., N.A.T., P.A.T., Stout, and Varney all were placed under a management company to coordinate their expanded activities. On 1 July 1931, United Air Lines was formed.[37]

Concurrent with the growth of United Aircraft was the passage of crucial federal legislation which changed the face of commercial aviation.

On 29 April 1930, the Third Amendment to the Air Mail Act of 1925 was passed. Named after Republican Senator Charles D. McNary of Oregon and Republican Representative Laurence H. Watres of Pennsylvania, the bill, known popularly as the McNary-Watres Act, offered any contractor a ten-year route certificate in exchange for the previous contract, which was due to expire soon, provided the airline had at least two years of operating experience. The rights of the pioneering companies would be respected. Furthermore, the postmaster general could expand or consolidate any route if, in his judgment, such an action was in the public interest. The bill was the brainchild of President Herbert Hoover's ruthlessly determined new postmaster general, Walter Folger Brown.[38]

Assuming office in 1929, Brown sought to bring rationality to the rapidly growing air transport industry. Many small airlines had been created too quickly and flew haphazard routes resulting in disorganized service in many areas of the country. Passenger traffic in particular was confused and sporadic. The existing situation offered little chance for improvement if left uncontrolled, and was strikingly similar to that of the railroads in the nineteenth century. After studying the problem for several months, Brown took action. He realized that by exercising dictatorial control over airmail contract awards, he could force the airlines to do his bidding. Brown's desire to reshape the air transport map was brought to full force in 1929 when he forced TAT to merge with part of Western Air Express to create a practical transcontinental line paralleling B.A.T. and N.A.T. The "shotgun marriage" produced a new airline, Transcontinental and Western Air, better known as TWA, the primary competitor to United.[39]

In Brown's opinion, much work was yet to be done. He required additional tools to realign the air routes to his satisfaction. Other large corporations, such as the Aviation Corporation (AVCO), and North American Aviation operated a plethora of unrelated schedules and routes which ignored the needs of much of the country. In early 1930, Brown persuaded the administration to back his plan to foster improved airmail service and promote passenger travel with appropriate legislation. He was assisted by representatives of the airline industry, including Philip Johnson of United.

Accordingly, between 15 May and 9 June 1930, Brown held a series of open, though unpublicized, meetings to award the new contracts. Representatives of the leading aviation enterprises were invited. The small operators were not officially asked to attend. Brown reasoned that only the large corporations had the resources to fulfill his ambition to fashion a coherent and cohesive transport system. This assumption would later prove his undoing. Twenty of the twenty-two prime routes were divided

Walter Folger Brown, postmaster general under President Hoover, created the network of air routes across the U.S. *Courtesy Smithsonian Institution.* (*SI 87–11946*)

between the major operators. Boeing Air Transport preserved its routes but did not acquire additional contracts.[40]

A third and most critical element of the McNary-Watres Act directly affected the future of aircraft development. The previous method of payment by weight of mail carried was replaced by a system of payment by total available volume. A price of $1.25 per cubic foot per mile would be paid to the contractor regardless of whether the space on the aircraft was filled. This new idea not only encouraged the airlines to fill any unused space with passengers as a profitable bonus, it stimulated both the airlines and the manufacturers to put into service larger aircraft that would earn higher subsidies because of their greater payload.[41] Other incentives encouraged the use of multiple engines, two-way radios, and the latest navigation and safety equipment. These provisions were a conscious effort by the Post Office to develop sophisticated passenger aircraft in the support of a national air transportation system. Ignoring the political ramifications of blatant favoritism and willingly creating aviation oligopolies at the public's expense, Brown hoped to encourage the airlines to spend the money they received through subsidies to modernize their fleets with a new generation of commercial airliners. This was one of the most important steps leading to the creation of the Boeing 247.

With the formation of United Aircraft and United Air Lines, and the creation of a national network of air routes by the federal government, Boeing was poised to take the bold step of building an aircraft so radically different as to change the shape of aviation.

2

New Technology and New Aircraft:
Origins of the 247

Boeing and United Aircraft were the first companies to act following the initiatives of the Post Office. A technical revolution was sweeping the aviation industry and United Aircraft was in the vanguard. Several important breakthroughs promised to increase greatly the capabilities and efficiency of future aircraft. The Boeing Airplane Company was among the first to take advantage of the situation by producing several radical designs which led directly to the most significant advance yet in air transport technology—the Boeing 247.

Of greatest importance was the introduction of all-metal, monoplane, monocoque construction. In an effort to streamline aircraft designs and to reduce the drag resulting from the external bracing of the wings, the Germans, particularly Hugo Junkers, had pioneered the internally supported, cantilevered monoplane wing during the First World War. Aircraft produced by Junkers and other farsighted designers in the immediate post-war years were very successful because of the relative efficiency of their clean and strong wings.

In the eternal struggle to reduce weight while increasing the strength of aircraft structures, Adolf Rohrbach built the first all-metal stressed-skin wing for his remarkable four-engined airliner, the E4/20 Staaken, which he designed for the Zeppelin company in 1920. By allowing the skin to carry part of the aerodynamic loads, eliminating the need for a complex internal structure, much weight was saved. Using a higher wing loading of over fifteen pounds per square inch, Rohrbach was further able to compensate for the inherently heavier metal structure at the expense of longer take-off and landing distances. Despite the structural benefits of this advanced design, the Staaken was too underpowered to take advantage of this breakthrough and its unprotected aluminum alloy construction was subject to rapid corrosion. Unfortunately, improvements to the E4/20 were not allowed to continue: the Allied Control Commission ordered its destruction in November 1922.[1]

Other advanced European aircraft also used a radical method of fuselage manufacture that gave a streamlined form, light weight, and great strength. First used by the French before World War I, monocoque construction (more precisely semi-monocoque), from the French term referring to single-shell boat hull manufacturing techniques, greatly increased the usable volume of an aircraft fuselage. In this manner, the plywood skin carried most of the load thereby reducing the weight of the structure. The Swiss Ruchonnet "Cigar" of 1911, the French Deperdussin racer of 1912, the Russian Sikorsky S.9 of 1913, as well as the Albatros and Pfalz series of German fighters of World War I employed this technique. In June 1918, the experimental German Dornier D-I fighter combined stressed skin with a metal monocoque fuselage. Beginning in 1920, the National Advisory Committee for Aeronautics (NACA), the U.S. government aeronautical research organization, became interested in the German work on airframe construction techniques and published numerous reports which were disseminated throughout the American aviation community.

Development of metal aircraft languished until the mid-1920s when methods were discovered which protected aluminum alloys from corrosion. In Great Britain, G. D. Bengough and H. Sutton of the National Physical Laboratory developed a technique of anodizing alloys with a protective oxide coating, while in 1927 in the United States, E. H. Dix, Jr. found a method of bonding pure, corrosion resistant, aluminum to the external surface of aluminum alloys. The resultant sheet metal was known as Alclad.[2] NACA approval and subsequent army and navy acceptance gave the green light to the industry to start work on new metal aircraft designs in the U.S.

Another technical innovation, that of the engine cowl, increased speed by smoothing the airflow over the exposed cylinders while retaining sufficient cooling of the engine. First used on the Lockheed Vega, the cowl was one of many products of the inventive minds of NACA, particularly that of Fred E. Weick. Experiments in the cowling of radial engines had been conducted as early as 1918 but with mixed results. Colonel Virginius Clark, using his knowledge of airfoils, developed a workable enclosed cowl in the early 1920s which unfortunately also caused engine overheating difficulties. Though Clark was unable to explain adequately the cowl's success in reducing drag, George Mead, realizing the potential of this device, hired him as a consultant to Pratt & Whitney, thus bringing firsthand knowledge of cowls to United Aircraft.[3]

The development of a practical engine cowl had to await successful results from NACA's research at its Langley Laboratory. Basing much of their research on the work of H. L. Townend of the British National Physical Laboratory, the creator of the successful "Townend Ring," NACA sought to improve this simple device which encircled only the top of the cylinder heads of radial engines. Intensive work on the ring began at Langley under the guidance of Weick during 1926, in response to requests received from the U.S. Navy's Bureau of Aeronautics and from industry. Weick and his research team at the Propeller Research Tunnel produced a practical full-cowl design by the end of 1928 and published their results, for which NACA received the coveted Collier Trophy.[4]

With the breakthrough in corrosion protection for aluminum alloys, the advent of the NACA cowling, and the increased awareness of new methods of aircraft construction, work began anew in the United States on all-metal, cantilevered monocoque aircraft.

One of America's most avid enthusiasts of metal stressed-skin construction was Jack Northrop, the designer of the sleek wooden Vega, who had left Lockheed in 1928 to start his own firm to produce metal aircraft. The first aircraft to be built under his own name was called the Alpha. This low-winged six-to-seven-passenger transport and mailplane blended a strong lightweight, cantilevered, stressed-skin wing with a monocoque, metal fuselage. So impressed was Bill Boeing by this aircraft that he purchased Northrop's Avion Corporation, adding it to the United Aircraft empire in 1929.[5] Northrop's fervent advocacy of all-metal aircraft had a lasting impact on the aircraft designs produced by the other members of the United Aircraft group. His influential voice was often heard in technical meetings, proffering advice.[6]

Building on this sound foundation, Boeing constructed a revolutionary aircraft of its own, the Model 200 Monomail, in 1930. Marking a major milestone in the development of modern aircraft design, the monocoque fuselage of the Monomail had a circular cross section. The result was a strong structure and a streamlined profile. The all-metal, cantilevered wing construction, which was completely new for Boeing, set the pattern for company designs for the next decade. Built from Duralumin alloy, the wing was of dual square-tube design with internal Warren truss girders and ribs, resulting in a complicated web of bracing which provided tremendous strength. The Warren truss was riveted to a corrugated Duralumin inner skin which was, in turn, riveted to a smooth outer skin. Fairings at the wing roots smoothed the turbulent airflow at the junction of the wing and the fuselage, further reducing drag.

John K. "Jack" Northrop (1895–1981) pioneered monocoque construction in the U.S. *Courtesy Smithsonian Institution.* (*SI 87–11948*)

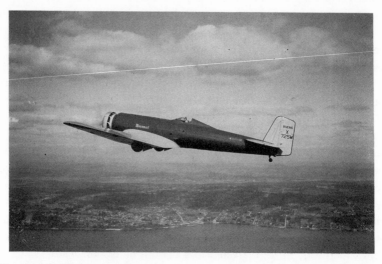

The Model 200 Monomail was the first all-metal Boeing. *Courtesy Smithsonian Institution.* (*SI 87–11906*)

This wing was attached to the lower portion of the streamlined monocoque fuselage which was designed to carry 220 cubic feet of mail while being flown by a single pilot, who sat exposed to the wind in an open cockpit midway down the spine of the craft. Power was provided by a single 575-horsepower Pratt & Whitney Hornet, the same engine used by the Model 40-B and Model 80-A. The Monomail was the first Boeing to be equipped with a semiretractable landing gear, which, though heavier than conventional gear, more than compensated for this handicap by greatly reducing drag.[7]

Despite its innovative design, the Monomail was hampered by the inefficiency of its ground-adjustable propeller. With the propeller set in fine pitch for takeoff and climb, the aircraft could not fly fast enough to take advantage of its streamlined form. With the propellers set in low pitch for high speed, the aircraft could not take off from short fields with sufficient loads to be of commercial use. Consequently, the Monomail was not placed into production. Only one Model 200 and one later version, the Model 221, were built, although the experience did convince Boeing of the superiority of the stressed-skin, all-metal configuration.[8] The company was forced to await further technological developments before a modern airliner design could be considered.

One of the last technical problems to be solved before the creation of a truly modern commercial transport concerned the question of multiple engines and the aerodynamics of powerplant placement. Previously, only single-engined designs had benefitted significantly from developments in aerodynamics. A successful long-range transport, capable of carrying a sufficient load of mail and passengers, would require additional powerplants for safety and reliability. The question remained as to how many engines would be necessary to provide both sufficient power and economical operation.

The location of the engines on the airframe was also a critical question. A three-engine layout, with one engine in the nose and one suspended beneath each wing, had been the standard for large transports, most notably the Ford Tri-Motor. This arrangement provided sufficient power, but was aerodynamically inefficient. Placing cowls on the engines failed to alleviate the problem because the turbulent airflow around the wings, the short, exposed nacelles, and the slab-sided fuselage still created much drag. In Europe, several twin-engine designs suffered from similar aerodynamic inefficiencies.

Beginning in 1929, Weick and other NACA engineers began to consider the relationship between engine placement and aerodynamic drag. After much experimentation, NACA discovered that drag could be reduced greatly and both the lift and engine efficiency enhanced if the engine was located on a line directly in front of the wing and the propeller placed far in front of the leading edge. According to NACA reports, the installation, if properly positioned, could actually increase the overall lift. The gains were so great that it was possible to eliminate the third, nose-mounted engine.[9] This discovery made possible subsequent breakthroughs in aircraft design which vaulted the United States into the forefront of the science of aeronautics.

The first aircraft to apply this new information was a Boeing product. Incorporating the lessons of the Monomail and assimilating the new data produced by NACA, Boeing used its own resources to build a twin-engined, all-metal monoplane bomber based largely on the Monomail. For maximum efficiency the cowled Pratt & Whitney Hornets were placed before the leading edge of the wing. For the first time on an American aircraft, servo tabs were installed in the control surfaces to assist the pilot in maneuvers by lessening the aerodynamic loads.

To minimize drag further, the monocoque fuselage was made as narrow as possible, thus dictating that the pilot and copilot sit in tandem behind the bombardier and in front of the gunner. Boeing's concession to convention left all four crew members in open cockpits. Semiretractable landing gear completed the design. When tested by the Air Corps, the advanced design of the B-9 enabled production versions of the bomber to fly at a maximum speed of 188 miles per hour and cruise at 165 per hour. To the astonishment of the military and the aeronautical community, this was as fast as the best pursuit aircraft in service.[10] Had the United States gone to war in 1931, no fighter aircraft in the world could have intercepted this bomber. During 1931, when the Army Air Corps was still flying World War I-style fabric-covered 100-mph Keystone bombers, the 188-mph B-9 came as a revelation.

By 1931, the Boeing Airplane Company had thus assumed preeminence as an aeronautical innovator and refocused its efforts towards the creation of a new airliner as radical as the B-9. The firm correctly perceived the positive political and technological climate which encouraged the production of a new generation of fast and efficient airliners.

The introduction of great numbers of Ford Tri-Motors, Boeing 80s, and other large transports during the 1920s, their projected life-span of several years, and the onset of the Great Depression, had all combined to eliminate the need for new replacement airliners until 1932 or 1933.[11] This gave the manufacturers sufficient lead time to evaluate the requirements for the next generation of civil airliners. For Boeing, much strategic planning was

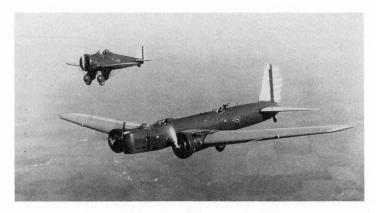

Incorporating modern construction techniques with the latest discoveries from NACA, the Boeing B-9, *foreground*, revolutionized bomber design. *Courtesy Smithsonian Institution.* (*SI 75–16036*)

A B-9 under construction clearly shows its metal structure. The other aircraft are F4B-4s for the Marine Corps. (*Boeing 5677-B*)

conducted at the high-level meetings of the Technical Advisory Committee of United Aircraft. In these meetings, held in Seattle in 1929 and in New York City in 1930 and 1932, the heads of United Aircraft's various companies, under the chairmanship of George Mead, decided the future of the giant corporation and the shape of a new generation of transport airplanes to replace the Model 40s and 80s then in service.

The ensuing spirited debates revealed deep divisions within the corporation between the advocates of large passenger aircraft and those of small. This disagreement would directly affect the subsequent development of the 247. George Mead and Igor Sikorsky were the staunchest supporters of larger machines. Mead, an engine man from New England who had been fascinated with automobiles as a youth, was educated at the Massachusetts Institute of Technology. His first job in aviation came in World War I when his poor eyesight kept him out of the military. Instead, Mead joined the Wright-Martin Corporation which built the famous French Hispano-Suiza engine under license. He came to Pratt & Whitney with Rentschler in 1925 and, with A. V. D. Willgoos, designed the first Wasp engine. Not willing to rest on his laurels, Mead was a driving force behind the development of the more powerful Hornet which brought even greater breakthroughs in aircraft performance.[12] Larger aircraft required the larger engines Mead wanted to build and Mead was emphatic in his determination to construct both.

Igor Sikorsky, one of aviation's great pioneers and the first to realize the potential of large aircraft, overcame his critics by building the world's first four-engined aircraft for the Tsar in 1913. His subsequent series of very large four-engined bombers operated with great success during World War I. Sikorsky later experimented with helicopters and monocoque designs before he emigrated from Russia after the revolution. In the 1920s he led the way in the creation of large multi-engined aircraft before turning his attention to a successful line of flying boats. Sikorsky Aviation had become part of the U.A.T.C. in July 1929.

As early as 1929, Mead was proposing, at least for the sake of discussion, the design of a fifty-passenger transport. Mead and Sikorsky reasoned correctly that only a large aircraft would be acceptable to the travelling public, for such a machine would offer comfortable seats, sufficient room, food, a lavatory, and other amenities. The ideal was to provide the Pullman car comfort and convenience of transcontinental rail service. Such a development would have to await production of much larger engines, but many of the more desirable features could be incorporated into transports in the near future.[13]

C. N. Montieth favored smaller transports and more conservative designs. (*Boeing 3097-B*)

The champions of the small ship, led by Boeing Chief Engineer C. N. Montieth, agreed with making more concessions to passenger comfort but vehemently disagreed with the construction of an aircraft larger than those currently in production. Educated at Washington University in St. Louis and at M.I.T., Montieth had come to Boeing Airplane in 1925 from the U.S. Army Air Service when he left the Engineering Division at McCook Field. He had worked with Boeing on the GA-X experimental ground attack bomber and the series of diminutive Boeing fighters.[14] A massive armored triplane, the GA-X was a notable Boeing failure while the small, high performance fighters were quite successful. With this object lesson in mind, Montieth argued the case on behalf of the airline pilots who wanted smaller, more maneuverable machines. He was blunt in his opinion:

> We are right up against the argument now as to what is going to be the future transport ship? A few big ones? We have got some big ones and [they are] getting to be whales [regarding] the size and unhandiness of them. In the first place, any ship bigger than the 80—and I think the 80-A is too big—is going to require housing facilities which we do not have and which are expensive in themselves . . . and we don't want to put a big investment in

housing facilities at terminals and intermediate points. And right now there is some question about how well we are going to be able to care for the 80-A on the line because they are too big to get into the hangars. We can talk all we want to about having these things outside and work[ing] on them, but [the mechanics] can't do it in cold weather.[15]

More importantly, smaller ships were thought to be safer, more cost effective, and more flexible in airline use:

. . . from the standpoint of weather, the pilots on the line want small ships because the minute they get into the least bit of thick weather with the big ships, they set them down. They don't even take small chances, because these fellows are so unhandy to have around. The pilots want a small ship . . . on account of the maneuverability.[16]

The numerous divisions of United Air Lines concurred with Montieth, adding that several aircraft could be operated more cheaply than one large one and that smaller machines could fly much faster. According to E. P. Lott of National Air Transport, "From the operators' standpoint, I don't think there is a bit of doubt but that the operator would rather operate a bunch of little ones than one big one. He can do it cheaper and do a better job of it."[17] According to Montieth, "You can build three six-passenger ships for less cost than one 18 passenger ship."[18] With the Post Office's emphasis on speed, the new machines should be able to cruise at least 150 miles per hour—50 percent faster than current types. Stated D. B. Colyer of Boeing Air Transport, "The Post Office is not interested in your capacity at all . . . they would just as soon fly two or three planes. What they are interested in is the speed at which you fly."[19]

The general consensus was for the small aircraft despite Mead's protests to the contrary. Given the economic and technical situation in 1931, this less expensive design appeared to be the correct path for Boeing and United Aircraft. The development of larger aircraft was postponed until the commercial climate changed in its favor. Design work would proceed on the smaller machines.[20]

Mead had his reservations. "We have reached a point now," he stated, "where we can't make a mistake and I would not want to get along four or five years from now and hear somebody had come along and disproved the theory of the big ship (being too large) and finding us wishing we had done something about it."[21] His fears were well founded.

Regardless of Mead's apprehensions, Boeing continued to work on a series of designs incorporating many different ideas. While the internal debate raged, Boeing engineers were working on a new trimotor, designated the Model 238. Using three Pratt & Whitney Hornet engines, one

Frederick B. Collins's inspired ideas for a twin-engine airliner led directly to the creation of the Boeing 247. (*Boeing 7120*)

in the nose and one each in the leading edge of the shoulder-mounted wing, the 238 could carry twelve passengers and a crew of three at a calculated top speed of 165 miles per hour. Gross weight was to be 20,300 pounds.[22] A more conventional trimotor, the Model 239, offered the same capacity but was designed as a biplane with fixed landing gear, in order to save weight. The maximum speed of this design was expected to be 152 miles per hour.[23] With the prevailing atmosphere of United Aircraft swinging towards smaller aircraft, Boeing proposed a nine-passenger high-wing transport, the Model 243. With two Hornets and retractable gear, it was expected that this aircraft would fly at a maximum speed of 169 miles per hour.[24] Although it seemed an excellent design, United Air Line pilots and corporate heads felt that this aircraft was still too large.

In the meantime, Frederick B. Collins, Assistant in the Sales Department, decided to go flying. Collins took leave from his post in 1930 and entered the Boeing School of Aeronautics in Oakland, California to acquire his Master Pilot's License and fly the routes of United Air Lines, and thus to become better acquainted with the needs of the airline divisions. After graduating, Collins flew with B.A.T. on the San Francisco-Chicago mainline where he gained much firsthand experience while at the controls of a Model 80-A.[25] As a member of the Boeing sales team, Collins was well aware of the significance to aeronautics of the B-9, which was under development at that time. His discussions with B.A.T. pilots convinced him of the need to replace the reliable, but slow 80-As in service. The solution was obvious to him—build a transport based on the new bomber. Full of enthusiasm, Collins approached Philip Johnson through William Patterson.

In February 1931, Collins drafted a detailed proposal for Johnson advocating a twin-engined, all-metal, low-wing six-to-eight-passenger monoplane to satisfy the needs of the airlines. This aircraft, with a 150 mile per hour cruising speed, would combine the inherent safety of a multi-engined machine with the speed of a streamlined single-engined type. If at least fifty were purchased, he calculated, the price could be held to a reasonable $45,000 and would result in a marked reduction of operational costs compared with trimotors. Designed to carry both passengers and mail, the new aircraft would satisfy the Post Office's desire for speed and would benefit from the government payment of three cents per mile bonus awarded to aircraft which could carry from six to nine passengers. Coupled with the McNary-Watres Act provision for a thirteen cent per mile payment for operating multi-engined aircraft with at least 78 cubic feet of cargo space, the aircraft could be quite profitable. The latest single-engined aircraft, like the Model 221, the six-passenger successor to the Monomail, were good, but forfeited the extra multi-engine allowance recently made available. The proposed transport would be very salable to airlines and also very attractive as a corporate aircraft. "In other words," Collins concluded, "the twin-engined plane is a potential all-purpose airplane besides [being] adaptable to strictly air mail and passenger line operation. It is felt," he continued, "that because of its superior merits . . . it is the logical type of airplane for this company to build."[26]

Encouraged by Johnson's positive response, Collins forwarded his recommendations to the Engineering Office. Chief Engineer Montieth reported back that such a twin-engined aircraft was feasible but, unfortunately, would have a ceiling of only 4000 feet with one engine out, which was insufficient to cross the Rocky Mountains. Temporarily shelved, Collins' idea was reborn after the transport division of United Aircraft, reorganized under United Air Lines as of July 1931, failed to agree on the 238, 239, and other proposals for the next generation of transports. With the backing of Thorp Hiscock, operations vice-president of B.A.T. and D. B. Colyer, the idea was again put forth to Johnson who

agreed to the proposal, with the provision that the single-engined performance be improved.[27]

Johnson, who had become president of United Air Lines, commanded
tremendous authority, second only to Rentschler. Though only thirty one
in 1926, the quiet, dynamic Johnson had become president of the Boeing
Airplane Company when Bill Boeing decided to enter semiretirement as
chairman. Johnson's parents had emigrated to the United States from
Sweden in 1889, only five years before his birth, and established a laundry
business in Seattle. Though respectful of his father, the young Phillip
Gustav Johnson avoided working in the family business at all costs, spend-
ing his summers instead sweeping floors in machine shops and learning the
intricacies of production shops. After high school P. G., as he was known
by his close associates, sold tires until he entered the University of Washington to pursue a degree in mechanical engineering. After he was hired
by William Boeing in 1917, Johnson rose quickly in the new company,
becoming plant superintendent in 1920, president in 1926, president of
Boeing Air Transport in 1927, and vice-president of United Aircraft and
Transport Corporation in 1931.

An unassuming individual of great integrity, Phillip Johnson was a
practical man who preferred informality to ostentatiousness. He was always Phil or P. G. to those who knew him as a youth and insisted that he
remain so despite his success as an adult. His unaffected demeanor belied
a sharp intellect which could quickly seize the essence of an argument
and swiftly analyze a lengthy report. Johnson's remarkable memory enabled him to recall names, facts, and figures months after reading them.
His always clean desk underscored his ability for rapid decision making
and an obsession with orderliness which could be seen in his aggressive
attitude towards work. Goal oriented, Johnson was more concerned with
the final result than with the numerous details and realized the importance of timeliness in production and the encouragement of new ideas to
improve business.[28]

In discussions with his friend Claire Egtvedt, who was now vice-
president of Boeing and in charge of the factory, Johnson further modified
Collins's suggestions. Instead of replacing the entire United Air Lines fleet
with one new type of machine, Johnson wanted a smaller, high-speed,
eight-passenger twin-engine airliner to supersede only the single-engined
transports currently in operation. The large 80-As and Ford Tri-Motors
would be replaced later by a bigger design.[29] Johnson announced his intentions in September 1931.

Frederick Rentschler was the ultimate authority on a decision so crucial to the fortunes of the corporation. Johnson addressed a detailed report to him outlining the specifics of the proposals on 30 September. The design, he stated, was the product of research conducted by Boeing and United Aircraft and "is a result of combined experience, as far as structure is concerned, of the (B-9) bomber and the Monomail." This low-wing, all-metal monocoque monoplane would be produced as "replacement equipment for the 40s, 95s, Douglases, Falcon, etc." Furthermore, "I believe we have now had sufficient experience with the Monomail and the bomber to safely launch a production program to replace the single-motor equipment in . . . approximately two years."[30]

Because of Boeing's experience with the B-9, no prototype would be necessary. Such an experimental aircraft would only be a "waste of time." Cost of each aircraft was estimated at $40,000. The gross weight, as equipped with night-flying equipment, would be 12,000 pounds with a payload of 2400 pounds. This would permit a maximum load of eight passengers and 800 pounds of mail. Electrically retractable landing gear was to be installed.[31]

Surprisingly, smaller Pratt & Whitney Wasp engines were selected for the new high-speed transport. Collins, most of the engineers, and especially George Mead, wanted the more powerful 575-horsepower Hornet used in the B-9, the Monomail, and the latest versions of the Model 40 and 80. But fearful of the larger 16,000-pound aircraft envisioned by Collins and enamored by the smoothness and reliability of the Wasp, pilots for B.A.T. argued successfully for the smaller engine in the smaller airframe.[32] In any event, the latest version of this supercharged powerplant could now produce 550 horsepower.

Performance projections were remarkable. In the age of hundred-mile-per-hour airliners, this aircraft promised a top speed of 173 miles per hour at 6000 feet and a cruise speed of 150 miles per hour at 75 percent power. Stated Johnson, "There is no doubt but this performance can actually be attained and if so would represent a desired step forward, not only in comfort, but in performance as well."

The aircraft would have stark appointments. This would permit the lightest structure possible combined with the greatest load-carrying capability. It would have no extraneous crew. "This airplane will provide for but one pilot," Johnson emphasized, "and will not have such facilities as lavatories, etc., which are included in the larger ship. It will merely be a high-speed, load-carrying ship to be used on the schedules carrying most of the mail and express, and the passenger arrangement is for purely accommodation reasons." In other words, the aircraft that would eventually become

Erik Nelson was the sales manager for Boeing and had served as a member of the historic around-the-world flight of the U.S. Army Air Service's Douglas World Cruisers. (*Boeing 7852*)

the 247 was to be built for the greatest performance with only the most spartan appointments for the passengers.

The development of a larger aircraft to replace the trimotors would come later and would require a prototype. "We expect to proceed with the construction of some type of multi-engined airplane of large capacity, [with] approximately a 4000 pound payload," he continued, "which would be the replacement for the 80-As and Fords. This design, however, should be developed in the usual manner of producing one or two experimental [aircraft] . . . because of the expense involved."

The tentative proposals for these two aircraft remained open for discussion. "At the present time," Johnson stated, "I am sending [Boeing Sales Manager] Erik Nelson to discuss not only this plane but the larger transport of which studies have been sent around, with our various operating officials and pilots. After he has accomplished this and settled any questions in their minds from a design standpoint, it is my intention to call a general meeting of all operating heads in Chicago and lay down the specifications to which this airplane will be built, as well as the larger and more luxurious liner.

"I have discussed this matter with Mr. Boeing," Johnson concluded, "and he is in full accord with my ideas." With this two-aircraft program firmly in mind, Johnson sent Rentschler copies of the general arrangement (preliminary) drawings of the small high-speed replacement for the Model 40 and 95 under separate cover, and included the performance estimates and the balance tables for "this particular airplane which we designate as Model 247."[33]

Rentschler was convinced. Engineering of the preliminary Model 247 design, which had begun earlier on 2 September, gathered momentum. Once the detailed specifications were drawn and sent to the United Air Lines divisions, Johnson received an unfavorable response which jeopardized the entire project. Asked to comment and recommend changes, the divisions returned the proposal with many negative remarks and proposed changes. As interpreted by Boeing engineers, the proposal as revised by United's reviewers had gained weight and lost speed. The aircraft had expanded from a gross weight of 11,600 pounds to 12,641 pounds. Combined with a lower-rated 530 horsepower Wasp, top speed had dropped to 156 miles per hour, with an according drop in cruise speed. Johnson and Nelson each sent terse letters to Egtvedt underscoring their concern. An irate Johnson demanded rectification:

> The detailed specification which we now have indicates an airplane with performance not much better than the present Fords. Under no circumstances can we afford to release for production this airplane or any other which will have a [cruise] performance of less than 150 mph at normal altitudes. I believe that the airplane as now designed is entirely too heavy.[34]

Nelson, a veteran army pilot and member of the famous flight of the Douglas World Cruisers in 1924, supported Johnson in full. "The Model 247 as it is at present," he stated, "has a gross weight entirely too high for the Wasp engine." Nelson felt that the geared Hornet would be more suitable but that "the operators are not so keen about these engines and would prefer a smaller airplane around the Wasp." He recommended an engine swap from the specified direct-drive Wasp to a geared Wasp which would produce the rated horsepower over a broader altitude range. Nelson was convinced that the airlines were "willing to sacrifice a certain amount of comfort for greater speed."[35] A necessary weight saving could be accomplished by the narrowing of dimensions. The width of the aisle could shrink from 12 inches to nine inches, thus saving three inches in the fuselage width. A maximum headroom dimension of only 5 feet 6 inches was acceptable, he reasoned. All of this would reduce weight and profile drag and therefore increase speed. If these requirements were not met, the 247 project would not continue. Johnson's determination was clear: "We cannot afford any quantity of new airplanes unless the specifications which we discussed in Seattle are made."[36]

Within two weeks, Egtvedt produced modified specifications. Gross weight was reduced to the original 11,600 pounds with eight passengers and one pilot, thereby restoring the desired performance. In replying to Johnson, Egtvedt was optimistic: "I believe that with the new set-up they [the Engineering Department] have made it possible to obtain the speed and climb performance which you outlined . . . and hope that when you have had an opportunity to look over the data you will find it more satisfactory than the original layout."[37]

One point did bother Egtvedt. The 247 was built primarily for speed and it appeared that the designers were willing to sacrifice passenger comfort, as mentioned by Nelson, for performance. To produce a design with the lowest possible amount of profile drag, the monoplane wing was placed midway up the side of the fuselage causing the wing spars to intrude through the passenger cabin. "There is one thing about this set-up which does not appeal to me," Egtvedt complained, "namely, the internal bracing, which is necessary to carry the wing loads through the fuselage. Apparently the only way to eliminate this would be to lower the wing to a position similar to that employed on the Monomail." He realized the problem this would cause since "this position on the wing would greatly increase the cross sectional area and consequently the drag of the plane."[38]

Ten days later, Egtvedt received the go-ahead from Johnson to proceed with the engineering of the new Model 247. After a lengthy conference at United Air Lines's Cheyenne maintenance base, the operating executives of the company agreed to recommend production of sixty of the smaller 247s to replace the current fleet of single-engined aircraft. Actual construction would begin after approval was received from Mr. Rentschler in New York. Writing to Egtvedt, Johnson stressed the need to prepare for rapid production, stating, "I will keep you advised relative to any new developments, but you should hold yourself in readiness to start this job and highball it through the shop more or less along the lines of what happened when the 40s were built after B.A.T. got their contract."[39]

On 14 November 1931, the mockup was ordered to be built without delay and would be so constructed as to represent the actual aircraft in as much detail as possible, particularly concerning the instruments and other equipment. Constructed of wood and covered in fabric, the fuselage mockup would be "sufficiently rigid so that the members of the [examining] board can move about the cabin and in and out of the cockpit without damage."[40]

Responding to an adamant request from Johnson, Plant Manager Gardner W. Carr assigned his best people to designing the 247. Overall responsibility for the entire project was placed in the hands of Robert J. Minshall, who was noted for his design talent. Minshall came to the company in

Boeing Plant Manager Gardner Carr was responsible for overseeing the actual construction of the 247. (*Boeing 3603*)

R. J. Minshall was given direct responsibility for the design of the 247. (*Boeing HS 3484*)

1922 where he first worked on the PW-9 pursuit project part time while studying aeronautical engineering at the University of Washington. As design engineer for the Monomail, his expertise in modern aircraft construction was critical for this new transport. F. C. Conner, whose organizational skills would be invaluable in the coming months, was named project engineer and assigned the task of coordinating the work of the subordinate designers. Detail design work, where cost supervision was paramount, was given to John Q. Dohse.

To speed production, a wooden jig was to be built, around which two sets of parts could be constructed as rapidly as possible. The first set would be used to build the first aircraft, which would then be flown as a test vehicle. The second set would serve as a model for the development of detailed engineering drawings to satisfy Department of Commerce regulations. Many of the parts were to be produced on the bench with the drawings made later from the parts in the second set. These plans would then be used for the preparation of tools and dies for production. The second set of parts would then be assembled into an airframe suitable for the required static tests. "It is believed," Carr wrote to Egtvedt, "that the above outlined practice will be both economical and sound inasmuch as it will give us the first airplane for flight tests before building parts for the full quantity to be produced. At the same time it will permit a reduction in engineering costs and will give the advantage of the practical shop viewpoint while the parts are being designed."[41]

Carr urged the determination of the production rate be made as soon as possible, for the decision affected the number of jigs necessary. He calculated a production capability of two aircraft per month for each set of jigs.

With the company tooling up for production, Johnson and others were beginning to have second thoughts concerning the matter of the single-pilot configuration. Apparently, as the size of the 247 grew, Johnson questioned the wisdom of his initial decision and was beginning to wonder if a larger 247 could fill United Air Lines's requirement for a replacement for not only the single-engined equipment, but for the larger trimotors as well. Egtvedt was left guessing. After assuming that he should proceed with the original plan, Egtvedt hedged his bets. "After our 'phone conversation the other day," he wrote Johnson, "a question came up as to whether we should make the mockup for a pilot and co-pilot or for just the single pilot. As we did not discuss this matter, I gave instructions to go ahead with the mockup on the basis of the single pilot arrangement and requested that the proper information and data be worked up to allow consideration for the pilot and co-pilot arrangement."

Boeing's chief designer was becoming uncomfortable with the expanding design. The original concept was growing so much larger and heavier, as a result of recommendations from the different divisions, stated Egtvedt, that "it appears to me that we are rapidly reaching a stage where we are falling into the tri-motor class of plane and diverging a long way from the original idea of obtaining a small, high-speed plane. . . ." The extra weight of additional equipment was his primary concern:

> When this design was originally contemplated, it was decided to use the single pilot and eliminate toilet facilities. With both of these additions, the payload efficiency is rapidly decreasing. . . . I question the advisability of incorporating too many desirable features in this smaller type of transport plane.[42]

Egtvedt made an uncharacteristically inaccurate assessment about airline passengers, fearful as he was about the loss of customers to the small but fast 150 mile per hour Lockheed single-engined machines which were entering the competition. In his opinion, United Air Lines was losing passenger revenue because "the public is willing to sacrifice a great deal of comfort to obtain faster travel." In sum, "possibly we are going a little too far when we include these desirable items which are not sufficiently appreciated to attract the business." Regardless of his stated reservations, preliminary designs to determine the correct size of the new aircraft continued, with Egtvedt's approval, on two versions of the 247.

Johnson grew more restless. In mid-December 1931, he circulated the specifications among the United divisions for the two configurations of the 247 and invited frank comments, particularly concerning the single pilot versus pilot and copilot debate. Opinions varied greatly. At a conference held in Cheyenne, members of B.A.T. fervently supported the original proposal. D. B. Colyer echoed Egtvedt's apprehensions primarily because the added weight decreased performance, dropping the crucial cruising speed to under 140 miles per hour. From Oakland, C. Eugene Johnson of P.A.T. also cast his vote in favor of the single pilot. The additional cost of redesign when added to the increased operational expenses did not justify the extra pilot, he felt. He did suggest the installation of a tandem skeleton control pit in the forward mail compartment which could be fitted quickly for a copilot, if necessary. Johnson also suggested the inclusion of a forward-stepped windshield.[43]

Colyer reluctantly agreed to the so-called straddle policy for an extra pilot. Fighting to the end, however, Colyer was emphatic in his opinion stating, "I would hate to see us lose 153 pounds of payload just to enable us to accommodate [the equipment for] a copilot, with a further loss of 170 pounds in payload when a copilot was carried."[44]

In contrast, a discouraged E. P. Lott of N.A.T. felt his was a lone voice in the wilderness. "It was perfectly evident to me following the Cheyenne meeting," Lott complained to Johnson, "that I was alone in my desire to have provisions for a copilot provided, the importance of this subject prompted me to urge that dual control with the pilots side-by-side and a proper entrance between the cockpit and cabin be provided. In my opinion, we will be making a serious mistake if these facilities are not provided." Deleting the second set of cockpit controls after the aircraft entered service would cost much less than adding a cockpit later.[45]

Erik Nelson offered a solution. He argued, as did Colyer, that the extra pilot arrangement could add up to 323 pounds and thus decrease the shrinking payload from 2200 pounds to 1877 pounds. This would leave the eight-passenger 247 with just 277 pounds of useful load for mail; an insignificant amount which was much less than the Monomail's. With the single-pilot, dual-control version, the payload would improve to 2081 pounds, which was still too small. Instead, Nelson proposed a redesign and enlargement of the original 247. "My suggestion would be," he stated, "should United Air Lines feel that they must have an airplane so arranged that a dual control could be installed to take care of the copilot, the airplane should be designed for two pilots with a payload of not less than 2400 pounds." This would increase the capacity to ten passengers with 400 pounds of mail.

Realizing, unlike Egtvedt, that the flying customer wanted the comfort and safety of having two pilots as well as speed, Nelson reasoned that a larger ten-passenger capacity was the minimum: "I feel that if the Air Lines are to cater to the public's demand and needs by giving them two pilots, two-way radio, toilet facilities etc., that the planes must have sufficient payload in passenger arrangements so that sufficient revenue at fifty percent capacity would make it feasible to operate with some slight revenue [profit]."[46]

A fifty percent load with the smaller two-pilot, six-passenger 247 would be just three persons. The revenue per mile would be a mere eighteen cents based on the standard Post Office rate of six cents per mile. A fifty percent load factor for a ten-seat 247 would produce thirty cents per mile, giving a net increase in revenue of twelve cents per mile over the smaller design. An additional yearly income of $144 million would result, which appeared to be crucial in the winter of 1931–32, the hardest period of the Great Depression.

After much debate, a two-pilot configuration was agreed upon for the 247 and the second mock-up built accordingly. *Courtesy Smithsonian Institution. (SI 87–8581)*

Philip Johnson was convinced. On 5 January 1932, upon his approval, supplemental work order #3 to revamp the Model 247 was issued by Boeing.[47] The new version was essentially the larger Wasp-equipped aircraft both Lott and Nelson suggested. Johnson now wanted to build a transport with seating for eight with two extra jump seats, a two-man cockpit connected directly to the cabin, a payload of 2400 pounds, a cruising speed of 150 miles per hour, and enough fuel for a flight of 300 miles with 35 percent reserves, 420 miles with extra fuel. Of importance to the traveler, the maximum headroom in the tight cabin was increased to six feet. Nelson hoped that this would help alleviate the problem of passengers tripping while stepping over the intruding wing spar.[48] He was wrong.

New drawings were completed by the end of January 1932, despite some sarcastic complaints from Colyer, who lamented that, as he and B.A.T. could not convince anyone else, "we must be wrong." He did concede that production should proceed with all due haste to beat the competition.[49]

Buoyed by the positive response from the other airline divisions, Nelson left Seattle for Hartford in February to get a commitment from Pratt & Whitney for an increased horsepower rating needed from the S1D1 version of the Wasp.[50] Boeing insisted on 550 horsepower. Anything less was unacceptable.[51] When queried by Nelson about the rating, George Mead was reluctant to agree. A staunch advocate of the larger 16,000-pound transport, Mead never abandoned his support for the Hornet engine. "From certain preliminary figures that I have made," Mead replied, "I very much doubt the wisdom of taking this much power out of the Wasp." Renewing his battle, Mead emphatically stated to Philip Johnson that "the best alternative powerplant seems to be the 1690 (Hornet) and we are, therefore, making a study of what can be done with this around the present design."[52]

Boeing's response was immediate. Reasserting earlier tests which verified the use of the higher-powered Wasp, an angry Egtvedt replied that the extra weight of the Hornet would reduce the payload. He doubted whether the operators would willingly agree to the change considering their positive experience with the Wasp-equipped Model 80s. Besides, the 247 was designed around "souped-up" Wasps.[53] What Egtvedt did not know was that Rentschler was firmly behind Mead and was determined to sell the larger powerplant.[54] Unwilling to concede, Mead, citing his vested interest in his partial ownership of United Aircraft, emphatically declared that he too had a voice in aircraft selection.[55] After a particularly heated discussion with Rentschler, Nelson left United Aircraft's New York headquarters totally discouraged, carrying orders to Boeing to start preliminary drawings for the Hornet installation.[56]

Egtvedt remained adamant and unswayed. On 15 February, he issued a work order calling for the installation of a 550 horsepower S1D1 Wasp.[57] Engineering analysis revealed to Egtvedt that, unless the Hornets could be uprated to produce enough power to compensate for the extra weight, the cruising speed would drop.[58]

Egtvedt persevered and won the argument, though as the future would show, it was to be a pyrrhic victory. Johnson urged Rentschler to have Pratt & Whitney speed the certification of the Wasp as soon as possible to hasten production of the transport.[59] Following final approval of the Wasp, Johnson opened negotiations with D. L. Brown, president of Pratt & Whitney, on 10 March for the purchase of from eighty to a hundred engines. The definitive powerplant was to be the supercharged, direct-drive Wasp series S1D1 which produced 550 horsepower at 2200 rpm at 5000 feet. This was with a compression ratio of 6:1 and a blower ratio of 10:1. The new engine would have the latest modifications to eliminate the

45

hot spot behind the engine block at the oil regulator. Weight was not to exceed 720 pounds. Significantly, Johnson insisted that the S1D1 be equipped for the eventual installation of a variable-pitch propeller.[60]

Propeller selection was critical. Early examples were fixed in pitch and designed for best performance either on takeoff or in cruise, but not for both. They were therefore inefficient. The blade angle of the ideal propeller could be changed from the cockpit to achieve maximum efficiency both in takeoff and cruise. Frank Caldwell of Hamilton-Standard, which had become a United Aircraft company in 1929, pioneered the first practical solution. Work on the variable-pitch propeller had been conducted by the British and Canadians as well during the 1920s. At that time, Caldwell was developing propellers for the army and had examined in detail a mechanical Hart-Eustis variable-pitch propeller. Realizing that a mechanical device was too unreliable because of excessive wear which often resulted in the disintegration of the propeller, Caldwell turned to a hydraulically actuated, hollow aluminum propeller using the engine's oil supply to assist in changing the blade angles.

Caldwell's first variable-pitch propeller was built in 1929 but was not perfected in time to assist the Monomail in improving its short-field performance. The initial type of variable-pitch propeller was designed for two positions and used centrifugal force and external counterweights to change the blade angle. The pilot manually selected the blade angle from controls within the cockpit. For this breakthrough, Caldwell won the 1929 Collier Trophy. By 1932, his two-position propeller had been perfected.[61] Later propellers were fully automatic and infinitely adjustable in flight, ensuring a constant engine speed.

Surprisingly, the Boeing Airplane Company was not at first interested despite the promised performance improvements. The device weighed too much and excessive weight was the nightmare of every engineer. "The controllable pitch propeller," C. N. Montieth declared, "is another item which will add weight to the installation and should be avoided if possible." The overly conservative Montieth believed the performance problems of the Monomail were caused by the bulky fuselage blanketing the tail and inhibiting takeoff and not by an inefficient fixed-pitch propeller. He believed that the more efficient placement of the 247's engines in wing-mounted nacelles, following NACA practice, would overcome the problem. For performance, he continued, "the big gain lies in the improved propeller efficiency gained by having two propellers in front of two small nacelle units instead of one engine in front of a big body."[62] Thus the unfortunate decision was made to fit a fixed-pitch propeller to the 247.

Fully aware of the potential consequences of this orthodox choice, D. B. Colyer offered a pragmatic and farsighted compromise which was accepted. He suggested that the 247 be designed to "take into consideration the possible eventual adoption of geared engines and/or adjustable pitch propellers." If so, sufficient propeller clearance should be specified. Colyer stated that he was "advised that the Hamilton Standard variable-pitch propeller decreases takeoff distance approximately 25 percent without adversely affecting cruising speed. There is also an increase in initial climb. However, it is hoped this plane will not need such special and expensive equipment. It won't hurt to be prepared for any eventualities if such preparation is relatively inexpensive."[63]

The final decision concerning the type of fixed-pitch propeller was made in favor of the three-bladed design which, though heavier and slightly more expensive than a two-bladed type, allowed for greater ground clearance, with a diameter of 9 feet 6 inches. The three-bladed propellers were also quieter as they revolved more slowly.[64]

With the overall specifications determined, and the engines and propellers selected, work could finally proceed in earnest. Under the leadership of Robert Minshall, the design team chose the same wing construction for the 247 as the B-9. The all-metal wing incorporated an expanded-truss, carry-through spar, with trussed ribs and wide-column construction. It was blended into a monocoque fuselage structure designed to carry ten passengers and two pilots who sat side-by-side in a completely enclosed cabin. A Wasp engine, surrounded by a streamlined ring, was in a nacelle in front of each wing. Only detailed work was required before production could begin. Tires were of new nonskid design made by the B.F. Goodrich company, which had the current contract with United Air Lines. Again for weight reasons, Boeing decided not to incorporate an automatic cutoff switch for the electrically driven retractable landing gear despite Nelson's recommendations for such a device. Nelson wished to prevent an inadvertent motor burnout if the crew forgot to turn off the mechanism after the gear cycled.[65] He was perceptive. One annoying problem discovered in service was exactly this motor burnout which forced the pilot to lower the gear tediously by a hand crank. A warning horn was provided to alert the pilot if the gear was not locked for landing.[66] Heavy internal engine starters were also deleted to save weight. Consequently, the Wasps had to be cranked by external inertial starters.[67]

With the design tasks complete, Claire Egtvedt asked Gardner Carr, the plant manager, for a cost estimate for the new transport. Originally Johnson had hoped to keep the price down to $35,000, but this was for the earlier design. Unfortunately, the cost of the updated 247 increased with the additions and modifications. Based on an anticipated order for sixty and assuming a delivery rate of four per month, a minimum price of $41,111.25 was calculated. This included a fifteen percent profit and a five percent handling charge. The selling price did not include the engines or the propellers.[68] Because of increased expenses for labor, parts and engineering, by January 1932 the individual selling price escalated to $52,700.[69]

The normally reserved Johnson was livid when he was told of the price. Enraged, he wrote back to Egtvedt, threatening to cancel the entire project:

> I am very much surprised at the selling price which you indicate, less engines. I will say immediately without any further investigation that you must find ways and means to be able to sell this airplane in quantities of approximately 60 and including engines and propellers but not radio (but provisions for same) for a sum of money not very much in excess of $45,000. If the Boeing Airplane Company cannot find ways and means of doing this, it would seem to us, from a transport angle, that it would be more desirable to negotiate with the Ford Motor Company to have them straighten up their particular airplane and install the 10:1–6:1 (Wasp) engines, and based on the performance of such a combination I believe we could satisfactorily use the airplane in our service. In other words, by doing so, we could buy an airplane with greater payload and at a price of several thousand dollars less.[70]

His anger was unrestrained. "I don't believe I have impressed on yourself and the people in Seattle," he continued, "the serious considerations which we must give to the cost of new ships, and we couldn't, for the sake of sentiment, place business in one of our own subsidiaries to our own monetary loss." Johnson had made it clear who was in charge and finished on a caustic note emphatically stressing to Egtvedt that "from your letter one thing seems to be apparent and that is there doesn't seem to be very much interest in this job. I judge so by the fact that you yourself do not take the trouble to sign your letters. I wish you would think this all over and let me have your reactions."[71]

Egtvedt's reaction to his friend's remarks was swift, yet remarkably restrained. Commenting first on the Ford proposal, Egtvedt agreed that "there would be no object in having this company design and build Model 247 unless this model could be purchased at a cost equivalent to that of a strengthened Ford with the *same performance and equipment*." Obviously that was impossible considering the elderly design of the Ford Tri-Motor and he was well aware of that fact. Egtvedt was particularly upset at Johnson's inference that Boeing did not need to make a profit on the sale of its products to the corporation. He drove his point home taking Johnson to task for his harsh remarks:

> No doubt in making your price comparison with Ford you are deducting from our estimates the possible profit this company might make on the basis that this company is merely a manufacturing subsidiary and any profit made will be returned to United.[72]

Johnson had questioned Boeing's 70 cent per hour wage scale as too exorbitant. Egtvedt countered explaining that 70 cents was fair as the average rate for the B-9 had been 72.9 cents. The lower 69 cent rate was paid to workers skilled in sewing and doping, which did not apply to all-metal aircraft requiring greater and more costly skills to build. Some labor costs could be trimmed, but it would be difficult because a desired order from the navy for twenty F4B-4 fighters had not materialized as yet. In addition, the Aluminum Company of America had unexpectedly raised their price for Duralumin, which was essential for the 247, thus driving up costs. Furthermore "we have made no attempt to negotiate for motors or propellers as it was my understanding that you planned to handle these items," he reminded Johnson.

Pointedly Egtvedt continued his offensive, stating "From the airline's standpoint, I hope you are successful in obtaining them at a cost plus fifteen percent profit basis. With a standardized product, they should be able to quote without any hazard of loss. I only wish our position of estimating a new model was so secure." He encouraged Johnson to defer his decision until the aircraft took shape when a valid assessment would be possible. The new mockup would be ready on 17 February and everyone seemed quite pleased with the new layout. Any further argument before-hand would be pointless as other alternatives might result from the mockup review.[73]

On Friday 17 February 1932, the Mockup Board convened to examine the latest version of the 247 in detail. Present were E. P. Lott and Walter Adams of National Air Transport, Harold Lewis of Boeing Air Transport, C. E. Johnson of Pacific Air Transport, and Leon Cuddeback of Varney Air Lines. Erik Nelson was in charge of the proceedings. After a lengthy meeting, the board was unanimous in its praise of the aircraft. "As far as I could tell," Nelson reported to Philip Johnson, "everyone was very pleased with the mockup. The cabin certainly looks nice with the additional height and the entrance to the pilot's cockpit is very well carried out with the split door." Passenger comfort was a great improvement over earlier aircraft. The new cabin arrangement provided individual vents for the cool air and the heater at each window together with a reading lamp.

The wood and paper mockup was examined and its design approved on 17 February 1932. The window line was raised 1.5 inches before production began. *Courtesy Smithsonian Institution. (SI 87–8586)*

Concern was voiced over the absence of any cabin lining, however. Though never specified, lining was considered vital to insulate the passengers from heat, cold, and noise despite Nelson's assertions that the 247 would be quiet enough because of its wing-mounted engines. The addition of cabin lining would exact a two-hundred-pound weight penalty, but the board insisted. Consequently, the Engineering Department was given the unenviable task of finding two hundred pounds to remove from the structure in compensation.[74] Inexorably, the 247 was growing into a luxury airliner, particularly when the board approved the inclusion of a lavatory.

Several other changes were suggested and approved as the final shape of the 247 emerged. Lewis of B.A.T. recommended that Boeing should raise the low window line by 1½ inches. "This change can be accomplished," remarked Egtvedt, "and, in my opinion, will be an improvement."[75] In the cockpit, the forward-swept windshield, designed to cut down daytime glare, was slightly revised and the pilot's side windows repositioned for better visibility. The cockpit roof was extensively modified by the installation of a small hatch with a clear "Plasticine" window with in it. For the roof, ahead of the hatch and above the pilots, the board requested the installation of another "plasticine" window equipped with a removable inner cloth cover, allowing the crew to regulate the exterior light level as well as permitting extra visibility when necessary.[76] The layout of the instrument panel was satisfactory but the emergency manual landing gear control was changed from a crank to an easier lever and ratchet device. To avoid disturbing the compass, the two-way radio equipment was relocated from the top rear to the bottom rear of the forward baggage compartment in the nose of the aircraft. Each control wheel would have three spokes with the upper third of the wheel removed to permit an unobstructed view of the instruments. In addition, the emergency exit, originally located on the left hand side of the cabin above the wing, was moved back to a position behind the wing, opposite the main cabin entrance hatch on the right hand side.[77]

For the first time in any commercial transport, trim tabs were fitted which allowed the pilot to adjust the flight controls from the cockpit while in the air. In all previous designs the tabs were set by the ground crew. This major advance, invented and patented by Boeing test pilot Les Tower and originally called "flaps," greatly reduced the flight loads on the crew.[78] One tab was fitted to the left aileron and one installed on the rudder. Surprisingly for such an advanced design, wing flaps, which allowed steeper and shorter approaches, were not employed. Boeing felt that the combination of a large wing and a low wing loading made the addition of flaps unnecessary.

With the final design approved by the board, Boeing anxiously awaited the go-ahead for production. Erik Nelson reflected the nervous anticipation around the factory, stating, "The most important thing, of course, is to get underway."[79] In March, Johnson, having cooled down from his earlier outburst, decided to proceed with purchase of fifty-nine Model 247s for the divisions of United Air Lines and authorized the expenditure of $3.5 million. One other 247 was to be built as an executive aircraft for United Aircraft and receive the designation of 247-A.

By this time, with the growth in the size of the 247, it was clear to Johnson that the new aircraft could replace all of the transports on the line, not just the Model 40s. Though smaller than the trimotors, the 247 could carry ten passengers and mail, the same mixed load as an 80-A, and do so fifty percent faster. Johnson realized that by replacing both the Model 40 and the Model 80 with the new transport, United Air Lines would have a chance to dominate the air travel industry, if the corporation acted quickly.

Johnson's approval was a major hurdle crossed. Now, the formidable task of building this new transport lay ahead. Speed of production was essential in order to place the 247 into service at the earliest moment in the hope of giving United the greatest possible advantage over its competitors.

3
The 247 in Production

Preliminary plans called for the roll-out of the first Boeing 247 production aircraft in September 1932. The second would follow in October, three additional in November, four in December, and six per month thereafter. This rate would tax the small Main Shop of the Boeing factory to the limit.[1] On 28 March 1932, Supplemental Work Order #2 was issued by Egtvedt for the release of purchased raw materials and equipment for sixty aircraft with initial delivery within three months.[2] The next day, Supplement #3 released construction for the fuselage, wing and empennage assembly jigs based on a production rate of six per month.[3]

Egtvedt, as vice-president and general manager of the Boeing Airplane Company, outlined the preparations to Johnson earlier in the month. With speed of production the key, Egtvedt had decided, in consultation with Montieth, to divide up the engineering shop to expedite detailed plans. He foresaw no problems in meeting completion dates unless considerable redesign was necessary. The company would do its best despite the other important contracts. "As you know," Egtvedt wrote Johnson, "we have Army and Navy work which will require the attentions of some of our best men in order to meet their requirement, however, Monty is planning to concentrate the maximum available talent on the transport project and overtime will be in force whenever there is something to be gained thereby."

Three complete sets of fuselage jigs would be built to increase production and maximize manpower. Egtvedt was realistic in his appraisal of the project. "Considering the problems to be solved and the work to be done," he concluded to Johnson, "I cannot be optimistic enough to believe the first plane can be properly constructed in less than six months' time, however, with no other serious complications, we will better our previous deliveries to 1 January. I can assure you that everyone will try hard to get as many planes to the lines in as short a time as possible."[4]

In another move to set up and speed production, Johnson urged Boeing to subcontract even more of the work than originally anticipated. Com-

A Boeing workman makes final adjustments on the jig for the left-side fuselage before actual assembly begins. *Courtesy Smithsonian Institution. (SI 87–8577)*

A completed cabin door and the jig around which it was constructed. *Courtesy Smithsonian Institution. (SI 87–8576)*

menting to Rentschler, Johnson stated, "My own reaction is that it will be to our interest to have as much of this work done outside as possible for two reasons. First, to speed up the job, and second, to eliminate the necessity of expanding our present equipment in Seattle."[5] The latter reason was most important: a new factory building and machinery would require a great capital investment and would drastically increase the costs of the project. Responding to Johnson's request, Plant Manager Gardner Carr prepared a provisional list of outside suppliers. For the steel inboard spar, he recommended the Metallurgical Laboratories in Philadelphia, which had wide experience fabricating heat-treated structures. United Aircraft partner Chance Vought could build control columns, various ratchet controls, and the complete tail wheel assembly. Pratt & Whitney had the machine shop for making the entire landing gear and retracting mechanism, the aileron control assembly, and the crucial large steel hinge fittings for the spars. Carr felt that major sheet metal items and all other fuselage and wing parts should not be subcontracted.[6]

Engineering work continued feverishly to remove all or most of the additional two hundred pounds produced by the installation of the cabin lining. The most important deletion was the internal electric starter. Since most of the airlines had sufficient electrical motors and facilities along their routes to drive external starters, Boeing decided to eliminate this thirty-four pound item. Thorp Hiscock urged the application of light-weight alloys in non-critical areas, particularly magnesium in the bulk-heads and radio compartment, the cockpit enclosure fairing, flooring, seats and instrument panel and even to hatches, doors and cowlings. Further savings could come from the use of magnesium mudguards, electrical conduits, boxes, and supports. Magnesium, though expensive, could provide sufficient strength if protected from corrosion.[7] This would trim ninety-seven pounds from the structure. Many, though not all, of these recommendations were accepted.

The refining of detail continued through the early spring of 1932. In a radical departure from all previous designs, the 247 was not to receive a coat of paint. Additional weight could be saved if the exposed Duralumin was chemically anodized to protect the finish.[8] This novel feature gave the aircraft a distinctive grayish green appearance.

A shockproof and insulated panel was devised to house the complete set of Pioneer, Sperry, and Boyce instruments. The intricate design and layout of the electrical system, especially the lights in the cabin, was also completed. The aluminum seats were given cloth numbers affixed to the well-cushioned green upholstery. Also, except for the two auxiliary seats, each had a pocket on the back for folders.[9] Of great importance to the queasy passenger was the inclusion of sanitary cartons in place of paper motion-discomfort bags. In the lavatory in the rear of the cabin, there would be no mirror or running water. Instead, water would be carried in one small two-quart vacuum bottle carried in the lavatory bulkhead.[10]

On 7 April 1932, Work Orders #4 and #5 were issued for the production release of sixty Model 247 transports in the final approval for construction. These were to be built in three series; the first of ten aircraft, the second of twenty aircraft, and the third of thirty aircraft, all with spares. The production rate was also increased to six per month after the first machine was completed. Supplement #5 authorized the testing of critical parts to comply with stringent Department of Commerce regulations.[11]

With the 247 finally in production, the heads of United Aircraft and Transport Corporation assembled in New York City for the fourth meeting of the Technical Advisory Committee on Monday 2 May 1932. Not unexpectedly, the corporation's latest transport was the dominant topic of conversation. After an initial discussion concerning the superior strength of the 247's structure of Warren-truss wing spars and of the inherent problem of passenger comfort when the spar intruded into the cabin, the talk turned to the actual construction of the aircraft.[12]

Responding to questions posed by George Mead, Montieth explained that each fuselage for the 247 was being constructed in three pieces and then bolted or riveted together. This was done to speed production and simplify repair once the transport was in service. The design of the landing gear was superior to the Monomail's and the control surface hinges, mounted on ball bearings, were similar to the Monomail's. The control lines were grouped in the fuselage for easy access during maintenance and the control surfaces manipulated by a worm-and-wheel arrangement which dampened rapid flutter and allowed the pilot to sense the air loads in flight. Because of the 247's smaller landing wheels, compared to the Monomail's, the brakes would also have to be smaller, which unfortunately would later prove a constant source of irritation for the pilots.

The engine cowl ring was not attached directly to the cylinder head. This avoided damaging the engine as had occurred in earlier Boeing aircraft. The committee was generally pleased with the new aircraft and sensed the importance of this transport for the future of air transportation, aeronautics, and their corporation.[13]

Throughout the late spring and into the summer of 1932, Boeing engineers and workers rushed the construction of the first 247 and worked out numerous small changes. Most of the alterations were minor and con-

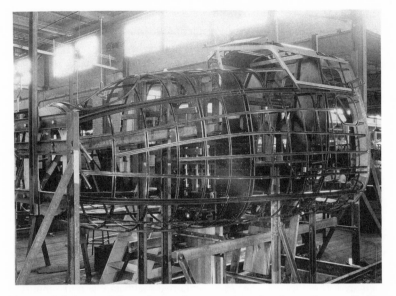

The metal skeleton of the cockpit and nose section takes shape. *Courtesy Smithsonian Institution. (SI 87–11950)*

cerned seat belt installation, cabin lights, ash trays, and the heating system requirements to maintain a constant seventy-degree cabin temperature. These were solved with little trouble. One minor item bothered Johnson. His desire for a mirror in the lavatory sparked a debate with Nelson.

Despite Johnson's request, Nelson declared the item unnecessary since there was no real need for it. "Inasmuch as women travelers will undoubtedly carry small mirrors in their bags," he concluded, "and as far as men are concerned, such an item is of no consequence."[14] Nelson prevailed, albeit temporarily.

In June, Philip Johnson approved the release for full production of the wing spar and authorized the Purchasing Department to place the order for metal forgings with a suitable subcontractor. A United Aircraft subsidiary, the Stearman Aircraft Company of Wichita, Kansas, instead of Pratt & Whitney or Vought as first proposed, was given the task of manufacturing the retractable landing gear assembly, the fixed tail wheel assembly, and the flight control columns.[15] A supplemental work order called for the completion of the first series of ten aircraft and sixteen of the second series by 1 January 1933.[16]

Encouraged by the apparent progress and anxious to see the aircraft in service, United Air Lines Vice-President William A. Patterson requested that Boeing inform him and United Air Lines when the first 247 was ready for assembly. At that time, he would send Ray Doherty of N.A.T. to Seattle to study the construction close hand and furnish weekly reports to the divisions outlining maintenance features.[17] Mr. Doherty was going to have to wait.

Everything was no longer proceeding smoothly, despite the fact that the static tests of the wing ribs had been completed successfully and most of the equipment and wing details finished. By August, production delays, caused in part by problems in the manufacture of the fuselage bulkheads, were forcing a postponement of the initial delivery date from September until December at the earliest.[18] The work dragged on for months and still no aircraft was forthcoming. The various transport divisions were becoming uneasy. In October, E. P. Lott of N.A.T. requested a realistic date for the first assembly. Responding for Nelson, F. B. Collins, the man who originated the idea of the 247, remained deliberately noncommittal: "Whatever date we might give you now will undoubtedly have to be verified at a later date so that instead of definitely committing ourselves at this time, we feel it would be more practical to keep your request in mind and inform you of the assembly when we have definite assurance that the date given you will be closely approximate." Collins did give Lott some idea of the delay involved, stating "a rough approximation, for your information, would place the date in the neighborhood of six or eight weeks."[19]

Collins confided to Nelson that the 247 work had finally crossed a major hurdle when the shop solved the problems with the fuselage forming dies. However, difficulties were continuing with one of the subcontractors. Stearman, manufacturer of the landing gear, had produced "somewhat careless workmanship . . . on the rubber piston seals installed in the oleo cylinders."[20] The problem was solved with the addition of correctly molded seals. Even Pratt & Whitney was making mistakes, having improperly installed primer connections in the wrong cylinders. This consumed more valuable time.

In November, the harried Plant Manager Carr was asked by his anxious superior, Egtvedt, to explain the reasons for the delay. Carr singled out, in particular, the total redesign of the aircraft which had occurred during the past winter. The purchase price and the delivery schedule had been set for the earlier version of the 247, which, like the B-9, was uniform in cross section. Since then, "the specification requirements were considerably altered and the problem entirely changed when two pilots were called for

The 247 begins to take shape with the riveting of the anodized aluminum skin to the fuselage center section. (*Boeing 5899-B*)

This close-up of the left nacelle shows clearly the ground-adjustable three-bladed propeller, the Pratt & Whitney S1D1 direct-drive Wasp engine and accessories, and the rugged construction of the engine mounts. *Courtesy United Technologies Archive. (UTC A-325)*

involving the wider cabin which had to be faired in." The debate over increased payload forced a redesign and "stepped up the necessity for saving every possible ounce of weight (which) became doubly vital." This caused a great deal of equipment redesign when steel dies were required to form the more complex bulkheads instead of simpler wood dies. Perfecting this equipment consumed much time and effort, driving up costs. In the wood shop, where the bulkhead dies were under construction, personnel levels were at the highest point since 1925. Of the eighty men working in the department, two-thirds were working on the 247. Furthermore, "for more than two months the men of the woodshop worked 12 hours a day. [This] program had to be discontinued because the men were breaking under the load and making more mistakes than the overtime would justify." Bad jigs were causing deformation of the Dural bulkheads after the metal aged briefly. This required redesign of the equipment. In addition, the spar tubing sent from the supplier failed to meet the required gauge and squareness tolerances. The tubing had to be remachined by Boeing or returned, either of which would cause more delay.

Because managers at the Boeing plant were getting nervous, Carr was forced to take drastic action to ensure completion. The November date for delivery had been postponed until the end of January 1933 and Egtvedt was understandably concerned. To allay his boss's fears, Carr lightened the load on his key engineers, telling Egtvedt, "Laudan has been relieved of all duties except those connected with the Model 247. We have likewise relieved Dohse and Leo Butler of all work except on that project."

An all-out effort was soon ordered by Carr. "We have issued instructions that all personnel working on the first transport are to go 12 hour shifts except where three shifts can be employed." Lysle Wood of the Engineering Department was reassigned to hammer out priorities and resolve disagreements between the department and the shop floor. With these changes, the production problems were finally overcome. The completion date for the empennage (tail assembly) was set for 1 December, the forward fuselage 15 December, and the final assembly for 1 January. Even after assembly there would be much detail work to complete. "It is on this basis," Carr hedged, "that we anticipate delivery before the end of January."[21]

The rest of December was spent making minor changes dealing with waterproofing, the fuel system, and the substitution of spruce, which was cheaper and easier to manufacture, for the metal cabin flooring. By the middle of the month, Mr. Doherty of N.A.T. finally arrived to start making his weekly reports.

Nearing completion, the initial order of 247s awaits the installation of the tail sections, outer wing panels, and propellers. *Courtesy Smithsonian Institution.* (*SI 87–8578*)

There remained only one problem that could not be overcome in time. As the first transport was taking shape, Carr was aghast at the color variation of the anodized finish. Earlier tests which led to the approval of the use of anodized Duralumin had demonstrated a uniform color consistency. In the meantime, however, the government changed the specifications for the anodizing. Carr was unsure whether this or the inherent difference in metal samples was responsible for the inconsistency. "At any rate," Carr wrote to Nelson, "it is now quite apparent that if anodizing is the only finish given the sheets, the airplane will have a very decided variety of color which would not be acceptable. Representatives of the Sales Department have already inspected the first rudder which has four distinct color stripes." Carr recommended the use of an aluminized Duco protective coat. This would provide an absolutely uniform finish with an acceptable increase in weight of fifty pounds.[22] Nelson forwarded Carr's memo to Johnson in hopes of a favorable reply.

Unpersuaded, an obstinate Johnson dismissed their concerns. "Speaking for United Air Lines," he declared "we have fully examined the samples of dural. . . . It is our opinion that there is just as much difference between the untreated metal as to shade as there is with the anodized metal. We believe further that anodizing is of sufficient value as a protective coating so as to offset any color variations." He firmly believed that if the panel were selected and matched carefully, the gradation would be slight. "Beyond that it is our opinion that after the airplane has been in service for a reasonable period it will assume a uniform color appearance."[23] The aircraft were to be left anodized and unpainted. Johnson was mistaken. Once the 247 entered service, the coloration did not change. In fact, United Air Lines would later report that many passengers feared that the aircraft they were boarding had been in accidents; the patchwork appearance looked as though it had been caused by repairs. Eventually, after several years, United Air Lines solved the problem by painting its 247s.

As the first Boeing 247 neared completion, another snag threatened the project. Late in December, the Army Air Corps had become concerned about reported Japanese interest in the transport. At that time, Japan was consolidating its recent intrusion into Manchuria and northeast China, posing a possible threat to America's interests in the Orient. The Air Corps was worried the Japanese might copy the 247 or learn enough about its revolutionary features to build modern bombers. Chief of the Air Corps Materiel Division, Brigadier General H. Conger Pratt, informed Boeing that the War Department's policy was not to interfere with the aircraft export trade "provided that no military secrets are thus divulged." Unfortunately, the 247 was heavily based on the B-9 bomber. "In this instance the commercial transport in question is a direct development of a military type which is still in a Service Test stage, and it incorporates structural and design improvements that are directly the result of developments of both your company and the Materiel Division. . . . In view of these considerations, the Air Corps must take the attitude that the release of the technical and structural details incorporated in the commercial design of the Y1B-9 is not to our best interests."[24]

Responding in his other role as president of the Boeing Airplane Company, Philip Johnson allayed the fears of the Air Corps through a liberal interpretation of the facts. First, he claimed, inaccurately, that the 247 was based solely on the Monomail designs and not on the B-9, especially in details concerning airline use and function. He was correct in stating that no 247 would be available for sale anywhere other than to United Air Lines "which will use the entire production first." Johnson stressed Boeing's policy not to negotiate any sales until the aircraft had passed its flight tests and received a certificate of airworthiness from the

Department of Commerce. No 247 would be sold abroad without government permission. "Boeing has never in the past entered into negotiations directly or indirectly for any type of aircraft before obtaining full approval from whatever Federal body had jurisdiction. It intends to follow this procedure in any future negotiations."[25] Johnson's remarks assuaged the Air Corps's fears.

This final obstacle overcome, the first 247 fuselage neared completion by Christmas Eve. Most important was that all the parts fitted. Except for minor details, the fuselage was ready for final assembly on 30 December. It was removed from its jigs, and allowed to rest on its landing gear.[26] Wing assembly was on schedule and set for 15 January. A relieved Gardner Carr reported that "there is every indication that the first airplane will fly before the end of January."[27] Only wing tests remained before the aircraft could be completed and flown.

The first two static tests revealed some buckling of the upper wing surfaces. Despite this Egtvedt authorized the installation of the complete wing set for flight tests and, "should additional difficulties be experienced in static test, (we) will use this set of wings . . . as they are perfectly safe."[28] The installation of continuous longitudinal stiffeners and thicker gauge metal on the upper wing quickly solved the buckling problem. On 27 January, the wing passed the Department of Commerce's tests without failure, stressed for a gross weight of 12,650 pounds in maximum overload condition. The addition of stiffeners later would allow the gross weight to be increased an additional 1000 pounds. The first flight was now scheduled for early February.[29]

At noon on Wednesday, 8 February 1933, an anxious crowd of Boeing officials gathered along the runway at Boeing Field. Present on that brisk winter day were Vice-President Claire Egtvedt, Plant Manager Gardner Carr, Sales Manager Erik Nelson, Engineer Fred Laudan and several others, all waiting nervously. C. N. Montieth was absent as he was attending the annual U.S. Navy cruise off the California coast. Shortly before noon, Chief Test Pilot Les Tower climbed aboard the first Model 247 followed by Louis C. Goldsmith, his copilot from United Air Lines. Tower fired up both Wasps and taxied to the end of the runway. At 12 o'clock, the sleek mottled gray-green transport roared down the strip, its tail quickly lifting off the surface, and swiftly took wing after a takeoff roll of only 800 feet. A relieved audience watched as Tower and Goldsmith, in their words, "felt it out" in the skies over Seattle. After a trouble-free flight, Tower brought the 247 back to earth and to the exultant throng below. Tower wore a broad smile as he emerged from the cabin, revealing his delight with the

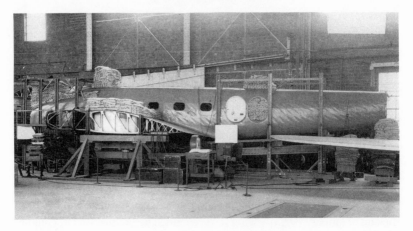

In January 1933, the first 247 underwent extensive static tests to confirm the strength of the airframe. In this view, bags of lead shot strain but do not buckle the fuselage and skin. *Courtesy Smithsonian Institution. (SI 87–8584)*

The Boeing 247 first flew on 8 February 1933. Here, the aircraft is being inspected after its flight. The mottled skin and the temporary "X" (experimental) registration are visible. Note also the mud guards on the wheels and the absence of the tail wheel fairing. (*Boeing 6127-B*)

handling and performance of the new machine.[30] After all the trials and tribulations of the past 18 months, Boeing had a winner. *

So pleased was the company with the aircraft, that Boeing employees were offered exclusive models of the 247 for purchase at cost. An attractive model cost $9.15. For an additional $1.35, the model would be equipped with working retractable gear.[31] Despite the relatively high cost and the pressing hardships of the Depression, the metal models were quickly snatched up.

After the successful first flight, the 247 was put through a rigorous testing program to determine its actual performance. Happily for Boeing, the 247 exceeded most, though not all, expectations. Maximum speed at a gross weight of 12,650 lb was recorded at 182 mph. The cruising speed of 161 mph was 11 mph better than expected, and the aircraft landed at a comfortable 58 mph. Range with a standard 203 gallon load of 87 octane fuel was 485 miles at 75 percent power. Maximum fuel load was 273 gallons and twenty gallons of oil were carried. The aircraft possessed an absolute ceiling of 20,500 feet, a service ceiling of 18,400 feet and could climb at 1070 feet per minute from sea level. Single-engine ceiling, at which altitude could be maintained, was a disappointing and surprisingly low 2000 feet, less than that on which Johnson had based his decision for original approval, although this would be corrected within a few months. Empty weight was 8375 pounds and maximum payload was 2372 pounds, 28 pounds fewer than hoped. The 247 had a power loading of 11.5 pounds per horsepower and a wing loading of 15.13 pounds per square foot. The light wing loading gave the aircraft excellent handling characteristics, but also provided a rather bumpy ride through rough weather. This was typical of contemporary aircraft, however. The Boeing 247 stood 16 feet high, including its tall radio mast, was 51 feet 4 inches long and had a wingspan of 74 feet.[32]

Most important, the question remained how well the 247 fared against its competition. A comparison with the Ford 5-AT Tri-Motor, the finest airliner then in service, is revealing. Despite 12.7 percent less horsepower,

---

*Naturally excited and interested, Boeing and United Aircraft employees were also encouraged to give the 247 a proper name. Boeing felt that an official appellation would be a more advantageous marketing tool than an emotionless numerical designation. In a "find-a-name" contest, begun in September 1932, Boeing offered $25 as the prize for the winning entry. Over two hundred entries were received by February. Mr. Cloyde L. Hoover of B.A.T. in Cheyenne was the winner with his suggestion of "Skymaster." Surprisingly, the name was not used, though it did appear on a later Douglas-made airliner. At the last minute Johnson decided against the name as it broke with Boeing tradition, but Hoover did receive his $25. *Boeing News*, September 1932, November 1932.

The prominent wing spar is visible in this view facing the front of the cabin. The steps in front of the spar house the heater. The cockpit door was placed directly over the front spar. *Courtesy Smithsonian Institution. (SI 77–8857)*

the modern Boeing could cruise 26 percent faster than the 135 mph absolute top speed of the Ford while carrying a similar load over slightly less range. Effectively, the difference in speed was more than fifty percent as the Ford normally cruised at 100 miles per hour at best. The 247 was also safer and more comfortable. Unlike the Ford, the Boeing was equipped with the latest navigational devices, could fly at night, and had two-way radio and autopilot. Its quieter, sealed, heated cabin was also more comfortable for the passenger.

Amidst the joy of the 247's triumph, a serious controversy reappeared. With full-scale production and testing under way, Johnson was becoming increasingly concerned about rumors of an advanced competitor from Douglas and postulated whether or not the Hornet, despite all of the arguments of the previous year, could still be installed in some of the later production 247s. On 23 February, he asked Fred Rentschler if this change would interfere with the production at Pratt & Whitney. Johnson was worried "because of the competition which is creeping in," and felt it might be "advisable to go to a larger engine earlier than anticipated."[33] A delighted Rentschler and Mead felt redeemed. For a time it appeared, in their opinion, that Boeing and United Air Lines had finally come to their senses. Rentschler immediately replied that half of the S1D1 Wasp order could easily be canceled and replaced by Hornets. He instructed Mead to contact Egtvedt at once to determine the necessary changes and suggested that the latest geared Hornets be used to extract the greatest power possible to maximize the performance gain. "My own feeling," Rentschler stressed, "is that even if we have to delay the second half of these transports, it might be well worth our while to do so."[34]

Claire Egtvedt was not so enthusiastic. A thorough consultation with Gardner Carr convinced Egtvedt that virtually a complete redesign of the 247 would be necessary to accept the Hornet. The price would be exorbitant. Retooling alone would cost almost $39,000, engineering expenses $9000. The process would result in an additional seven-month delay. Propeller clearance would also be a problem as the larger engine required bigger airscrews. Armed with these facts, Egtvedt was adamant. "In my opinion," he reiterated, "the installation of the geared 1690s is entirely out of the question." A better solution would be to use this powerplant as the heart of the next generation of Boeing transports under consideration. Furthermore, and of significance for the development of the 247, Egtvedt pointed out that the same degree of performance enhancement would result if the present direct-drive Wasps were modified to power a geared propeller, instead of the more expensive 625 horsepower Hornets. "The way things stand at present," an exasperated Egtvedt replied to Johnson, "I would suggest that you take the planes with direct drive engines as this will give excellent performance for a low operating cost. Beyond this, the only change that I could advise would be to have the engine company modify these engines at some later date to use a 4:3 gear ratio. This would improve your performance at no greater increase in operating costs."[35]

The vacillating Johnson agreed with Egtvedt's arguments and withdrew his proposal. Nevertheless the idea was born which would eventually lead to the production of the second version of this aircraft, the 247-D, the following year. The question of geared engines set Johnson to thinking about the next generation of Boeing aircraft. "In our future designs of transports," he stated, "we should so locate the engines with reference to the fuselage that we would not have to redesign and rebuild the entire airplane in order to use geared engines. This should be borne in mind in the design which we now have under contemplation as a replacement type for the 247."[36] After discussions with United Aircraft, a disappointed Rentschler agreed with Johnson's decision to stay with the Wasp.[37]

At this point, the infighting over the 247 came to an end, the engineers at Boeing Airplane and the pilots of United Air Lines, prevailing over the objections of corporate management. With Philip Johnson as the driving force, the 247 was readied for service after its difficult gestation, in the form envisioned by Claire Egtvedt, not by Fred Rentschler or George Mead. For the short run this was a good decision, enabling the 247 to take immediate advantage of its technological and economic superiority over its competitors. In the long run the choice was not so wise. Though integrally involved with running the huge U.A.T.C. combine, Johnson, Rentschler, and Mead were not aloof bankers or accountants, but trained engineers who also understood the aircraft and airline business. Though persuaded by Egtvedt and Montieth to stay with the smaller aircraft, their reservations were well founded. Within a year of its introduction into service, the 247 was to be superseded by a larger, more powerful, and successful aircraft, that could have been designed by Boeing but was not.

For one brief, triumphant year, however, the Boeing 247 reigned supreme. By 16 March 1933 the 247 had won its certificate of airworthiness—ATC #500—and was approved by the Department of Commerce for commercial service. Even the government inspector R. B. Quick was impressed. "We are satisfied that for performance, strength, and safety, this plane is a marvelous development and undoubtedly will prove one of the most outstanding contributions to air transport for 1933 and probably any other year."[38]

On 30 March, the first 247 for the airlines was handed over to B.A.T. Production tempo increased rapidly. Johnson anxiously encouraged swift manufacture so that United Air Lines could exploit the advantages presented by the aircraft as quickly as possible over the competition. Ironically, the much greater speed of the 247 was causing considerable scheduling problems. Johnson was faced with a pleasant dilemma and needed more airplanes to solve it. "It was our original thought that it would be possible to equip one schedule at a time with the new airplanes. However, because of their speed this is impossible and impractical inasmuch as they overtake preceding schedules operating with our older equipment before these airplanes reach their destination. Therefore, it has been decided to hold off using the new airplanes until we have sufficient to completely equip the New York-Chicago run and the Chicago-San Francisco run on all schedules with the Model 247."[39]

Twenty-one aircraft were the minimum considered necessary. Johnson asked Egtvedt to step up production so that Pacific Air Transport and Varney Air Lines as well as Boeing Air Transport could be expeditiously reequipped. Fourteen 247s were delivered in April. By 3 May, the eighteenth transport had left the factory. Gardner Carr was quite pleased with the effort, commenting to Johnson, "Frankly, I think the plant has done a splendid job in getting these airplanes out within two days of the schedules." There was a price to pay, however.

The payroll had to be increased to 2200 men working in three shifts to make the deadline. New and untrained workers created headaches. "There is no question but that our costs have gone up because of this fact," he remarked, "but we had no alternative if we were to make the delivery schedule which we felt was more important in order to give the lines equipment rather than save money on costs at the expense of a delay in the program."

Carr calculated a unit price of $53,000 for each 247. He was close. The actual costs had soared to almost $77,000 for each of the first ten aircraft because of numerous last-minute changes. The unit cost for the entire run of sixty was calculated to be $56,400, well over Johnson's target of $45,000. The eventual unit cost was $68,000.[40] With luck, Boeing figured to break even on the venture. The high production rate was overtaxing the factory. Carr requested that the plant build only six in May and backlog four instead of building ten. In this way, United Air Lines would get its twenty-one aircraft and the factory would be relieved somewhat from its backbreaking pace.[41]

Regardless of Carr's request, production continued unabated. Ten more 247s rolled from the factory in May, ten in June, eleven in July, and the last ten of the initial order in August.[42] Johnson's wishes obviously prevailed while the 247 was entering scheduled service along United's main line in spectacular fashion.

4

The 247 Enters Service

Boeing Air Transport Captain John McCullough Hodgson, a twenty-four-year-old reserve pilot, delivered most of the first twenty-five Model 247s during April and May. Boeing Chief Test Pilot H. T. "Slim" Lewis had asked him to accept this envious task in late March. Within a day, Hodgson was packed and on his way to the Washington Athletic Club in Seattle where he would live for the next two months.

Hodgson's rigorous flight schedule required him to fly these transports to the various headquarters of the United Air Lines division across the country, including Oakland, Salt Lake City, Cheyenne, and Chicago. Most of the flights proceeded smoothly. Some did not. Several of the new features of the 247, which gave the aircraft its remarkable performance, also contributed a fair share of problems.

The pilot-adjustable trim tabs were an initial source of trouble causing Hodgson considerable consternation on one delivery flight. The tabs themselves were a welcome addition as they greatly reduced the flight loads on the pilot by balancing the rudder, elevator, and ailerons. But the choice of location of the controls for the tabs within the cockpit left something to be desired, as Hodgson discovered rather dramatically.

On one of his flights to Portland, Oregon, both engines suddenly and mysteriously quit. "On the delivery flight between Portland and Seattle there was no available line pilot to go along so I took the Seattle Station Manager along as copilot. He had a beautiful red-haired secretary he wanted to take along and, as there were no other passengers, I said O.K. After takeoff, I let him fly, as it was a clear day and he knew the route. After a while it was obvious he could fly quite well so I decided to go back and pay a visit to our one passenger—the pretty red-haired secretary.

"She was sitting about half-way back in the passenger cabin and I walked back and sat down across the aisle from her. Just as I started to describe the beauties of Mount Rainier, to our left, both engines quit cold! It was deathly quiet and I was awfully quick returning to the cockpit.

"I noticed that the gas tank selector had been turned off. When this

The instrument panel contained the latest navigation equipment and the controls were neatly laid out. (*Boeing 6245-B*)

valve was pushed back to feed both tanks, the engines started up again and all was well—except that it was still quiet in the cockpit while we tried to figure out why he had turned off the gas. It was soon quite plain! As I had walked back in the cabin, the center of gravity shifted aft and the nose started up. Les reached for the trim tab to adjust the horizontal balance, but he got hold of the gas tank selector handle instead of the trim tab handle and had rotated the handle far enough to shut off the gas to both engines." The station manager had been the victim of two design errors. The control for the trim tabs had been placed too close to the fuel selector lever and was also identical in shape and size. Upon landing, Hodgson promptly called the 247 project engineer who immediately redesigned the handle and changed its location, before the problem could recur.

Unlike previous transport aircraft, the 247 was equipped with internal locks on the control surfaces. Past practice required that wooden blocks with red and yellow streamers be affixed externally to the control surfaces to prevent damage from the wind when the aircraft was tied down. Under normal procedure, a ground crewman signalled to the pilot that the locks had been removed, thus freeing the aircraft for takeoff. Because the 247's controls were locked by hooks on the rudder pedals and the control column in the cockpit, this habitual step was unnecessary. New 247 pilots occasionally forgot and, with the ground crewman signalling "all clear" after removing the wheel chocks, attempted to fly. Hodgson witnessed one such "flight" at Boeing Field. Assuming incorrectly that the locks had been removed, one Boeing test pilot took off with all of his controls locked firmly in place. Through brute strength he managed to wrestle the transport back to the airport. Surprisingly, the pilot had not realized his mistake until after he had landed. Fortunately no fatal accidents were caused by the locks. More thorough indoctrination of the pilots helped to eliminate the problem.

Difficulty was also encountered with the low frequency (LF) four course radio ranges installed by the federal government along the major routes, which were first used by the 247 for navigation. "These first LF ranges had some unfortunate characteristics," Hodgson reports. "Their signals were subject to phenomena called "fading," "skipping," "interference," "bending," and "displacement." But worst of all, the signals would fade because of rain or snow, and were drowned out by thunderstorms. The static problem was eventually solved by a specially equipped 247-D modified and flown by United Air Lines.

"With the 247 we found out that the design of the aircraft antenna was vital to flying the radio ranges. I discovered this while delivering a 247 to Chicago. The antenna that was used was located on top of the fuselage and was a long straight wire running from a mast in front of the cockpit to the vertical stabilizer. This provided a good strong signal but was directional."

The range emitted Morse code signals which, when the aircraft was on course, was a continuous tone. "The whole system worked fine with the "V" shaped antennas on the Boeing 40-Bs and the 80-As, but the long straight antenna on the 247 did not [work well]." The 247's antenna displaced the on-course signal which gave a false reading. "This characteristic made for zigzag flying while trying to bracket the beam. It made it impossible to fly the range on course with any degree of accuracy or comfort." Thorp Hiscock and Russ Cunningham quickly devised a successful "V" antenna for the 247 which replaced the characteristic mast on the early models.[1]

Once the twenty-five aircraft were delivered, Hodgson returned to Boeing Air Transport to fly the aircraft in service. In the meantime, in appreciation of their diligent services, ten Boeing shop foremen were flown in a new 247 before it was delivered so that they could experience the product of their labors.

The third 247 was delivered to Varney Air Lines, a division of United Air Lines. *Courtesy Smithsonian Institution.* (SI 86–4348)

For 45 minutes the delighted passengers were given a first-hand look at their work as the aircraft was put through its paces. All the foremen were pleased. Frank Wallach from the sheet metal shop remarked favorably on the smoothness. "A better ride than I'd ever had before," he commented, "I particularly noticed its quietness and lack of vibration." To Leo Butler of the body shop, the 247 was "the best Boeing commercial plane thus far. It's less noisy, more comfortable, and better ventilated. A fellow can take a real pride in having had a part in the 247's production." The ten were most impressed by the transport's single-engine performance. J. L. Carter of the cable shop was "surprised to see the ship do as well as it did on one motor with 13 people on board. It's much superior to anything I've flown in before." "The one-motor performance provided me the biggest thrill," stated Charles Thompson from the welding shop. Al Walloch, from the control surface shop summed up the group's feelings when he remarked that the 247 "was quite an improvement over the 80-A. I was mighty impressed to observe the manner in which the plane kept its balance with one motor cut."[2]

Boeing Air Transport personnel were not so thrilled. During their preliminary tests, B. A. T. discovered the same problem that the manufacturer had discovered earlier: the 247 had a disconcerting inability to maintain altitude with one engine out. In this condition, the aircraft could hold a

Single-engine performance with the fixed-pitch propellers was disappointing. *Courtesy United Air Lines. (UAL 37-B1)*

maximum ceiling of only 2000 feet. To B.A.T. officials based in Cheyenne, Wyoming, 6131 feet above sea level, this problem was critical. Takeoff and cruise performance also suffered at this altitude. The manufacturer was aware of this difficulty although not overly concerned. Egtvedt confided in Phil Johnson that recently "tests were conducted with full throttle conditions and . . . with a load of 12,650 pounds, the rate of loss in altitude was very small at 5000 feet, yet we are unable to show a definite ceiling where there was no loss in altitude until we approached the 2000 foot elevation specified by the Department of Commerce."[3] This small loss provided a barely adequate safety margin over the mountains.[4] More effective measures were required especially if Boeing were to increase the gross weight to 13,000 pounds as planned earlier.

The Research Division of United Aircraft was more concerned and was working on a solution. Detailed tests were conducted in the spring at Rentschler Field in Hartford. A new 247 was equipped with a pair of Hamilton-Standard two-position variable-pitch propellers designed by Frank Caldwell. The results were impressive. Takeoff distance and time improved twenty percent to 740 feet in 15.2 seconds. Climb rate grew twenty-two percent and cruising speed increased 5.5 percent to 171 mph. Of greatest importance to B.A.T., the one engine ceiling improved a staggering one hundred percent to 4000 feet, still lower than Cheyenne, but a vast improvement nevertheless.[5] So impressed was Boeing that the last thirty aircraft built were delivered with the two-position Hamilton

Standard variable-pitch propellers beginning in June 1933. This made the Boeing 247 the first airliner in the world to be so equipped. Quickly, the other aircraft already in service were also retrofitted with these propellers.

On Sunday, 12 June 1933, at 1:30 in the afternoon, a Boeing 247 left Newark Municipal Airport on the aircraft's first transcontinental commercial flight. At the controls of National Air Transport's NC13308 was Captain Warren Williams.[6] On board were reporters from major New York newspapers, anxious to see for themselves the wonders of this highly touted aircraft. They were not disappointed. For the same Boeing 80-A price of $160 one way or $260 round trip, the Boeing 247 carried its wealthy passengers through to San Francisco in only 21 hours. Prevailing winds on the return journey sped the travelers home in a record-setting 19 3/4 hours. Travel time was cut by an remarkable seven hours.[7] The New York *Herald-Tribune* was ecstatic:

> The arrival at San Francisco of a new commercial air liner after a scheduled flight from New York of 21 and 1/2 hours will open the eyes of every one who has not been following the extraordinary development of commercial aviation in this country in the last few years. . . . So here we are at the fulfillment of a dream which seemed so fantastic even after Lindbergh flew to Paris. . . . In the matter of speed, the transports of yesterday averaging 100 miles per hour are now obsolete. What, eight hours to Chicago?! The new liners make it in 4 3/4 hours, so that one may leave Newark Airport after the theater and a leisurely midnight repast and be in Chicago for breakfast. And if San Francisco be one's destination, . . . the Pacific by bed time sounds so much more economical of life's fleeting moments.[8]

United Air Lines recorded an immediate rise in passenger traffic in all of its divisions, aided in no small way by an aggressive advertising and public relations campaign. Advertisements appeared in most of the major aviation and popular journals touting the "new FAST schedules," and the "fastest regularly operated transportation service ever offered the public." Repeatedly the theme of the "three-mile-a-minute" Boeing was drilled into the public's consciousness. "Every day . . . 47,600 miles." One advertisement proclaimed, "Dawn to Dusk, Dusk to Dawn, sixty of the new Boeing 247 transports carry their loads of mail, passengers and express over the coast-to-coast and other routes of United Air Lines." A Boeing announcement read: "Pioneers of the new era in high-speed, deluxe air transportation—surpassing every claim made for them—they have definitely proved themselves tomorrow's transports today." Night flights could be conducted now with ease: "Across the continent in a single night" and "A flight of 2600 miles between twilight and early morning." United's 247s traveled in all

Frank Caldwell's two-position variable-pitch propeller greatly improved the 247's overall performance. *Courtesy Smithsonian Institution. (SI 75–15176)*

NC13309 loads passengers at Newark for the flight west. *Courtesy Smithsonian Institution. (SI 87–11907)*

kinds of weather: "Fly over winter," another advertisement suggested, "Flying is no longer seasonal, you know, the spacious cabins of United big twin-engined transport planes have controlled heat; are equipped with wide adjustable reclining chairs."[9]

Having a cabin attendant cater to the needs of the passengers was a comforting attraction. "Other niceties of service include the thoughtful attention of attractive stewardesses; delicious complimentary lunches and chicken dinners aloft. (The advertisement failed to mention the attendant's bruised shins, acquired when attempting to step over the intruding spar, or the resulting spilled coffee.)

United's pamphlets and brochures publicized the 247's safety features. The public was invited to "study the powerful wing span," and the "cushioned landing gear." Photographs illustrated the "bridge-like construction of one of the spars and the wing." The aircraft was especially strong "because the sturdy metal construction of its fuselage is braced three ways "which make it more than half again as strong as the Department of Commerce requires." Safety was assured because the aircraft was equipped with "*two* engines with the power in reserve, *two* pilots, whose average flying experience is a half-million miles; virtually *two* sets of instruments; an airplane with sixty percent surplus strength!—operated by an airline with 70,000 miles experience." Each flight was supported by a team of 1400 United Air Lines employees, including pilots, cabin attendants, mechanics, and technicians. Two-way radio was installed to keep the crew in constant contact with the ground and the vast network of weather reporting stations. All of these salient points were made in free handouts, postcards, colorful booklets, and even cartoon drawings.[10]

Coupled with this intensive advertising was an equally ambitious sales and promotion campaign designed to appeal to the well-heeled public. One pamphlet suggested taking a swift Boeing to "fly out West to the National Parks via United Air Lines" because "it's the interesting, fast, time-saving way for vacation travel." "You can leave later, arrive sooner, stay longer" while enjoying "the cool clear comfort of air travel to the National Parks this summer." United Air Lines kindly offered to make all of the travel arrangements.[11]

In an interesting, though patronizing, commentary on generally-accepted social attitudes at the time, United claimed that flying in the new Boeing 247 was so safe that even women could fly with ease and take their children safely with them as well. The airline offered several travel suggestions for female passengers. Tweeds, knits, and rough silks, which do not easily crumple, were the best clothes to wear, along with a close-fitting hat and a warm coat for exiting the well-heated aircraft. Women were asked to pack lightly and keep the weight of the bag to thirty pounds. "Have powder and lipstick and clean handkerchief in your handbag; there's no chance to fiddle with your major luggage after it's packed away."

Stimulating discussions were possible in the quiet cabin. "Conversation may be carried on with ordinary Bostonian modulations and you will find interesting, congenial fellow travelers aloft." A restful sleep was possible because "unless your past sins keep you awake, there's no reason why you shouldn't slumber." The ride was claimed to be as smooth as a train and the ventilation system "changes the air in the cabin every 45 seconds." In addition, "food appears out of nowhere. You'll probably be hungry and enjoy it thoroughly . . . dilly-dallying across the sky in a three-mile-a-minute plane is apt to whet your appetite to an appreciable edge."

The new Boeing was said to be so safe that even the smallest children could come along. "You can stow the little darlings into a plane and as soon as you've started, you're practically there. . . . United's stewardess-nurses provide the food the youngsters need and amuse them as well."[12]

Of course, these rosy pictures painted by United's promotions masked the economic realities of air travel in the 1930s. Though claiming to cater to all, the airlines only carried the privileged. The $160 one-way fare was the equivalent of approximately $2000 in today's money. Only business-men, who were willing to accept the high cost of a ticket in return for a savings in time, and the wealthy could afford to fly on the airlines. When the general public travelled, which was infrequent during the Depression, they either drove, took the bus, or rode the train.

The year 1933 marked a major turning point in American history, even as the nation struggled to overcome the deprivations of the Great Depression. In March, just at the time when the first 247 was delivered, Franklin Delano Roosevelt was inaugurated as the 33d president of the United States. His avalanche of new programs and ideas—some successful, some not—had in aggregate a positive and invigorating effect on the nation's morale which, coupled with his cheerful demeanor, imbued the public with new hope and courage. This new optimism was reflected in the record attendance at the "Century of Progress International Exposition," commemorating Chicago's first hundred years. The fair presented to the country a bright picture of the future based on the assumption that science would triumph over nature, to the benefit of mankind.

Clever United officials seized this opportunity to show their new aircraft to an anxious public. Because of the unfavorable economics of air travel, it was necessary to explore every possible avenue to demonstrate the advan-

In the 1930s, commercial flight was the domain of the businessman and the wealthy. Pillows and hats could be carried in the overhead nets. These women chose to wear their furs. *Courtesy Smithsonian Institution. (SI 75–12099)*

NC13310 was the star attraction in the Travel and Transport Building at Chicago's Century of Progress International Exposition in the summer of 1933. *Courtesy Smithsonian Institution. (SI 87–8582)*

tages of the latest aircraft and to encourage as many people as possible to fly. An appearance by the 247 at this most popular exposition was seen by the company as an ideal way to win additional favor and customers. The enthusiastic throngs were entertained by the arrival of the transatlantic formation flight of Italian General Italo Balbo, the staging of the first All Star baseball game, the scandalous fan dancing of Sally Rand, and the numerous international displays. The crowds were treated to a panoramic sky ride, a set of George Washington's false teeth, a miniature zoo, a million dollar Chevrolet assembly line and, highlighted in the great windowless Travel and Transport Building, a sleek Boeing 247, representing the epitome of modern travel.

The 247 registered as NC13310, and later replaced by an updated NC13360, sat dramatically perched on steel pedestals above the floor. A catwalk was erected over one wing, thus allowing the thousands of visitors a close-up look at the interior. Loudspeakers broadcast a typical two-way radio conversation between the pilot and the ground. Beneath the aircraft stood a Wasp engine behind which was a smaller theater showing a continuous film. This and several static displays stressed the speed, safety, and comfort of this new airliner.[13]

United Air Lines's 1933 summer brochures highlighted the company's presence at the exposition and offered several package deals to potential travelers. One such arrangement encouraged Seattlites to fly to Chicago by 247 in only 17 hours, visit the Century of Progress, and take a leisurely six-day "easy drive home" after "getting a 1933 Chrysler or Plymouth that you've been waiting for at the lowest prices in automobile history." The traveler did not have to pay until he returned home.[14] By the end of the exposition, almost 61 million visitors toured the show and went home impressed by the latest shining example of America's industrial genius.

Another clever promotion involved a leading aeronautical journal. In the hopes of convincing the youth of America to become more air-minded and to encourage their acceptance of the new transport and United Air Lines as the leaders in the industry, Popular Aviation sponsored a 247 model-building contest in October 1933. The contest closed on 15 December. By November, 4500 of the 6000 available sets of plans had been distributed. The purpose was to highlight the many advanced features of the 247. "Model builders should bear in mind that this contest will be won by the model builder who will be able to duplicate in detail as many features in miniature as possible." Successive articles and issues published photographs and drawings of important features along with helpful construction hints. The grand-prize winner received an all-expenses paid, two-day, 6000 mile vacation to either Seattle, San Francisco, or New York City. Second place was a similar 3000-mile trip and third place was a one-day 2000-mile journey, all on the 247. Other valuable prizes included a silver model of the 247, authorized inspection tours of the nearest United Air Lines facility, gold medals and three-year subscriptions to the magazine.[15] The campaign was an immense success. With this and the innumerable other promotions, combined with the massive public interest generated in the popular press, United's ridership and profits soared.

Throughout the latter half of 1933, the full fleet of fifty-nine Model 247s were carrying passengers, mail, parcel post, and air express with speed and regularity. A typical trip was delightfully described by Briton E. G. Gordon England in *Popular Flying*. Wishing to visit an ailing acquaintance in Chicago, England chose to fly, on the suggestion of friends, on one of United's 247s, because this was the quickest possible way.

Even with flights almost hourly, the 247 service was so popular that tickets had to be booked well in advance. England received a seat on a reserve flight that left on the half hour to accommodate the extra loads. He began his trip in a chauffeur-driven seven-place Cadillac limousine, provided by the airline, which whisked him to Newark Airport. Despite the effortless drive, he was quite annoyed at having to pay seventy-five cents for the privilege. "Why isn't this included in the ticket?" he queried.

Swiftly, England was shepherded into the comfortable waiting room, his ticket processed and his baggage checked. Outside, the crew was completing its final preparations on his aircraft, impressing him with "the air of quiet efficiency about the whole organization." Once called, he and his fellow eight passengers boarded the 247 at 4:30 P.M. "While we were taking our seats, a small electrically illuminated notice was shown at the front end of the cabin, prohibiting all smoking and asking us to fix our seat belts. . . ." When completed and checked by the attendant, the pilots opened up the engines "and in a surprisingly short run we were up and away." The performance of the aircraft was quite noticeable. "The rapid rate of climb was most impressive and, as we did a half circuit of the aerodrome, I heard the retractable under-carriage being wound up." The extinguishing of the "no smoking" notice was the "signal for our air hostess to busy herself handing round copies of the latest evening papers, magazines, and cigarettes, and fuss around each one to make sure that his or her particular wishes were being met." England heartily approved. "Somebody behind the organization was a good psychologist and it was obvious that everything was done to make you feel that this was the most ordinary, normal, and delightful way of travelling." Soft, clean pillows were provided by the attractive Miss Kiddoo who impressed England with her efficiency, well-trained manner, and the fact that she was a hospital nurse.

England also approved of the 247's ride and comfort. "The ventilation seemed excellent in spite of the smoking; the arrangements for the heat control were admirable, but the temperature kept too high for a Briton. A cruising machine carries her tail very high, so, in spite of the low wing, one gets a reasonable view." Flying over the mountains was disconcerting, however. "The weather was bad and the ceiling was low—indeed, disagreeably low—as we had to fly over the dreaded Allegheny Mountains, and there was enough movement to call it rather bumpy; but the high cruising speed, therefore, gave one a feeling of a certain stiffness in the air."

After an hour aloft, night fell as the 247 droned onwards over the crest of the ranges "with certainly not much more than fifty feet below us at certain points. It soon became extremely dark and little or nothing could be seen of the surrounding country except for the lights of cars on the roads and the habitations as we passed, but with almost boring monotony, we seemed to pass the flashing beacons along the air route. It reminded me rather of going up a long sea channel at night and passing the flashing buoy lights. In the different parts of the route they are as close as ten miles apart."

Cleveland, Ohio, was the first stop. "As we approached the aerodrome, it was floodlit with a projector using what is known as the shadow beam. Down the center of the flood-light is a dark shadow just about the width of the machine and down this the pilot lands, so that while on each side of him the aerodrome is brightly lit with a flood-light, he is himself landing in absolute darkness, so there is no dazzle of any kind." Immediately upon landing, the passengers were discharged into a waiting room to stretch and enjoy a small buffet while the aircraft was serviced with fuel, oil, and fresh batteries. Thirteen minutes later, they were again airborne. At this point, Miss Kiddoo offered dinner to each passenger. "She appeared to have a wonderful selection of daintily prepared light meals. The Americans are past masters at attractive salads, sandwiches, and food of that kind. One could have either hot coffee and cream, or chocolate and cream, or the inevitable iced water if that were preferred." The coffee was excellent though England was a bit nonplussed while attempting to balance his tray on the pillow placed on his lap for that purpose. "I still feel that small fixed tables would be a great advantage." After a brief stop in Toledo, the 247 flew on uneventfully to Chicago after a flight of 5 3/4 hours. Upon landing, England thanked Miss Kiddoo, hopped into the waiting Cadillac limousine and drove off to the St. Stephens Hotel. That cost him another seventy-five cents, which he paid under gentle protest.[16]

Adjusting the aircraft compass. *Courtesy Smithsonian Institution.* (*SI 87–8571*)

This and thousands of other United 247 flights introduced the advantages of modern high speed air travel to thousands of fortunate passengers, although the overwhelming majority of the American public could not afford it. Safety was the key and was relentlessly pursued. Unfortunately, not all of the flights were as happily uneventful as Mr. England's

On the evening of 10 October 1933, a National Air Transport 247 cruised steadily above the tranquil farmland of Chesterton, Indiana on its way from New York to Chicago. At 8:49 P.M. over Liberty, Indiana the pilot, Captain Terrant, completed his routine radio transmission, reporting "everything okay." Shortly thereafter his Boeing 247, NC13304, exploded and plunged to the earth below. Terrant, his copilot, flight attendant and all four passengers were killed.[17] Alice Scribner, the stewardess, was the first United attendant to perish in the line of duty.

Initial press reports offered only unfounded theories as to the cause. Quoting Mr. B. M. Jacobs of the Department of Commerce, the International News Service concluded that the accident was caused either by pilot error forcing the aircraft into a hill or an on-board fire which somehow triggered an uncontrollable tailspin. I.N.S. stated that "officials surmised a motor or a gas tank exploded." United Press quoted an airline official who believed that the aircraft blew up after an unexplained forced landing. To eyewitnesses, the aircraft appeared to have burst into flame while flying at 1000 feet and then plunged into a grove of trees.[18] Rumors spread of severe flutter in the elevator or rudder, or perhaps a weakness in the whole tail structure. Boeing and United officials feared a major structural defect might exist. There had been an accident earlier in May when a 247 had inadvertently flown into a blind canyon wall near Provo, Utah, on its delivery flight. That was simply a case of pilot error which had killed no one. This was another matter.

Slowly the clues were pieced together. Porter County, Indiana, coroner Carl Davis stated that there were "some curious aspects" about the accident that required further investigation. "It was brought out in the inquest yesterday that there was an explosion in the air" which blew the tail off the aircraft but "was not followed by fire" until the transport struck the ground, igniting its fuel tanks.[19]

On 13 October, the Associated Press published an intriguing story. Apparently parts of the wreckage and a bottle fragment bore traces of gun powder or nitroglycerine. Department of Commerce officials were quoted speaking of "considerable evidence of an explosion," referring to holes in the metal and excessive damage in the remains of the baggage compartment. The investigators had already concluded that there was no explosion of the fuel tanks in flight. When the official report was issued, Boeing officials breathed a sigh of relief. D. B. Colyer, now a vice-president of United Air Lines, made the announcement confirming the report. Apparently, a bomb of unknown origin had been placed in the lavatory or the cargo hold which blew off the aircraft's tail. There were no clues as to why the bomb was on board although a Chicago gangland murder of one of the passengers was suspected. Boeing and United officials, and particularly engineers and designers, were relieved to learn that there was no inherent flaw in the 247's design. Speaking for the airline, Colyer concluded that there was "no structural failure of the aircraft until the explosion."[20] The crime remains unsolved.

Several other 247s crashed during the service life of this aircraft. In every case, weather, pilot error, or some other unforeseen incident conspired to cause the accident. Its advanced features enabled the 247 to fly at times when older aircraft would have remained grounded. Paradoxically, however, the speed of the aircraft, together with the fallibility of "modern" navigation equipment, sometimes led unwary pilots into difficult situations. The great strength and structural integrity of the 247 never failed and on several occasions successfully withstood forced landings which would have destroyed lesser machines.

In part to allay the fears of the public caused by the crash in Indiana and another fatal accident in Oregon in November, the Army Air Corps was

NC13319 was operated in the northwest by Pacific Air Transport. *Courtesy Smithsonian Institution. (SI 87–11936)*

asked to test a 247 to destruction so as, first, to determine how much punishment the transport could withstand and, second, to provide an objective opinion of the aircraft's handling characteristics. In early December 1933, Boeing 247 NC13322 was turned over to the Air Corps Materiel Division at Wright Field, Dayton, Ohio. The fuselage was subjected to a severe static test. The structural strength of the aircraft exceeded the requirement, buckling only after load factors of 5.25 on the rear and 5.5 on the front fuselage section were reached. Failure occurred only after loads 8.50 and 8.70 times the weight of the structure were placed on the respective fuselage halves. The anodized Alclad 17-ST aluminum alloy met all specifications and there was no evidence of intercrystalline corrosion which would weaken the material. Comparative tests with a second 247, NC13334, confirmed these secret findings, particularly in the satisfactory torsional frequency tests of the baggage compartments.

The first trial was a sixty-five minute test flight. The two pilots reported nothing unusual. No flutter or vibration was observed in the ailerons or other control surfaces at every speed between stall and 180 miles per hour. Furthermore, there was no flutter in the wings nor any other structural member. Only normal skin wrinkling was seen during heavy load conditions. In fact, "the airplane handles easily and responds well to the controls." Control forces were considered normal for an aircraft of the size of the 247 though the elevator seemed somewhat heavy. The engines were very smooth and completely vibrationless. The aircraft was very comfortable. "With the windows closed it is very quiet inside the cabin and pilot's compartment. Further vibration tests were satisfactory."

Flight tests on NC13334 were equally satisfactory. Outside vision was good though the pilot sat too close to the window, and could strike his shoulder on the window rails. The passenger seats were comfortable and ample leg room was provided. As experienced by most travelers on the 247, the intruding wing spars "necessitated steps at both spar positions and is not a very desirable feature." Cabin heating and ventilation were considered very satisfactory.

The 247's takeoff characteristics were good with little or no tendency of the aircraft to swerve off line because of propeller torque. Loading was satisfactory although a great deal of elevator trim was required when the aircraft slowed for approach. The test crew noted that "the airplane can be landed using the trim tabs without touching the control column." The aileron action was easy and effective through all speeds, although the rudder and elevator movement did not meet Air Corps's specifications. "The airplane was dived with power on to a speed of 200 miles per hour and at this speed the stick forces on the elevator and rudder became so excessive that it was practically impossible to maneuver the airplane without resorting to the trim tabs." This was a maneuver beyond the designed flight envelope of the aircraft, however. Stability and maneuverability were both more than sufficient. The pilots could report nothing wrong with the aircraft when operated normally. Lieutenant Hill thought it a "sweet flying airplane which was much better than the B-9."[21]

The New York Times was impressed with the results and announced that "the only commercial airplane in the United States [that] has been completely statically tested—that is tested to destruction by load—has emerged from the ordeal with flying colors. A 10-passenger Boeing 247 . . . has been flown in observation tests, studied with vibration machines, tested for torsion and harmonics and, finally, its fuselage was broken down under a load of 52 tons of lead; an overload of about 60 percent."[22]

Such national recognition confirmed the reliability of the 247 and reassured the public. The aircraft was remarkably free of major problems although, throughout the course of thousands of hours of commercial service, several minor complaints did surface. Modifications were made following failures on some engine mount diagonal cross members, aileron trim tab motor shafts, and especially in the lavatory door lock. Apparently on several occasions, embarrassed patrons had been locked in the "blue room" when the lock malfunctioned. Erik Nelson suggested an external

Air freight was an important source of revenue along with airmail payments and passenger air fares. *Courtesy Smithsonian Institution. (SI 87–11908)*

handle for the door be fitted to permit the flight attendant to open the lavatory door in emergencies.[23] This, too, was approved.

Of more far-reaching importance were several reports of control column failures while in flight. An urgent wire was sent to the Boeing factory by Boeing Air Transport after two failures were reported at Omaha similar to an earlier incident at National Air Transport in Kansas City. Immediate action was urged before a serious accident could happen if both columns failed in flight. Acting quickly, C. N. Montieth and his engineers devised a suitable reinforcement that could handle strong gust loads and recommended the development of forged steel hinges to correct the problem.[24] After these steps were taken, no further difficulties were reported.

United Air Lines and Boeing officials recommended a number of changes for the next production series of 247s. An improved and updated 247 was urgently required if Boeing was to maintain its lead until the planned new luxury airliner would be ready, several years in the future. Time was running short. The competition was catching up.

5

Improving the Breed: The Boeing 247-D

Boeing became more and more sensitive to reports of a new transport under development by Douglas, for which Boeing was indirectly responsible. In 1932, United Air Lines's competitor Transcontinental and Western Air was faced with a quandary. Following the well-publicized death of famed Notre Dame football coach Knute Rockne in the crash of a T.W.A. wooden-winged Fokker F-10 in March 1931, the government required all operators of similar equipment to perform more frequent—and expensive—examinations of their aircraft. This, among other reasons, pushed the airlines towards the complete acceptance of all-metal aircraft and forced T.W.A. President Jack Frye to approach Boeing in the hope of ordering some of the new 247s then under development. In a classic example of marketing nearsightedness, Boeing informed Frye that T.W.A. could not purchase any 247s until after the entire order had been completed for United Air Lines.[1] Boeing, from United Aircraft's narrow viewpoint, should not jeopardize the fortunes of its corporate brother.

Faced with the prospect of maintaining in service an expensive and obsolete fleet while a competitor built an insurmountable lead, Frye turned to other manufacturers for a solution. He needed an aircraft as good as or better than the 247. T.W.A. wanted a transport, preferably of metal construction, with three 500-550 horsepower engines. The required maximum speed of 185 miles per hour and cruise speed of 150 miles per hour was similar to the Boeing's. The proposed aircraft was to weigh 14,200 pounds and carry at least 12 passengers. It had to be capable of taking off from the highest and hottest fields on T.W.A.'s routes on one engine. Of the five manufacturers who received the famous "Jack Frye letter" of 2 August 1932, only Donald Douglas responded with a satisfactory proposal.[2]

In a bold move, the Douglas Aircraft Company of Santa Monica, California, rewrote and improved the requirement. Free from the corporate restraints which dictated engine selection at Boeing, Douglas chose the most powerful radial engine available, the 700-horsepower, supercharged Wright Cyclone. With so much power available, there was no need for a

Jack Frye, president of TWA. *Courtesy Smithsonian Institution. (SI 87–11923)*

third engine. Consequently, Douglas suggested a twin-engined, all-metal, low-wing, cantilevered monoplane equipped with retractable gear and, therefore, very similar in concept to the 247.[3] Aware of the problems as well as the advantages of Boeing's design, Douglas wisely decided to place the fuselage over the wing and accept the increased drag to avoid the need for intruding wing spars. One aspect of this development, humiliating in the extreme to United Aircraft, was that this aircraft, subsequently designated the DC-1, was essentially the aircraft that Rentschler and Mead had originally wanted Boeing to build.

The remarkably simple yet durable multicellular wing was of revolutionary structure and could have been used on Boeing aircraft had not corporate politics once again intervened. Designed by Jack Northrop and first used on his Alpha, this wing was composed of multiple spars which dis-

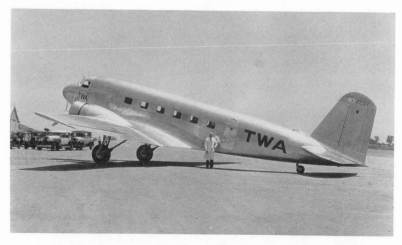

The Douglas DC-1 was essentially the larger aircraft design that Rentschler and Mead wanted Boeing to build instead of the smaller 247. (*Douglas 4982*)

persed the loads through the wing, producing a stronger, lighter, and less expensive structure. When Northrop left the United Aircraft combine after William Boeing tried to merge Northrop's small company with Stearman in Wichita, Douglas acquired the rights to his wing. Remembering the miserable Kansas winter weather, Northrop moved to warmer southern California to join forces with Douglas.[4] His wing was a primary reason for the success of the Douglas commercial transports.

At first, Boeing brushed aside reports of the new Douglas DC-1. According to Erik Nelson, army officials were not too impressed because it "looked like the airplane would be entirely too large for the powerplants they contemplate installing." The general consensus was that nothing much would come of this design unless Douglas received a satisfactory contract. Nelson was objective in his observations, however. "They have in mind a much larger airplane than our 247. The body is quite a bit larger, with an estimated ceiling throughout the cabin of about 6' 2", . . . the cabin would hold about 14 seats with a lot of leg room and also aisle space. . . . The fuselage is mounted above the wing so no spars will come through the cabin which will eliminate any interference from the same, giving a very nice looking cabin."[5]

C. N. Montieth had missed the first flight of the 247 because he was taking part in the annual U.S. Navy cruise. On 20 February 1933, on his way back to Seattle after a considerable time at sea, he stopped by Douglas's Santa Monica plant to examine the progress of the DC-1. Montieth had mixed emotions concerning the new transport. He was impressed by the size. "This transport is to be a huge affair about the size of our 80-A." The skin, which was made of 24ST Alclad aluminum, "will give a very pleasing appearance." He was not impressed by the structure. "It will be surprising if they do not find the fuselage to be considerably heavier than they anticipated. . . . The wing of the Douglas transport apparently will be a three spar construction, the spars being extremely deep plate girders with .60 webs and bent up angles for flanges. This does not appear to be extraordinarily good structure."[6] The Boeing Chief Engineer could not have been more mistaken. This Northrop-designed multicellular structure was immensely strong, superbly efficient, and, above all, economical. In addition, Montieth disliked the placement of the two wing-mounted engines behind and out of sight of the pilots.

It was at this time that Philip Johnson began to have second thoughts about the Wasp and asked Boeing to see if it was possible to install Hornets on the remaining twenty Model 247s. Daunted by the difficulties involved, Johnson encouraged the company to begin design work on the new luxury transport with all due haste while examining the possibilities of upgrading the present 247. Discussions between Johnson and Montieth revealed a new aircraft strikingly similar to the Douglas and to Mead's original idea. The new aircraft would seat twelve to fourteen passengers, weigh over 15,800 pounds, have the pilots sitting well ahead of the two engines, and be equipped with two 700-horsepower Hornets.[7] Work on the new Model 280 began in July 1933. Speed of design and construction was of the essence. The problems experienced in the development of the 247 could not be repeated. The race was on and Boeing was losing.

Boeing decided to upgrade the current 247 design to produce a stop-gap transport until the new aircraft could be built. Work could not begin in earnest until the fall of 1933, by which time the original order for 247s had been completed. Then, in September, Boeing received news that was shattering in content and far reaching in its effect. The Douglas transport had flown and had exceeded T.W.A.'s stringent altitude requirements.

The new DC-1, piloted by freelance test pilot Eddie Allen, flew with a full load from Winslow, Arizona, to Albuquerque, New Mexico on only one engine. According to Allen's statements, the aircraft climbed out of Winslow without much difficulty after an engine was stopped as soon as the transport was airborne, and flew to Albuquerque at an altitude of at least 1000 feet above the ground. The DC-1 handled so well that most of the passengers did not notice that an engine had been cut. Remarkably,

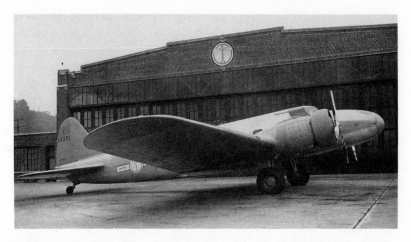

Designated the 247-E, the original 247 was used to test numerous cowling, engine, and tail arrangements which led to the production of the 247-D. *Courtesy Smithsonian Institution. (SI 87–11935)*

the single-engine flight time of 2 hours and 14 minutes was only five minutes slower than the regular Ford Tri-Motor schedule. In another single-engine test, the Douglas managed to maintain an 11,000 ceiling, well above the Boeing ceiling. Cruising speed with both engines was recorded at an average of 189 miles per hour, faster than the 247's maximum speed.[8] Clearly, Boeing was faced with a formidable challenge.

The most important question concerning the improved 247 involved engine selection. The Hornet was obviously out of the question because it would require a massive redesign of the airframe. As early as March 1933, Johnson suggested using a geared version of the trusty Wasp which could maintain its rated power at a much higher altitude. "I do feel, if Pratt & Whitney will play along with us," stated Johnson, "that we should attempt to use a geared Wasp in one or two of the airplanes in service so that we are fully cognizant of their performance."[9]

Work continued in Hartford throughout the year on refining this powerplant, known as the S1H1-G, while in Seattle numerous improvements were incorporated into the next fifteen Model 247s. Using the original 247, renumbered as X-13301, as a test bed, experiments were conducted on a completely new elevator to improve the flying characteristics. To dampen some slight flutter, the standard doped elevator fabric was replaced by a metal covering which alleviated the problem. After several experiments, a new rudder with a straightened hinge line was incorporated to reduce the heaviness encountered in flight and improve control harmony. The single trim tab on the rudder was augmented by another tab above it which was used as an aerodynamic balance for reducing rudder loads.[10] This device remained parallel to the fin by using a special linkage, thereby reducing pilot effort.

Responding to complaints from passengers, a redesign replaced the old direct-air heating system which drew warmth from engine exhaust baffles with a more efficient ethylene glycol radiator. Individual ventilators were eliminated as was the window above the cockpit. In addition, the wheel wells were strengthened after several failures had been reported while in service.[11]

The most striking visual difference was the return to a conventional aft-sloping windshield.[12] The former forward-sloping windscreen tended to reflect ground lights at night especially during landings. The aft sloping-design also reduced drag marginally.

By October, the first geared Wasps were installed in a 247 for trials. The extra weight and increased length of the engine shifted the center of gravity too far forward, exacerbating the aircraft's already sensitive nose-heavy tendency. Claire Egtvedt was worried and wrote to Johnson that "to date, the tests on the long engine mounts for the transport have been most discouraging in that the main thing, which we set out to correct, namely, the stability of the airplane, has not been solved by moving the engines forward. In fact . . . the stability is not quite as good as with the planes you now have." With a power-off glide, the aircraft was unstable, unlike the direct-drive 247. Egtvedt believed the problem stemmed from a change in the air flow around the longer powerplant and mount. After tests on the United Aircraft's executive 247-A, which had a geared twin-row Wasp Junior, Egtvedt felt that the standard engine mount would be required to improve the balance and stability. Apparently the same problem had been encountered by Douglas and was one common with low-wing designs. Ballast was therefore necessary. "It does not appear, even with the use of the geared Wasp," Egtvedt declared, "that we will be able to completely eliminate all ballasting." The geared Wasp version would require some counterweights in extreme loading conditions "but that the amount of ballast would be considerably less than half of that at present required." Johnson authorized wind tunnel tests to confirm Egtvedt's theory.[13]

Boeing wished to install a three-bladed variable-pitch propeller and place the engine in the latest streamlined NACA-inspired cowling. The propellers were quieter than the older two-bladed versions, were larger in diameter, and more efficient. The cowling, designed by Chance Vought

The 247-D incorporated a straightened hinge line and an additional tab to balance the heavy rudder forces. (*Boeing 7782-B*)

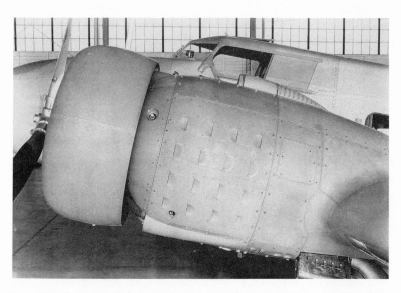

Several cowl and nacelle variations were tested during 1933 before the final design of the 247-D was determined. (*Boeing 6216-B*)

and the Boeing Research Division, was much smoother and cleaner in appearance than the ring it replaced and covered the entire engine, thus eliminating the need for the nose shutter.

Ice formation had always been a major fear of pilots and engineers. During certain atmospheric conditions ice can form on the wings and tail, dangerously increasing weight and decreasing lift. The problem was first examined in 1929 by Dr. William C. Geer, a chemist at Cornell University. Using funds awarded by the Guggenheim Foundation, Geer, working with N.A.T., devised a system of pneumatically expanding boots which could break off the ice that formed along the leading edges of the wings and empennage. After successful tests, he won the support of C. W. Leguillan of the B. F. Goodrich Tire and Rubber Company and moved to that firm to continue research on his deicers.[14]

Aware of the significance of this device, Thorp Hiscock urged that deicer boots be fitted to all Boeing aircraft. Montieth objected because he was concerned about potential corrosion formation where moisture might be trapped between the rubber and the Duralumin leading edge. He was eventually overruled.[15]

By 1933, Hiscock and Goodrich had perfected the deicer boot to such a degree that it was then possible to install this equipment on a transport aircraft. Writing to C. H. Hatfield of United Aircraft and Philip Johnson, Hiscock summarized his recent activities stating:

> For your information, we have directed a redesign of the Goodrich over-shoe, so it has been lightened to approximately 30 percent of its original weight. This would place it in a reasonable class as a commercial installation. They (Goodrich) are quite optimistic in their new unit and have made us a comparatively attractive quotation for a test installation. Since the theory has not in any way been altered from their original model, there is practically no question as to whether it will work or not.[16]

The device was approved for installation in the latest production Boeing transports. Once again the 247 was used to pioneer new technology, this time in flight safety.

In all previous correspondence, the updated version of the 247 had been referred to as only the "15 additional aircraft" of the series. On 29 November 1933, Erik Nelson requested that, to avoid any possible confusion with the new transports under development, these machines be designated as the Boeing 247-D.[17] Throughout the winter of 1933 and 1934 Boeing engineers worked diligently to perfect the installation of the geared S1H1-G Wasp, with its newly developed automatic valve lubrication system, and the numerous details of the improved 247-D.

The S4D1-G geared Wasp was used on X-13301 as a prototype installation for the more advanced S1H1-G. *Courtesy United Technologies Archive. (Boeing 7139-B)*

B. F. Goodrich rubber deicer boots were first fitted to the leading edges of the wings and tail of the 247-D and helped solve the problem of rime ice. *Courtesy Smithsonian Institution. (SI 86–12111)*

While the Boeing Company struggled to maintain its tenuous techno-logical lead, political events were unfolding which would permanently change the shape of the American aviation industry. Boeing, as part of the United Aircraft and Transport combine, would be directly affected as steps were being taken by the federal government to disassemble the huge aviation holding companies.

President Roosevelt entered office at almost exactly the same time that the 247 was introduced to the nation. With the zeal of a reformer and the mandate of the American people to correct the injustices of the past and revamp the U.S. economy, the Roosevelt administration initiated a campaign to expose the perceived abuses in government and industry, including the airline industry. One of the first targets was the Post Office and former Postmaster General Walter F. Brown.

The Democratically-controlled Congress began the attack. On 28 September 1933, the Senate opened hearings to investigate airmail and ocean mail contracts. In January 1934, Senator Hugo L. Black, the chairman of the Special Committee, responded to the pleas of the smaller airlines, which had felt cheated by Brown's apparently arbitrary awarding of contracts to the major carriers. Anxious to expose Republican misdeeds to an outraged public, the Black Committee publicized Brown's high-handed dealings and his support of the giant aviation holding companies. As the crisis spread into February, the new Postmaster General James Farley approached Roosevelt with the committee's findings.[18]

The spirit of the law—if not the letter—had been broken. There was little the president could do when faced with the evidence unearthed by the Black Committee. On 9 February 1934, Roosevelt canceled all of the airmail contracts and turned over the responsibility to the Army Air Corps. Ten days later, one of the saddest episodes in Air Corps history began when, ill-prepared and ill-equipped, it began to deliver the mail. Despite performing well, and on some routes even better than the airlines, the Air Corps effort was blemished by a series of operational and training accidents which killed ten pilots. Responding to the resultant public outcry, which was fanned by opportunistic criticism from representatives of the airlines, especially Eddie Rickenbacker and Charles Lindbergh, the president was forced to suspend the operation temporarily in March. Limited service was resumed in the better weather of April, while Roosevelt reluctantly announced the return to the contract system of mail delivery under new legislation.[19]

Late in April, Farley gathered together the representatives of the airlines to award new airmail contracts, this time to the lowest bidder. There was one provision. No company or individual who had participated in the so-called "spoils conference" of 1930 was allowed to bid. Furthermore, in the future, no aircraft manufacturing firm could control an airline.[20]The nation had been appalled by the profiteering of a handful of individuals who appeared to be living too well in a period of economic depression. Fred Rentschler, who had turned a $253 investment into many millions of dollars through astute stock transactions, was the primary target of these accusations. His corporation had profited from the lucrative airmail subsidies awarded by Brown and was by far the largest of the three aviation holding companies. While not illegal, his actions cast an unfavorable light on the operations of United Aircraft at a time when millions of Americans were homeless and hungry. By breaking up the massive, oligarchic holding companies, F. D. R. hoped to prevent the recurrence of past excesses and better regulate the industry. In this he succeeded. Being the consummate politician, he also realized that trust-busting was always popular with the voters.

All the giant holding companies were disbanded. The airlines were reformed under slightly different names but with vastly different corporate structures. United Aircraft was split apart, with Pratt & Whitney divorced from the other founding company, Boeing. Boeing took the opportunity to change its name to the Boeing Aircraft Company. Though already in semiretirement, William Boeing left the business entirely out of anger over recent events, taking with him the coveted Collier Trophy of 1934 in belated recognition for the creation of the 247 and his other aircraft.

United Air Lines became independent and, on 1 May 1934, altered its function from that of a management organization to that of an air carrier by officially absorbing its constituent divisions. This also meant that Philip Johnson, the driving force behind the airline and the 247, was forced to leave his post as president of U.A.T.C. Though he had never committed a crime or even been accused of any wrongdoing, Johnson was pushed out under a cloud of suspicion by the government. He was forced to carry this unwarranted burden of guilt until 1939, when new legislation allowed him to return to the industry, thus clearing his name. Into Johnson's place moved William "Pat" Patterson as president of the new United Air Lines.[21]

These reorganizations threw the aviation industry into turmoil. In 1933, most of the major airlines had managed to eke out a small profit, despite the Depression. Barred from government contracts for much of 1934, however, these same companies registered huge losses. United Air Lines lost approximately $300,000 per month in early 1934.[22] Ironically, when the dust settled, essentially the same airlines flew essentially the same routes as before. The small contractors, who had instigated the investigations to improve their chances of receiving federal subsidies, benefitted little in the long run.

Boeing was left in a precarious economic position. Without the resources of United Aircraft and Transport, Claire Egdtvedt, now the president and general manager of the Boeing Aircraft Company, was left almost empty handed. Only a contract from the Army Air Corps for the design and construction of the XB-15, a secret four-engined, long-range bomber, provided money. In August 1934, desperate to find a way out of the economic doldrums, Egtvedt took a huge gamble and risked all of the company's available funds on a new bomber proposal for the Army Air Corps. Known as the Model 299, this graceful four-engined bomber owed much of its design to the 247 as well as the XB-15, and eventually rescued the company from collapse. The 299 became better known as the B-17 Flying Fortress of World War II fame.

While decisions crucial to the future of the company were being made, Boeing continued to work on the 247-D. Time was short. Just before the cancellation of the contracts, Jack Frye and Eddie Rickenbacker flew the Douglas DC-1 across the continent in an astounding 13 hours, over six hours better than the 247's time.[23] But as no airlines were in a financial position to buy new aircraft until the contracts were renewed, Boeing was given a grace period for the 247-D. The respite was brief.

On 11 May 1934, the larger Douglas DC-2 made its first flight. Seating two more passengers than the prototype DC-1, the latest Douglas entered service with T.W.A. only three days later. With this, Boeing's competitive advantage disappeared. Rushing the first 247-D to completion, Boeing managed to finish X 13301 and deliver it to United in August. This aircraft was actually the very first 247 built. After having been used as a test bed, and being given the unique designation of 247-E for this purpose, it was modified into the first 247-D. The first of the production 247-Ds was scheduled for delivery to United in late September 1934 with all ten to be completed by late November.[24]

The performance was dramatically improved over the earlier 247 and was comparable to that of the DC-2s. Maximum speed was now 200 miles per hour, an 18 percent increase. The cruising speed of 189 miles per hour was 7 miles per hour faster than the top speed of the earlier version. Range at 75 percent power was 750 miles and 840 miles at 62 percent. Fuel capacity remained at 273 gallons, thus indicating improved fuel efficiency. The absolute ceiling was raised almost a mile to 27,200 feet and the service ceiling increased to 25,400 feet. Most significantly, the single-engine ceil-

More spacious than the 247, the cabin of the DC-2, with its flat floor, allowed passengers more freedom of movement without the risk of tripping over the wing spars. *Courtesy Smithsonian Institution. (SI 76–3141)*

Though designated as the 247-E, X-13301 was upgraded and delivered to United Air Lines as the first 247-D. This photo was taken before the fin and rudder were changed. *Courtesy Smithsonian Institution. (SI 87–8587)*

ing was raised to an astounding 11,500 feet, a 7599-foot improvement, and more than a match for the DC-2. Gross weight meanwhile grew to 13,650 pounds with a 182-pound payload increase.[25] The 247-D represented a remarkable developmental achievement considering that there was no increase in horsepower. The enhanced performance was the direct result of greatly improved streamlining of the cowlings, more efficient geared engines, and the three-bladed, variable-pitch propellers.

Despite the improvements, the new 247-D was still hampered by its small capacity and relatively uncomfortable cabin, when compared with the DC-2. The intruding spars remained. To the discerning public, the cabin of the Douglas aircraft looked far superior, with ample headroom and space to move about in the cabin. Before the first production 247-D entered service, however, it was earmarked for a very special assignment. Number 1953, just off the construction line, was destined to compete in what was billed as "The World's Greatest Air Race."

6

The MacRobertson Race

One of the most important contributions of air transportation was the linking together of countries and continents which had previously been separated by time and distance. Great Britain, as well as other colonial powers, successfully used the airplane to improve communications with its overseas dominions. Separated by over 11,000 miles, Great Britain and Australia especially sought ways to bridge the vast distance that separated them. Many brave individuals had attempted to fly this far-flung route but managed after great trials to reveal only the potential and not the reality of practical commercial service. The enterprising Dutch had managed to open regular scheduled service between the Netherlands and Batavia, the capital of their colony in the East Indies, in 1931. The French had also extended air service to Saigon in the same year. But the British had yet to reach Australia. One adventurous Australian sought to encourage a solution to this problem.

In 1932, Sir MacPherson Robertson, an Australian millionaire candy manufacturer and noted philanthropist, dreamed up a competition to promote ties with Britain and to highlight the centennial of Melbourne and the state of Victoria. Robertson offered a large sum of money to the winners of an England-Australia air race. After announcing his intentions in 1933, he began to organize the massive event, scheduled to start on 20 October 1934. The prize was $10,000 (about $500,000 in 1991 dollars) to be divided between the top three finishers in an all-out speed category and a handicapped division. Although aircraft could be registered for both, only one prize would be awarded for each winning entrant.[1]

When announced, the contest generated immense international interest. Under the aegis of the Royal Aero Club, the race was open to all competitors and types of aircraft, provided the aircraft met the stringent safety requirements concerning weight and performance. Each machine was required to conform to the certificate of airworthiness from its country of manufacture and to be equipped with proper instruments and maps. The closing date for entrants was 30 June 1934.[2]

Many of the fifty-nine applicants were internationally known, including the famous American racing pilot Roscoe Turner. Turner had just won the prestigious Thompson Trophy at the National Air Races and had shattered the U.S. transcontinental speed record. Intrigued by the tough challenge offered by MacRobertson, he began a search for a suitable aircraft.

Aware of the performance of the 247 and of the added capabilities of the 247-D, Turner selected the new Boeing for the race. "I chose it because it has been in service and tried out longer than any other fast transport on the market. It has proven its ability to stand up in regular day and night operation. Speed isn't the only thing essential to success in this race. Dependability has to be there too. This ship has plenty of both."[3] Since Boeing was not an official participant, Turner arranged an agreement with United Air Lines to lease its first new 247-D for the race.[4]

With the aircraft officially entered and approved in the speed category, Philip Johnson, in one of his last acts as president of United, wired Boeing on 12 July with instructions to proceed with the preparation of Turner's 247-D.[5] The aircraft was essentially stock. The only major modifications entailed removing the ten cabin seats for the installation of eight extra tanks to increase the fuel load to 1125 U.S. gallons of 80 octane fuel. Range was thereby increased to approximately 2500 miles with no significant performance penalty. Other changes involved the installation of a fifty-two gallon oil system, the replacement of the airliner radio with equipment preferred by Turner, the inclusion of a modified vacuum system, and revised fuel line plumbing.[6]

Early in September, the aircraft was ready. In the meantime, Turner had recruited Clyde Pangborn as his copilot. Pangborn was a famous aviator in his own right, having flown with Hugh Herndon in the Bellanca Pacemaker Miss Veedol on the first nonstop flight from Japan to the United States almost three years earlier. At noon on 10 September, Turner and Pangborn accepted their 247-D and flew it from Seattle to Los Angeles, setting a new record of 5 hours and 33 minutes for an auspicious beginning.[7] Before the flight, Turner had only 75 minutes in the aircraft.[8]

The aircraft bore only Turner's personal markings. On each side of the nose was a red ball with a white "57" within. An avid showman and also an astute businessman, Turner had convinced the sponsor of his other racing efforts, the Heinz Corporation, to support his latest endeavor. At that time, Heinz was marketing its first and only dry breakfast cereal, Rice Flakes, and was using Turner as the center attraction of a massive advertising campaign.[9] With Colonel Turner's face appearing in magazines across

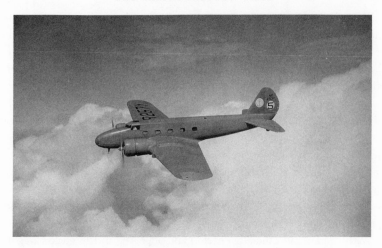

The first production 247-D flies above the clouds on a test flight before the MacRobertson Race. The aircraft is adorned with its race number and special registration, NR257Y. *Courtesy Smithsonian Institution.* (SI 75–12085)

Turner inspects the additional tanks that increased the total fuel load to 1124 U.S. gallons. *Courtesy Smithsonian Institution.* (SI 87–11910)

the country hawking Heinz Rice Flakes, the 247-D, with the "57" company logo emblazoned on its nose, was an ideal flying billboard.

The aircraft carried a restricted registration number of NR257Y (the "57" another allusion to the sponsor) the race number "5" and, after the visit to Los Angeles, several more markings. After picking up Warner Brothers' sponsorship, Turner allowed an elaborate design to be painted on the rear of the fuselage proclaiming the aircraft the "Warner Brothers Comet." Actress Bebe Daniels christened the right and left engines, "Nip" and "Tuck," a prophetic commentary on the risks of the upcoming journey. These names appeared beneath large American flags which were painted on the outboard side of the engine cowlings.[10] After Los Angeles, the aircraft was flown to New York City where it was dismantled, crated, and shipped to England on the S.S. *Washington*. Turner and Pangborn arrived with NR257Y at Southampton on 7 October, reassembled their aircraft and flew to Heston Airport, London for race preparations. On the 16th, they moved to Mildenhall, some seventy miles northeast of London, where the other competitors were gathering.[11] At this time Turner added another crew member to his team, Reeder G. Nichols, an experienced radioman.

Among the fifty-nine entrants and twenty-one aircraft were four machines of special interest. The primary British entries were three sleek, all-wood, two-seat de Havilland D.H.88 Comets, powered by two de Havilland Gypsy 6 engines, designed and built exclusively for this competition. These beautiful racing aircraft, flown by the R.A.F.-trained team of C. W. A. Scott and Captain Tom Campbell-Black, the famous flying husband-and-wife team of James Mollison and Amy Johnson, and Lt. Cathcart Jones and Kenneth Walker, were the aircraft favored to win. The other aircraft was from the Netherlands and was entered by K.L.M. (Royal Dutch Airlines) and flown by the seasoned crew of Koene Dirk Parmentier and Jan Johannes Moll. The two Dutchmen were flying a American DC-2, named *Uiver* (Stork).[12] Unlike Boeing, Douglas did not restrict the sales of its new transport. Aware of the advantages of this aircraft, K.L.M. wisely ordered the first DC-2 for use in Europe and, eager to exploit the machine's speed and range, put it in service on the important route from Amsterdam to Batavia, Dutch East Indies.

The correspondent of the *Aeroplane* aptly summarized the rivalry between these competing designs while the aircraft were on public view in a Mildenhall hangar:

> Almost next to the Douglas and just beyond Melrose's Puss Moth was the Turner-Pangborn Boeing which offers a most interesting comparison with

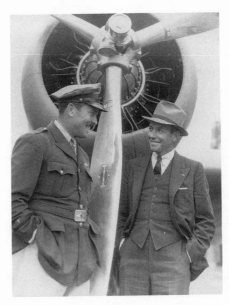

Turner chose distance flyer Clyde Pangborn as his copilot. (*Boeing 7575-B*)

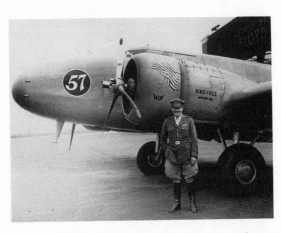

The red and white "57" reflected the sponsorship of the Heinz Corporation. Turner stands next to "Nip," the left engine. The other Wasp was appropriately named "Tuck." *Courtesy Smithsonian Institution.* (*SI 72–8419*)

The *Warner Bros. Comet* is loaded aboard the S.S. *Washington* for its voyage to England. *Courtesy Smithsonian Institution.* *(SI 87–11912)*

At Heston Aerodrome, Middlesex, the 247-D was tested before it was flown to Mildenhall. Turner and Pangborn pose with their mechanic, Don Young. *Courtesy Smithsonian Institution.* *(SI 87–11913)*

the Douglas. Boeing was the first to produce this particular form of twin-engined, high-speed airliner, and when it came out, that particular version must have looked the cat's whisker. Now the proximity of the Douglas makes it look a trifle *démodé*. . . . [13]

As the starting date of 20 October rapidly approached, the contestants were concerned with completing last minute preparations. Turner and Pangborn's efforts were frustrated by a decision of the Royal Aero Club judges. Turner had flown the Boeing over to Martlesham for the verification of its U.S. certificate of airworthiness. Unfortunately, the inspectors discovered that the Boeing was 300 pounds too heavy. A detailed search revealed no explanation for this extra weight until the inspectors realized that an error in converting the weight of U.S. gallons to Imperial gallons was the culprit, compounded by the cooler weather which caused an even greater fuel density. Roscoe was in a quandary though his sense of humor remained intact. "Our ship's fine and the weight is O.K. She's absolutely grand and perfectly ready for the trip. . . . But she'll have to fly without us."[14] A more practical solution was fortunately found. Because a new certificate of airworthiness with a greater gross weight limit could not be acquired in time, it was agreed to empty and seal off tanks number two, seven, and eight.[15] This restriction would force Turner and Pangborn to make an extra fuel stop along the route.

The course was to be flown in regulated stages. All participants were required to stop at Baghdad, Iraq; Allahabad, India; Singapore; and in Australia at Darwin, Charleville, and finally Melbourne. Additional fuel stops were permitted at any checkpoint along the way, although each contestant had to make his own arrangements for fuel there.[16]

On 20 October, a Saturday morning, twenty aircraft lined up on Mildenhall Aerodrome, Suffolk, for the start of the MacRobertson Race. Bearing race number "5," Turner's 247-D took off for the first stop, Athens, precisely 45 seconds after 6:30 and following the Comet "Black Magic," flown by the Mollisons.[17] Crossing Europe, the crew enjoyed the scenery but was grateful for their reliable equipment, as recorded by Reeder Nichols in his radio log:

> Through holes in clouds [we] can see the wonders of the Swiss Alps. . . .
> All high peaks are visible and believe Turner is altering course to go through pass. Most of higher peaks are on same level as us and our altimeter is reading 15,000 feet. Motors running very sweetly for which we thank Mr. Pratt and Mr. Whitney as this certainly is no place to set down.[18]

Turner, Pangborn, and Nichols, landed ten hours and 11 minutes later at Athens for fuel after an uneventful flight. One hour and fifteen minutes

Fuel is added to Turner's 247-D just before dawn on race day. *Courtesy Smithsonian Institution.* (SI 72–8425)

later, they took off for Baghdad, 2551 miles from their original starting point. They were then in fifth place overall. Among those ahead was the DC-2. After stopping to refuel at Karachi, they headed for Allahabad. They almost did not make it. For four hours, as Nichols radioed the airfield and received scant assistance, all the while the DC-2 was forging ahead:

> 1640 GMT Allahabad coming in with bang. . . . Called him but no soap. He opens up and gives Dutchman buzz. Hear Dutchman faintly and assume he has already left Allahabad. Can't seem to get much service from Allahabad and Calcutta is also hogging the air.
> 1730 GMT Haven't sighted Allahabad as yet, can't get bearings from Allahabad and every time I ask him for a few minutes of key so I can take bearing he answers with same old story about beacon being visible 60 miles. Would like to get that operator around neck. Have been up front for last ten minutes helping Roscoe look for beacon. No soap.[19]

Two hours later, the situation was becoming desperate. The 247 was running dangerously low on fuel and, by this time, the crew realized that they had overshot Allahabad. At 1935 GMT Nichols broadcast an S.O.S. Nichols' log describes the tense situation:

> After sending out the S.O.S. Allahabad apparently realized the urgent need of his radio and gave us his undivided attention from there on. Several times we established a course but it didn't exactly agree with the terrain we were

flying over and inasmuch as our gas was running damn low we were constantly on the lookout for a decent place to land.

To the north of us were hills and small mountains and altogether a very
uninviting spot to have to set a ship down in. Pang's (Pangborn's) maps
showed so many rivers and they all looked so much alike that it was very
hard to tell one from another, however, we had overshot Allahabad something like 150 miles and over 50 miles to the south so we had no definite
idea of exactly where we were and how far from Allahabad.

For over two hours we flew with throttle back just beyond the stalling
speed in order to conserve gas and Pang was constantly searching the country for landmarks. No doubt the radio helped to confirm Pangborn's navigation and we were on the verge of deciding whether or not we would jump
when we discovered a flash on the far horizon to the north. Pang had already
decided that we were south of the course and in the meantime, Allahabad
had arranged a crude makeshift loop and were attempting to take bearings
on us. Allahabad informed me that we were in a southerly direction from
them and I told Pang about this, he had already decided to go north where
we picked up the lights.

After sighting the lights, I asked Allahabad to turn them on and off so
that we could definitely establish whether or not we were right on our belief
that we had sighted Allahabad. They turned them on and off for a minute or
so and we knew that we were headed in the right direction but whether or
not we had enough gas to get there was the question in all of our minds. The
auxiliary tanks were completely dry and the right wing tank was also dry.
The gas gauge showed that we had about five or ten gallons left and 60 or 70
miles to go. We then decided that if we did crash to go down with the ship
rather than risk the chance of being separated if we jumped in parachutes
and being eaten by tigers or other wild animals.

We kept the airport constantly advised of our position so that if we did crash
they could have sent a rescue party out for us. It was awfully hard to judge
distance in this country due to the excellent visibility which we are not used
to in the United States. The air is very clear and one can see for miles. I did
not reel in my antenna until we were just about ready to land. During the
excitement of reaching the airport, I forgot to turn off my dynamotor and
when I grabbed the antenna to reel it in, I touched 2000 volts which gave
me a nasty jolt and paralyzed my right hand and arm for 15 or 20 minutes. I
reeled it in with my left hand which was a pretty hard job due to the location
of the reel under the operating table, and Roscoe set her down like a fly
lighting on a juicy morsel of food. Believe me we were damn glad to get
down and a couple of stiff shots of whiskey sure felt good.[20]

The error cost them an unexpected 5½ hour delay. Luckily, they still
managed to gain fourth place.

Turner and company quickly added fuel, took off, and flew across the Bay of Bengal to Alor Setar, Malaya, and then south to Singapore. They increased power to improve their time and, according the Nichols, had the motors, "stretched out . . . to overtake the Dutchman."[21] Their steady pace advanced them to third position and they were closing on the rival DC-2. The 247-D crossed the Dutch East Indies, stopped at Koepang, and proceeded to Darwin, the first stop in Australia.

Along the way, they experienced their first mechanical difficulty. Above the Timor Sea, the strain on the engines began to tell when "Tuck," the starboard powerplant, began to lose oil pressure. Turner managed to bring the aircraft in safely to Darwin where he removed its cowling and read-justed the oil pressure relief valve. Nichols had to crawl into the tail of the aircraft to replace the antenna weight which had broken off earlier. It was during their two-hour stay that the trio were informed that they had lost the race. "Learned Scott and Black had landed in Melbourne," wrote Nichols in his log, "so that leaves us out of the first money but the Dutchmen are still going strong and while there is life there is hope."[22]

They took off again and headed across the Gulf of Carpenteria towards Charleville. Again the oil pressure dropped, but this time on both engines, forcing Turner to cut power again. Despite this continuing problem, the trio flew directly to Charleville. Confident in their ability to overtake the DC-2, they left Charleville for their final destination, just 780 miles away. Hopes were high for an excellent second place finish as *Uiver* had been delayed at Albury, just 158 miles north of Melbourne.[23] Nichols was encouraged:

> Landed Charleville after helluva night spent over the Australian jungle. Everybody is tired and sore and we had just learned that the Dutchmen had a forced landing at Albury and was stuck in the mud, so this gives us fresh encouragement to push along. . . . Old "Nip" and "Tuck" both need some serious attention but it seems such a shame to have to tear into them when we are only a hop, skip, and a jump from home base. We gassed up and took on a bite of sandwich and some hot tea.[24]

Unfortunately, the oil problems appeared with a vengeance along the final stages. One hour away from Charleville, "Nip" began to act up so Turner again reduced power and flew on his other engine. Soon, smoke began to pour from "Tuck." Fearing the worst, Turner anxiously brought the aircraft down at Bourke, New South Wales. Upon examination, Tur-ner and company discovered that a small leak in an oil line was dripping directly on the hot exhaust manifold. They had hoped to remove the cowling and thus redirect the airflow around the leak but were forbidden

Roscoe Turner, Clyde Pangborn, and Reeder Nichols arrived tired but happy in Melbourne on October 26. *Courtesy Smithsonian Institution. (SI 86–6491)*

by race officials to leave the cowling behind. On the ground the three "tightened up all of the rockerbox nuts and then found out that the cowling couldn't go in the cabin so we put it back on again. Roscoe was so damned tired that he was swaying back and forth and the heat was not helping the situation either."[25] Exhausted and fearful of fire, Turner, Pangborn, and Nichols courageously decided to press on regardless of the danger. Surprisingly, once airborne, the oil line sealed itself, restoring pressure, thus allowing Turner to open the throttle to try to overtake the Dutchmen.[26]

His efforts were in vain. Despite their trouble in Albury, Parmentier and Moll had crossed the finish line behind the winning Comet of Scott and Black. Less than three hours later, at 3:36:08 GMT and 1:36:08 in the afternoon local time, the Boeing landed in third place. The flight of 11,323 miles had taken 92 hours 55½ minutes in elapsed time.[27] A relieved Nichols noted his feelings in his last log entry:

> Passed over the finish line at Melbourne and 15 minutes later landed at Laverton airport where a big reception awaited us. Most welcome thing to my mind was American cigarette offered by American Vice Counsel [sic] and

four tall drinks of White Horse scotch. We were all very tired and showed the effects of (almost four days) racing.[28]

It was symbolic of the future that Turner's aircraft placed just behind the Douglas. What made the Douglas feat all the more remarkable was the fact that the aircraft carried passengers and mail as part of K.L.M.'s regularly scheduled service. Because of the rules allowing an aircraft to win either the speed or handicap event, but not both, Turner officially finished second in the speed category, behind the victorious Comet. Parmentier and Moll opted for the handicap first prize of $2000 rather than the $1500 for second prize for speed, which was given to Turner.[29]

Regardless of the outcome and the remarkable achievement of Scott and Black, the aeronautical community was far more impressed by the outstanding performances of the two American-made airliners. These aircraft dramatically demonstrated the superior capabilities of the current state of American aeronautics. Despite defensive reactions in some of the British press, attacking the "belittling of an achievement" of the Comet,[30] the London *Morning Post* realized the implications:

The results of the England-Australia air race have fallen like a bomb in the midst of British every-day commercial and military aviation. Preconceived ideas of the maximum speed limitations of standard commercial aeroplanes have been blown sky-high. It had suddenly and vividly been brought home that, while the race has been a triumph for the British de Havilland 'Comet,' British standard aeroplane development, both commercial and military, has been standing still while America had been going ahead. It has been realized with astonishment that America now has in hundreds standard commercial aeroplanes with a higher top speed than the fastest aeroplane in regular service in any squadron in the whole of the Royal Air Force.[31]

Flight perceived the salient issues:

Three types, it may be said, were entered with definite objects and policies—the 'Comets,' the 'Douglas,' and the 'Boeing,'—and each of them has made good and practically proved what their entrants set out to prove. The 'Comet' was designed specifically to fulfill the conditions of the race, and it has fulfilled them completely. The other two set out to prove that the new types of fast commercial aeroplanes which have been developed in America . . . could make a brave show even in such a race as this. They, too, have proved their point. . . . Parmentier and Moll in the 'Douglas,' Roscoe Turner and Clyde Pangborn in the 'Boeing,' all did magnificently, but the race was actually between the ideas and execution of the designers.[32]

Although he finished behind the Comet and the Douglas, Turner was, nevertheless, quite pleased. Upon his arrival in Melbourne, he sent Boeing a congratulatory telegram stating "Every member [of] your organization should be proud of such a wonderful aircraft as we used, Regards."[33] Boeing, too, was pleased. Awaiting Turner's arrival was a telegram stating " . . . the boys are all proud of your outstanding accomplishment and fully appreciate what you and Pangborn have done by successfully completing such a lengthy flight over strange terrain. We also appreciate that you were flying a commercial transport plane where dependability was first consideration in design. Cable plans when convenient."[34] Egtvedt had an idea planned for Turner's return.

If acted upon quickly, the vast international publicity of Turner's achievement and the capabilities of the 247 could be a marketing bonanza for Boeing and for United. Smarting from the victory of the rival DC-2 and the Douglas's transcontinental speed record set by Jack Frye of T.W.A. and Eddie Rickenbacker of Eastern Air Transport in February, Boeing cast about for suggestions in the hope of seizing the advertising initiative from the competition. The most promising idea involved an attempted record flight by Turner from Vancouver to Agua Caliente, Mexico. This idea, which was gaining favor at Boeing, concerned a 1383 mile flight along the Pacific coast which would highlight United's service and shatter Rickenbacker's north-south speed record if an average speed of 180 miles per hour could be maintained. A round trip could be touted as the fastest international flight on the American continent and would emphasize the utility of the P.A.T. route. Before the flight, Turner could stop at every major city served by United and announce his intentions thus boosting public interest.[35] Turner, the inveterate showman, was agreeable. Others at Boeing were not.

The ever conservative Montieth was having second thoughts. Writing to Egtvedt after discussions with other Boeing executives, Montieth stated, "We were unanimous in our opinion that we have nothing to gain and every thing to lose by continuing in this project. . . . We particularly object to Crary's idea of having Turner make a tour of P.A.T. announcing his intended record flight. If he does so and then flops, everyone get a black eye. Let him make the flight first and talk about it afterward."[36] His cautious reasoning was persuasive. The flight could in no way boost aircraft sales because, in his words, "we have no more 247s to sell." Production was ending. Boeing knew that its advanced airliner was unfortunately approaching obsolescence. It was critical to produce a new transport superior to existing types as soon as possible.

Freed from its corporate entanglements, Boeing initiated work on an airliner based on new, secret technology pioneered by Boeing for the U.S.

Repainted, Turner's 247-D entered regular commercial service as the flagship of United Air Lines's fleet of Boeings. *Courtesy Smithsonian Institution.* (*SI A42344-E*)

Army Air Corps, with the intention of leaping over the successful Douglas commercial transports. Based heavily on the four-engined B-17 strategic bomber, this new aircraft would eventually become the Boeing 307 Stratocruiser, the world's first pressurized airliner.

In the meantime, Montieth and company recommended a safer way to take advantage of Turner's exploits. "What we would like to do," Montieth announced, "is dispose of the plane immediately upon return of the conversion (back to airliner configuration) and let United Air Lines do what they wish afterward." "Let them worry about the extra insurance," he concluded, "we cannot see why we should continue to carry the lion's share of the burden when we have the least to gain by it."[37]

Egtvedt soon agreed and turned the project over to William Patterson and United.[38] After the extra fuel tanks were removed and the seats reinstalled, the aircraft was delivered to its owner. For the first flight of the 247-D in United's colors, Roscoe Turner flew his former racer from Seattle to Chicago, on 1 January 1935, with suitable accompanying fanfare.[39] This 247, reregistered as NC 13369, became the pride of the fleet, its racing heritage emblazoned on its fuselage. On the right side, aft of the passenger door, was proudly painted "This Plane Carried the Stars and Stripes Across the Finishing Line in the World's Greatest Air Race." A colorful map with the route traced in black graced the aircraft just below the inscription.

If the markings failed to catch the traveler's eye, an informative brochure was distributed to each passenger. Printed on a pale purple leaflet was a poetic reminder that "this very plane flew from England to Australia in the great international air race" and was "the only U.S.-built and U.S. flown plane to finish the race." This aircraft "is now the flagship of United Air Line's fleet of fifty-five sister Boeing air liners, flying on regular frequent schedules. . . ." Furthermore, this rugged yet luxurious Boeing had overcome enormous obstacles and was now able to give the public "every advantage Turner and Pangborn lacked as well as every advantage they had."[40]

With the introduction of the Boeing 247-D, United was able to keep pace with the competition until its initial investment in the aircraft could be paid off and more modern equipment purchased later in the decade. In the meantime, during the course of 1935, United returned at least thirty-two of the original 247s to Boeing for conversion. At a cost of $1 million, these aircraft were upgraded to 247-D standard with the installation of Wasp S1H1 engines and all of the related changes. Only the forward-sloping windshield was retained on most of those aircraft previously left unmodified, thus differentiating the rebuilt aircraft from production 247-Ds.[41]

True to Boeing's tradition, the new and rebuilt 247-Ds continued to provide sterling service for the airline. The enhanced performance cut transcontinental travel time from 19 hours and 15 minutes to 17 hours and 5 minutes.[42] United, still the largest airline in the U.S., touted its vast experience, the directness of its routes, and frequency of operation as reason enough for passengers to fly the "Mainline." The routes were correctly said to be the shortest between New York and the West Coast and, with the "1935 Boeing," still faster on some routes than T.W.A. The new 247-Ds were advertised as quieter aircraft because of the geared engines and three-bladed propellers and were "especially built to fly at *comfortable* altitudes" even on one engine.[43] Nevertheless, actual operations could still be adventurous.

One of the many significant new features introduced on the 247-D was the addition of the B.F. Goodrich deicer boot. This equipment, the first successful technological innovation to address the problem of in-flight ice formation, met with mixed acceptance. While effective against the rough rime ice which formed on the leading edges of the wing and tail, the boots were ineffective against the formation of the more dangerous clear ice which could coat the entire aircraft and greatly increase weight and drag. In general, pilots did not have much confidence in the deicing equipment. Maintenance was also a problem. The rubber dried out quickly, forcing frequent replacement. In summer weather, the rubber often bled, becoming sticky and making routine maintenance a chore.

When working, the devices could produce disconcerting reactions with the nervous passengers. According to Helen Huntley Brumley, a former flight attendant on United 247-Ds, "The only times I was really frightened were on several occasions when ice formed on the wings so fast that the device on the wing's leading edges could not take care of it and we were unable to gain enough altitude to get out of this condition—the chunks of ice would fly off the wing onto the fuselage—quite an eerie feeling!"

Caring for passengers in the early days of air travel was often arduous. Mrs. Brumley flew on United 247-Ds from 1935 to 1939 and was well acquainted with the rigors of flight. Flying eighty hours a month for $125 a month, United's attendants were often called upon to exercise their training as registered nurses. The 247-Ds and other transports were unpressurized and had to fly through bad weather at lower altitudes. Airsickness was common, particularly with apprehensive passengers on their first flight. Mrs. Brumley's experiences were typical of other attendants on 247-Ds.:

> As we carried 10 passengers and most of our flights were at least of four hours duration, it gave us a lot of time to talk with our passengers and to point out places along the route. We supplied strip maps for each passenger. . . .
>
> Many businessmen made frequent trips and it was nice to get to know them. One of the features of the 247-D we disliked was the bulkhead half way up the aisle we had to step over. We were always fearful of tripping over that step while serving trays. The plane was quite noisy and the heating system did not always provide sufficient heat.
>
> At times the weather would cause the airport in Newark to be fogged in and, instead of returning to Cleveland, we would land at a small airport on top of a mountain at Kylertown, Pennsylvania. We would then take our passengers by car (most of the time we used large funeral limousines) down the mountain roads to Altoona, Pennsylvania and send them by train on into New York. This made it difficult for businessmen to arrive in time for morning appointments and caused much grumbling—we tried to tell them that it was necessary to do so for their safety—but sometimes it failed to work. During the car trip to Altoona, it was our job to make out refund checks for each passenger for the unused portion of their ticket—many had flights on to other East Coast cities.

As we had limited storage space, the meal service was meager but ample—mainly it consisted of box lunches—sandwiches, celery and carrot strips, olives, fruit and either cake or cookies. We served coffee, tea, or hot chocolate from large thermos bottles. Later, pieces of fried chicken were added. The lunches were put on board most of the time in Cleveland. (A very friendly Italian gentleman was the caterer and often would include a snack for the pilots and the stewardess.)[44]

Maintenance of the 247-D was straightforward because the aircraft and its component parts were readily accessible. As there was no internal starter, an external inertial flywheel was used to start the engines. An electrically-driven motor wound up the flywheel which was connected by a gear-driven device to the engine. According to former United mechanic Dick Wood:

When the flywheel spun rapidly, the ground mechanic would pull a "tee" handle on the side of the cowling to engage the spinning flywheel with the engine, turning it over. This cranking was good for [only] a few seconds so it was important for the man in the cockpit to position the throttle and mixture and to prime properly. On a cold morning, the ground mechanic could get frustrated if the man in the cockpit failed to start the engine. This "winding up" was done by a large starting motor connected to a 220 volt power source in the hangar or gate position at the terminal. Strapped inside the nose compartment door of each plane was a hand crank for emergency use.

Mechanics did have to be careful on wet days because the starter was not adequately insulated and could give a nasty shock to the unsuspecting.

Once started, the aircraft was taxied by the ground crew to the gate or hangar. Care had to be taken to keep the 247-D from flying inadvertently. The Boeing was extremely tail-light, particularly with no passengers or baggage on board. Even slight bumps would bounce the tail into the air if full "up" elevator was not held. For Wood, flight was tempting:

One job I had for some time was delivering a 247 to the terminal for the first flight of the day to Oakland. After engine warm-up and magneto check, I'd get control tower clearance onto a runway for a run to the terminal. Though I had not received my pilot's license yet, it was a temptation during a beautiful dawn. The tail wanted to rise and I would think "all I have to do is to push a little more on those two throttle knobs and I'd soon be flying in this smooth air." I always managed to control the impulse, of course.[45]

By 1935, United Air Lines was fighting an uphill battle to preserve its place as the nation's foremost transcontinental carrier. The inroads made by T.W.A. and their DC-2s were beginning to hurt. Whereas in the first six months of 1934, United carried 43.7 percent of all airline passengers,

The 247 and 247-D were started by an external electric motor which spun an inertial flywheel. Note the forward-swept windshield of this converted 247-D. *Courtesy Smithsonian Institution.* (SI 87–11955)

the ridership declined to 37.9 percent in the second half after the introduction of the Douglas.[46] All-out efforts were made to boost ticket sales with new travel offers and polite downplaying of the competition.

Once again United promoted all-expenses paid package tours of the parks and resort areas of the West, the "Nation's Greatest Playgrounds."[47] The airline had even more ambitious plans. In July 1935, the first arrangement of its kind between an American carrier and two European companies was reached when United and Imperial Airways pooled their resources to give the American tourist greatly enhanced traveling flexibility. Under this agreement United, in conjunction with the French Line steamship company, could take a traveler from anywhere along the airline's routes to New York City where they would board the S.S. *Normandie* ocean liner, which would sail across the North Atlantic in five days. Once in Europe, Imperial Airways could take them across the Continent as well as Africa and the Orient. The brochure made it clear that United was the best way to travel in the U.S. The "Mainline" was said to have the most popular direct route

NC13312, the *City of Des Moines*, formerly the *City of Seattle*, makes its approach. Note the Hamilton Standard Hydromatic propellers. *Courtesy Smithsonian Institution. (SI 87–11918)*

and offered the best scenery. As to the question of which airline had the better aircraft, United sidestepped the issue stating that "all of the major lines have splendid planes" but only United flew the sturdy Boeing. As for speed, "several airlines are about equal. There is only a matter of minutes difference, usually—even on long distance flights. Between many cities, United's flights are the fastest due to the Mid-Continent Route and fast planes." In a prophetic reversal of their former position, United attempted to make a virtue of a vice, claiming that "mere speed is never allowed to interfere with passenger comfort. . . . It is generally more important to pick a convenient time of departure and arrival and to fly at smooth comfortable levels than to save a few minutes of flying time."[48]

United Air Lines even went into the movie business to promote the 247-D. Returning an earlier favor by the airline, Paramount Pictures decided to make a film highlighting the safety and professionalism of air travel. Entitled *13 Hours by Air*, the picture followed the transcontinental flight of seven passengers in a United 247-D flown by a senior captain played by Fred MacMurray. The well-paced melodrama developed around several mysterious travelers, a hunted killer, a diamond robbery and the inevitable love interest between MacMurray and costar Joan Bennett. Throughout the film, the tall, lanky, MacMurray had surprisingly ample headroom while on board the 247-D and never tripped over the exposed

NC13301, the original 247 and, after modification from its 247-E status, the first 247-D, is seen at Oakland, California, 1941. (Peter M. Bowers collection) *Courtesy Smithsonian Institution.* (SI 87–11917)

spar, which was conveniently absent from the set. By the time the story was resolved, the audience had been treated to a well-documented study of the intricacies of airline operations and particularly of the strength and excellent characteristics of the Boeing 247-D, which survived a forced landing during a blizzard in the High Sierras. The latest facilities of United were prominently displayed as was NC13342, one of the original aircraft which were later modified to 247-D standards. Surprisingly good for its genre, *13 Hours by Air* was a commercial success when released in 1936.[49] The misleading title, however, chosen for its dramatic ring, was indicative of United's dilemma. In normal operations, the 247-D took at least seventeen hours to cross the country, not thirteen. Only one transport could fly as fast as claimed in the movie's title, the Douglas DC-2. The 247 also appeared, though in lesser roles, in several other movies including *Without Orders, Men With Wings, Stunt Pilot, Flying Blind,* and *Sherlock Holmes in Washington.*

United continued to fly the 247-D until World War II, but on secondary routes and as instructional aircraft. In 1940, the older two-position, three-bladed counterbalanced propellers were replaced by Hamilton Standard Hydromatic constant-speed, three-bladed, variable-pitch propellers. An attractive white with blue trim livery was adopted, covering the gray anodized finish, thus standardizing the colors of United's mixed fleet of 247-Ds and DC-3s.

Symbolically perhaps, the future arrives at Boeing Field, Seattle. United's 247-D, NC13326, waits on the ramp in 1940 behind its rival stablemate, the Douglas DC-3, NC16070. (Gorden S. Williams collection) *Courtesy Smithsonian Institution. (SI 87–11933)*

In an effort to attract more business with the 247-D, United offered the first low coach fares to the public, on 10 April 1940. Flying between San Francisco and Los Angeles with intermediate stops, the 247-Ds provided scheduled service for only $13.90 one way. Known as the "Sky Coach," this low-cost operation was possible because the aging Boeings were fully depreciated and therefore cheaper to fly. The less comfortable accommodations, when compared with the DC-3, were deemed acceptable considering the very reasonable fare. The service flew successfully until 23 April 1942, when it was terminated because of the war.[50]

Despite United's determined efforts, the Boeing's days of glory were rapidly drawing to a close. By 1937, more modern aircraft had forced the 247 off the mainline service and onto the secondary routes throughout the country. Nevertheless, the sturdy transport still had many years of useful service ahead of it.

7
Secondary Airline Service

Desperate promotional and sales efforts could not compensate for business lost in the face of superior competition. Though moderately successful, these efforts at rearguard actions could not overcome the merits of the better-designed DC-2. When the further improved Douglas Sleeper-Transport appeared in December 1935, United was forced to take drastic measures. The day version of the D.S.T., known as the DC-3, could carry from twenty-one to twenty-four passengers in unrivaled speed and comfort. The diminutive Boeing could no longer compete. On 6 April 1936, United Air Lines placed its first order for the DC-3.[1] The only concession to the airline's corporate heritage was the specification of 1000-horsepower Pratt & Whitney Twin Wasps in place of the Wright Cyclones, and the location of the passenger door on the right side of the aircraft. Deliveries began in the autumn of 1936, marking the beginning of the end of the 247 era with United.

The first steps to dispose of the Boeings were taken in 1934 with unmodified 247s.[2] United wisely did not dump the surplus early versions of the 247 on the open market but made these sound aircraft available for purchase or lease to those smaller airlines whose routes fed directly into United's network. This clever idea was designed to solve United's immediate cash flow problems by increasing revenue at once and lowering operating costs, thus allowing the airline to purchase more modern equipment. William Patterson summarized the situation aptly:

> With the fall-off of passenger business in 1934 there was a surplus of at least 12 airplanes. The depreciation of this equipment was a heavy burden. The theory was that we could possibly convert some of this equipment into cash to be used for the purchase of new equipment and we could operate more economically through the purchase of larger airplanes without a relatively increased cost per mile as compared to total seat miles flown. In addition, in view of the fact T.W.A. in their long non-stop flights had affected our through business, it seemed logical to build up certain feeder lines into productive territory with more modern equipment in the hope that this

would result in increased short haul business of feeder lines into United to offset that loss to T.W.A. on the long-haul business. This theory was put into practice.[3]

The first unmodified 247s disposed of in this manner went to three airlines. Leasing and sales agreements were signed with National Parks Airways, Western Air Express, and Pennsylvania Airlines and Transport on 31 October, 6 December, and 26 December 1934, respectively. Other sales and leasing agreements were concluded with these airlines after the DC-3 entered service with United. On the whole, the terms of the deals were generous and mutually beneficial.[4]

National Parks received its first of three Boeing 247s in November 1934 on a one-year lease with an option to buy. These aircraft were used on routes covering Montana, Idaho, and Utah, until the airline was purchased by Western Air Express on 1 August 1937.[5]

Western, in fact, was the largest operator of the 247 after United. Returning to its old name after a period as General Air Lines, Western Air Express bought nine Boeings in January 1935 and leased another twenty-four at various times until 1940. As United Air Lines was forcibly divorced from United Aircraft, so Western was split from General Motors. The terms were harsh, forcing Western to turn over its fleet of new DC-2s to Eastern Air Lines, in which G.M. still retained an interest, pending the sale of its assets, leaving Western with no aircraft. The lease of second-hand 247s saved the airline from extinction. The arrangement worked well as Western Air Express grew into a virtual subsidiary of United with complementary routes and equipment.

Western's experience with the Boeing was, however, mixed.[6] It lost twenty-five percent of its initial fleet when NC13314 crashed on 1 September 1935 on a delivery flight from Burbank to Saugus, California. The pilot, copilot, and flight attendant were killed when the aircraft was flown into the ground during heavy fog. Fortunately, there were no passengers on board.[7] Nevertheless, with its 247s feeding into United's routes, Western was able to turn a small profit of $50,000 in 1936. The achievement, which brought the company back from the brink of extinction, was blemished by two accidents which involved passenger fatalities in the following year. On 15 December 1936, Trip two left Burbank for Salt Lake City in the late evening. After stopping at Las Vegas, the 247-D continued on into the early morning hours until radio contact was lost after 2:23 A.M. The aircraft had vanished. An intensive search failed to locate the 247-D until, well into June 1937, the wreckage of NC13368 was discovered. The aircraft had struck a mountain peak, strewing fragmented parts over the

Western Air Lines was the largest operator of Boeing 247s after United. NC13337 is at Pocatello, Idaho, in 1935. (*Boeing HS 3289*)

mountain and at the base of cliff. The fatal crash was Western's first ever involving passengers, ruining a perfect safety record. Pilot error, compounded by radio static, was to blame.[8]

On 12 January 1937, during this tragic winter for many of America's airlines, Western Trip seven clipped another mountain peak, this time near Newhall, California and plummeted into the ground. Half of the occupants were killed, including noted explorer and film maker, Martin Johnson. His wife Osa, survived. Once again the pilot was faulted for exercising poor judgment during severe icing conditions.[9] Not long after the accident, Western acquired National Parks Airways and its two 247s, which came as welcome replacements. In all of these instances, the 247 was not to blame.

Another operator of the Boeing 247 was Pennsylvania Airlines, which acquired its first 247 from United in December 1934, for the Detroit-Washington route. Pennsylvania's experience with this aircraft was more positive. The shorter stages of its network were ideally suited to the characteristics of the Boeing, which could easily operate into the smaller airfields along the airline's routes. Quickly the 247 replaced Stinson A and Ford Tri-Motors. After merging with Central in November 1936, the new Pennsylvania-Central Airlines, better known as P.C.A., acquired additional Boeings to serve the added routes. P.C.A.'s routes linked the major cities of the Middle Atlantic states with the Great Lakes and, as the line expanded during the late 1930s, with the South. The primary route linked Milwaukee with Washington via numerous intermediate stops.

With P.C.A., the Boeing 247 enjoyed a rebirth, providing reliable service until 1940. It was rapidly introduced throughout the system with great success and was very popular with flight crews. [10] One route, however, required a special modification before the Boeing could be used. The popular 39-minute flight between Detroit and Cleveland was not particularly difficult but most of the distance lay over the open water of Lake Erie. Federal authorities, heedless of the demonstrated reliability of the Wasp engines in the 247, required trimotors to fly the route. Obviously, the 247 could not meet this requirement unless a compromise was reached between P.C.A. and the government. Consequently, P.C.A. arranged with the Walter Kidde Company to install inflatable flotation gear on the 247 in case of a forced alighting in the lake.

According to former P.C.A. Captain Edward P. O'Donnell, the pilots were not fond of the device. "We had a great mistrust of this type of installation," he states. "It was manually operated from the cockpit with just a cable which went through the housing of the exterior of the airplane which contained the inflatable bag. We had a great fear of these bags being inadvertently deployed in the air, so we carried forty-fives [45 caliber pistols] with us just in case, so we could fill the sack with holes." The pistols, which pilots were required by the government to carry to protect the mail, would be fired from the cockpit window. Fortunately, neither the bag nor the pistols ever had to be used because the aircraft was so dependable. "We had no qualms about being forced down in the water," O'Donnell states, "the engines were extremely reliable."[11] Safety was also enhanced by the requirement of flying the route at a 5000–6000 foot minimum ceiling which supposedly would allow the aircraft to glide back to shore.

The Boeing 247's short-field performance was ideally suited to P.C.A.'s "Tobacco Road" route between Norfolk, Virginia and Knoxville, Tennessee, with numerous stops across North Carolina. Despite the absence of flaps on the aircraft, the 247's landing run was remarkably short. According to another former P.C.A. Captain, William "Tex" Guthrie, "You couldn't use the 'Three' because several of the fields were too small for the DC-3." The 247 "could land a heck of a lot shorter" than its larger rival. [12] The "Tobacco Road" provided several perquisites for P.C.A. passengers, according to Mrs. Mary O'Donnell, a former flight attendant for the airline. Meals were served in paper boxes with a roll, an apple, and always "good southern-fried chicken, especially out of Knoxville."[13] When flying

A Pennsylvania Central 247-A starts up in front of its hangar in Grand Rapids, Michigan. *Courtesy Smithsonian Institution.* (*SI 87–11958*)

Two cheerful PCA pilots in 1938: *left*, Edward O'Donnell; *right*, Ralph Read. (*SI 86–12273*)

through the heart of tobacco country in North Carolina, complementary cigarettes were passed among the passengers in Winston-Salem.

The exemplary flying characteristics of the Boeing 247 actually prevented an accident in Knoxville. In the early 1940s, the Knoxville airport did not have a control tower. All aircraft approached the field at their own risk, hoping to see any other traffic in time. Tex Guthrie was making a routine landing when, looming dead ahead, was a larger Delta DC-3 flying down the other end of the runway. Quickly, Tex banked his 247-D, standing it up on one wing, thus narrowly averting a collision.[14] On less dangerous occasions during normal landings, P.C.A. 247s would routinely turn inside the less maneuverable DC-3s on approach and land before the Douglases.

P.C.A. pilots found the 247 a stable and forgiving aircraft that had a very gentle stall and would not fall off in a spin. Pilot Ralph Read recalls that he "felt safe" in the aircraft since he and others "could wrap the Boeing" around obstacles in difficult maneuvers. The 247 was ideal for flying into airfields such as Baltimore's Logan Airport which was surrounded by dangerous power lines.

The transport could even be looped, a feat performed by several unnamed pilots on ferry flights.[15] Edward O'Donnell, who later flew in World War II, found that the famous Boeing B-17 heavy bomber "had much the same characteristics as the 247," of which it was a direct descendant. The only feature found wanting on the 247 was the brakes. Captain O'Donnell, echoing the voices of most who flew the 247, felt that the brakes "were rather inadequate." A pilot "had to stand on them," states Captain Read.

The Boeing 247's reputation for strength and ruggedness was demonstrated clearly on the two occasions when P.C.A. Boeings went down. Flying from Hoover Field, Washington, D.C. to Pittsburgh during the winter, a 247 crewed by Budd Baker and Johnny Tilton began to pick up clear ice immediately after takeoff. When the deicer boots were activated to no effect, Baker decided to turn south in the hope of finding warmer air. All the while the ice continued to build. As the weight and drag increased, the aircraft began to lose altitude. Baker kept the aircraft at the edge of a stall for as long as possible but was eventually forced down in a corn field near Orange, Virginia. Despite clipping the tops of a grove of trees, Baker made a smooth, uneventful landing. The passengers and crew walked away unhurt. The tough aircraft was crated, sent back to Boeing for repairs and later reentered service although, O'Donnell notes, "we never felt it flew quite right after that."[16]

Tex Guthrie poses next to his PCA 247-D at Knoxville, Tennessee, in 1941. (W. C. Guthrie collection) *Courtesy Smithsonian Institution.* (*SI 86–3276*)

PCA flight attendant Marion McClintock converses with an interested passenger while flying in a 247. She later became the wife of PCA pilot Edward O'Donnell. *Courtesy Smithsonian Institution.* (*SI 86–3786*)

The second incident was more serious. On a flight from Charleston, West Virginia to Pittsburgh, a P.C.A. 247-D flown by Captain Russell Wright crashed on take-off after a rare engine failure. With a load of six passengers, the aircraft could not gain enough altitude immediately on one engine to clear the approaching mountains. The ensuing crash into a forest tore off the wings of the Boeing but left the fuselage intact. Once again the remarkable strength of the 247 saved all on board from death. The only serious casualty was flight attendant Irene Coates, who injured her back because she sat in the small jump seat for attendants that was bolted to the rear bulkhead.[17]

The 247s flew several special flights while in service with P.C.A. During the bitter winter of 1936, severe flooding isolated Pittsburgh from food and medical supplies. P.C.A. was one of several airlines that flew relief missions into the city, delivering yeast cakes, water, and typhoid serum. P.C.A.'s 247s were fitted with special tires with chines (ridges) to deflect water away from the aircraft. For a time, P.C.A. Boeings were the only aircraft that could fly into and out of the city.

Until 1938 and the arrival of the airline's first DC-3, the 247 served well as P.C.A.'s flagship, opening many new routes and providing notably trouble-free service well into the 1940s. According to Charles Baptie, who was often involved with public relations at P.C.A., the 247 was also used on a number of publicity flights, including Easter sunrise services broadcast in flight by radio station KDKA and "high-flying birthday parties."[18]

United Air Lines concluded a fourth arrangement, this time with Wyoming Air Service on 31 January 1935, in which United provided sufficient aircraft to operate three daily round trips between Denver and Cheyenne. United paid for all the ancillary costs except for personnel, receiving in turn twenty cents per scheduled airplane mile flown and two-thirds of the passenger revenues.[19] Wyoming used a total of six 247s at various times, continuing to use the aircraft after it sold some of its routes and changed its name to Inland Airlines. Inland continued to fly 247s until 1943, when the airline merged with Western.[20]

Boeing 247s remained in service with United and the four airlines which fed into United's network until the onset of World War II. The war greatly curtailed civil air transport as the entire airline industry was mobilized. Beginning in 1942, the airlines operated skeleton fleets on limited routes as transport aircraft and trained personnel were absorbed into the military. As part of the commitment to the war effort, twenty-seven Boeing 247s were commandeered and purchased by the U.S. Army Air Forces, including all but one of United's remaining fleet of twelve. Designated the C-73,

The crash of NC13359 into the West Virginia mountainside on 16 April 1941. Remarkably, all survived as the fuselage remained intact. (W. C. Guthrie collection) *Courtesy Smithsonian Institution. (SI 86–3280)*

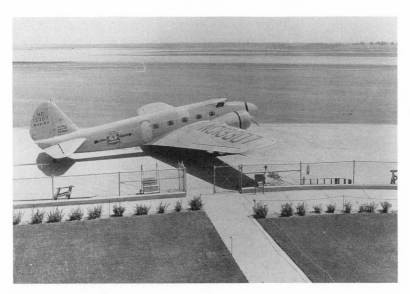

Wyoming Air Service flew six 247s at various times between Denver and Cheyenne. *Courtesy Smithsonian Institution. (SI 86–5933)*

131

these aircraft were eventually given more powerful 600-horsepower Pratt & Whitney R-1340–53 Wasps, similar to those used on North American T-6 trainers, and assigned to the Air Transport Command. During the war four C-73s were wrecked and four were used as instructional airframes. Two were transferred temporarily to Eastern Air Lines for general testing along its routes. After the war, one was sold to a broker and the remaining eighteen returned to commercial airlines.[21]

With the massive surplus of C-47s (DC-3s) after the war ended in 1945, and the entry of the larger four-engined DC-4 and Lockheed Constellation into trunk-line service, the trunk airlines had little need for the diminutive, aging 247. The robustness of the Boeing, however, was an endearing trait to several smaller commercial operators.

During the course of the war, eight 247s were in use in Canada. Sold by P.C.A. and others in 1940 to the Canadian Department of Munitions to aid the allied war effort, these Boeings were assigned to the Royal Canadian Air Force. After limited service with the R.C.A.F., the eight aircraft were sold or leased to commercial firms. Maritime Central Airways purchased one and Canadian Pacific leased five for its own use and for associated Quebec Airways and Yukon Southern Air Transport.[22] The Boeing's great strength and excellent short-field performance made it ideal for the harsh northern environment.

One Canadian Pacific aircraft created a minor record by carrying a unique cargo on one flight in December 1944. Though designed to transport just ten passengers, it carried twenty-six—all babies. The infants, all under the age of five months, were being sent from an orphanage at La Crèche Saint Vincent-de-Paul in Quebec to one in nearby Chicoutimi. The tiny passengers were placed in specially-built cribs and loaded on board under the care of one attendant. The babies slept through the flight, awakening only upon landing.[23] The 247s served only for a brief time with Canadian Pacific before returning to the United States at the conclusion of the war.

Another Canadian Boeing was assigned to the British Royal Air Force for significant wartime experiments. Given the serial number DZ203, this 247 was transferred to the R.A.F. in July 1941, assembled at Speke and flown in August in a display of blind bombing as part of the R.A.F. Special Duty flight. In November 1941, the S.D.F. was renamed the Research Section of the Telecommunications Flying Unit. It used the 247 for a variety of tests, particularly the development of an instrument landing system after April 1944. Using an autopilot designed to interact with I.L.S. signals, DZ203 completed the first successful ground-controlled

The 247-D was redesignated the C-73 after twenty-seven were acquired by the Army Air Force. *Courtesy Smithsonian Institution.* (*SI A4450*)

Quebec Airways also used the 247. This D model is parked at Montreal Airport. (*Boeing P42191*)

133

This Canadian Pacific Air Lines 247-D flew a unique cargo of twenty-six babies in December 1944. (*Boeing P44927*)

Formerly NC13344 of National Air Transport, this 247-D was transferred by Canada to Great Britain where, as DZ 203, it pioneered ground-controlled automatic landing systems. *Courtesy Smithsonian Institution.* (*SI 87–13090*)

automatic landing while flying from Defford in October 1944. Some three hundred hours were flown with the automatic approach and landing experiments.[24]

According to Group Captain John A. McDonald, "We were able to home the Boeing from fifty miles, orbit the field at a selected range, line him up with the runway and land, all on the auto-approach system—results not previously achieved in any sphere of aviation."[25] The aircraft completed the war as part of the Blind Landing Experimental Unit at Martlesham Heath and received a modified nose during its tenure with the R.A.F.[26]

Three of the Canadian Pacific 247-Ds were purchased by Burt Zimmerly and placed in operation with his small Idaho airline on 28 July 1945. With these aircraft, plus two others purchased later, Zimmerly Airlines was able to expand its route network and changed its name to Empire Air Lines in 1946.[27] In two years of service, the five aircraft amassed a total of 3.5 million accident-free miles before they were replaced by the ubiquitous DC-3.[28]

Farther north, the 247-D soldiered on in the unforgiving Alaskan wilderness. Founded in 1927 to serve the people of the isolated regions of Alaska, Wien Alaska Airlines found the 247 well-suited for its diverse tasks and purchased two former C-73s from the U.S.A.A.F.[29]

One of the aircraft, NC13313, a veteran of over 16,000 hours, was extensively modified. In 1945, Northwest Air Service, an aircraft maintenance company, installed a large cargo door on the aircraft. Simultaneously, in 1946, Boeing instituted a service program to help its customers and to encourage business during the postwar economic slump. According to Wellwood E. Beall, vice-president of engineering-sales, "Now that the wartime pressures are off, Boeing is again in a position to assist all operators of Boeing aircraft, including owners of earlier models such as the 247. . . . Such assistance will include not only the routine resupplying of data on operations and maintenance, but also design of structural revisions to suit new users and in some cases actual factory modifications and special overhaul of delivered aircraft."[30] Sigurd Wien was the first and only operator to take advantage of this opportunity and sent NC13313 to Seattle for further work.

While it was at Boeing, four additional fuel tanks totalling 276 extra gallons were installed in the wing extending the range from a modest 580 miles to almost 1200 miles. To improve navigation, the latest automatic radio direction finder and communications equipment were installed, changing the profile of the aircraft above the cabin. The 247 was also

Burt Zimmerly stands by the door of one of the Boeings used by his Empire Air Lines. (*Boeing P6164*)

NC13313 was extensively modified for Wien-Alaska Airlines. Note the bulged cockpit roof. (*Boeing P44658*)

given an attractive paint scheme designed by Boeing. The second Wien aircraft, however, was never updated as originally planned.[31]

The 247-Ds adapted readily to the rugged 7000 miles of Alaskan routes, most of which were north of Fairbanks and included service to Point Barrow. Wien's traffic manager Charles V. West favored the 247-D because "it is ideally suited for the short fields we use. To take off we turn up the engine with the brakes on, pull the wheel back and give her full power. We've taken off from 1200 foot fields this way." The strength of the landing gear and the capabilities of the high-lift wing were other impressive features. In fact, Sig Wien was so pleased, he wrote Boeing "a letter of praise and appreciation . . . for building an airplane with the sturdiness and dependability . . . of our Boeing 247-Ds." The aircraft could successfully carry difficult loads into and out of the poorest of fields in the worst weather with cross winds of over thirty miles per hour and temperatures of thirty-five degrees below zero. Wien recalled a particularly difficult operation:

> The landings and takeoff were made easily enough and much to my surprise—you see the ship was still new to us as was bush flying with any kind of multi-engined ship in Alaska. By now the performance, sturdiness, and dependability of our Boeing has been realized . . . a seemingly dangerous operation is now just a routine operation. . . . The 247 is tops.[32]

Other Alaskan operators included the Civil Aeronautics Authority which flew a 247-D for utility work after the war, and Woodley Airways. Renamed Pacific Northern Airlines in August 1945, Woodley flew two 247-Ds for just seven months after the aircraft entered service on 20 June.[33]

The 247-D also served two prominent airlines in South America. The Sociedad Colombo-Alemana de Transportes Aéreos (SCADTA) operated 247-Ds. After its organization by Colombian nationals and German emigrants, Pan American Airways acquired financial control of SCADTA in 1931, and, in an effort to modernize and consolidate the fleet of assorted Junkers, Fords, and Sikorskys, purchased SCADTA's first three 247-Ds directly from United Air Lines on 5 December 1936.[34] The short-field capability and compact size made the 247-D an excellent aircraft for service across the Andes and the Colombian rain forests. The first ten Boeings were SCADTA's flagships and pioneered several new routes throughout the country. Routes were also blazed into the llanos, or plains, of eastern Colombia where new airfields were built to link these remote areas to the outside world for the first time.[35]

Through pressure from the U.S. government and the rising fear of the German threat to the Panama Canal, SCADTA was nationalized in 1940

This well-worn 247-D flew for Woodley Airways in the immediate post-war years. (*Boeing P27450*)

A 247-D of White Pass Airways. (Keith T. Petrich collection) (6600790)

and renamed AVIANCA, Aerovías Nacionales de Colombia. The new airline dismissed its employees of German origin and was officially acknowledged by Pan American, although Pan American had been in legal control for several years. In reorganizing AVIANCA, Pan American replaced the 247-Ds with DC-3s on the primary intercity routes, performing well, though four were lost in accidents. By 1947, all the 247-Ds had been replaced by DC-3s.[36]

The other South American operator was Viacão Aérea Bahiana of Brazil which flew one 247-D, PP-BHC, in the state of Bahia from 1945 until the airline folded in 1948.[37] C.R. Holck acquired the Boeing, then sold it to Raymundo Duarte Muniz in 1953. In turn, Muniz became the primary stockholder of SAVA, (Servicos Aero-Taxi e Abastecimento do Vale Amazonica, Ltda.), which acquired the aircraft on 30 October 1958. SAVA was a charter firm that served the Amazon region. Reregistered as PT-APO, the 247-D Boeing flew until 24 April 1963, when an engine fire forced the aircraft down in a swamp on a flight from Almeierim to Prainha. PT-APO was then taken by barge back to Belém where it was eventually scrapped and stricken from the register at the end of 1971.[38]

Farther north, in Mexico, the 247 enjoyed considerable popularity and success. At least eighteen 247s operated with no fewer than thirteen companies. The first four 247-Ds in Mexico were seized by Mexican authorities in March 1937 as they were being readied for shipment to Republican Spain. As the fortunes of the Republicans were in doubt, the 247s and the other aircraft and equipment which were slated for delivery were taken by the Mexican government at the request of the Republicans in order to prevent the aircraft from falling into the hands of General Franco and the Nationalists. The four Boeings were auctioned off soon thereafter, to raise money for the partial repayment of the republican war debt to Mexico. Mexican Air Force Captain Juan José Sixto del Rio bought them and sold them to C.M.A. (Compañía Mexicana de Aviación, S.A.). After Pan American gained partial control of Aeronaves de Mexico, two 247-Ds were used to augment the service between Mexico City and Acapulco in September 1941 until replaced by former U.S.A.A.F. Douglas C-39 versions of the DC-2. During the war Aeronaves de Michoacán flew one 247-D and LAGOSA (Lineas Aéreas Guerrero-Oaxaca, S.A.) flew one in freight service in 1946.[39]

One of the most important Boeing 247 operators in Mexico was LAMSA (Líneas Aéreas Mineras, S.A.), founded by U.S. citizen Gordon Barry in 1934. LAMSA struggled until 1943 when United Air Lines bought a controlling interest in the hope of expanding internationally.

Passengers board one of SCADTA's flagships. *Courtesy Smithsonian Institution.* (*SI 87–11960*)

Brazilian PT-APO of SAVAG lies derelict on a Belém airfield after a tiring career flying supplies up the Amazon. It was scrapped in 1971. *Courtesy Smithsonian Institution.* (*SI 87–11963*)

XA-BEZ was one of four 247s operated by Compañía Mexicana de Aviación (C.M.A.) *Courtesy Smithsonian Institution. (SI 87–11940)*

The distinctive red, white, and green markings of LAMSA's 247-D *Estado de Chihuahua* were patterned after the markings of United Air Lines, after the latter company revitalized the struggling Mexican carrier in 1944. *Courtesy United Air Lines. (UAL P 374)*

After changing the name to Líneas Aéreas Mexicanas, S.A., United transformed LAMSA almost overnight into a carrier of substance with the injection of money, technical assistance, and equipment. In October 1944, five United 247-Ds were transferred to LAMSA resplendent in the Mexican red, white, and green national colors, patterned after United's current livery. By December 1946, only one was left in service, carrying freight between Ciudad Juarez and Mexico City.[40]

Also in 1934, Italian immigrant Carlos Panini founded Servicios Aéreos Panini, S.A. As he expanded his airline outward from central Mexico, Panini added two 247s and one 247-D to his fleet in 1947 to replace the Buhls in service. In 1948, Panini sold out to Aerovías Reforma, S.A. By this time, another four 247-Ds were in operation.[41] In addition, three more 247-Ds were flown briefly by Aerovías de Michoacán, which changed its name to Aerovías de Michoacán-Guerrero after the acquisition of the Boeings permitted expansion of its routes.[42] Other Mexican commercial operators were Servicio Aéreos de Chiapas, S.A.; LAUSA (Líneas Aéreas Unidas, S.A.); Aeronaves Oaxaca; Taxis Aéreos Nacionales, S.A.; ATSA (Aero Transportes, S.A.); and Líneas Aéreas del Pacifico. Five of the Mexican Boeings were eventually returned to the United States. These were modified as crop dusters by Jesse Bristow in Miami and flown between 1956 and 1960 throughout the country.[43]

A few Boeing 247s also continued in passenger service for a few years in Central America and the Caribbean until attrition, the lack of spare parts, and the availability of the DC-3 and other more modern aircraft brought the 247's airline career to a close. Founded in 1944 as a Pan American subsidiary, LANICA (Líneas Aéreas de Nicaragua) briefly operated 247-Ds, opening service on the airline's first routes. Across the border in Costa Rica, AVO (Aerovías Occidentales, S.A.) flew two 247-Ds from 1947 until 1951, when the airline folded. One of the last airlines to operate the venerable Boeings in regular service was RAPSA (Rutas Aéreas Panamenas, S.A.), which earned an enviable reputation for safety throughout Panama.[44]

In Haiti, James O. Plinton, a black American who was a flight instructor and former employee of T.W.A. and Eastern, formed Quisquiya Ltd. in March 1948. For three years he flew a 247-D, along with a Lockheed Lodestar, from Port-au-Prince to Miami and to all of Haiti's island neighbors. He was the first to serve the Turks and Caicos Islands.[45]

Thus, as time passed, what had once been the pride of United Air Lines were forced into far lesser roles. Until the early 1960s, the ten or so remaining Boeings hauled cargo in remote places and performed other

Despite the U.S. registration, this 247-D flew in Mexico for Líneas Aéreos Del Pacifico. (W. T. Larkins collection) *Courtesy Smithsonian Institution.* (SI 87–11920)

Nationwide was an irregular operator flying NC1060M from Detroit to points within Michigan. (Museum of Flight) *Courtesy Smithsonian Institution.* (SI 87–11943)

duties for which they had never been intended. Jesse Bristow's ten crop-dusting aircraft were equipped with smaller Pratt & Whitney Wasp Junior engines of 450 horsepower, salvaged from surplus Air Force BT-13 trainers. Outfitted with these powerplants, BT-13 cowlings, and the appropriate plumbing for dispensing insecticide, they were flown by several crop dusting companies in the U.S., including Robertson Aviation and Central Aircraft of Yakima, Washington. Nationwide Air Transport Service flew one 247-D on irregular service from Detroit to points within Michigan during the late 1940s. This aircraft, c/n* 1692, had at one time flown for Varney and United, then for Pennsylvania Airlines, and eventually for AVIANCA before returning to the U.S. Other operators of the remaining 247s included Travelair Taxi of Cleveland, Ohio; Airspray Inc., of Orlando, Florida; Precipitation Control of Taft, California; Zig Zag; and California Standard, of Calgary, Alberta.[46]

One 247-D performed a unique service in the twilight of its airline career. Painted pink with champagne bubbles adorning the top of its fuselage, N-91R, the *Reno Champagne Cruiser* flew between Washington, D.C. and Colonial Beach, Virginia in 1956 and 1957. As part of a package charter, adventurous, wealthy Washingtonians and their female companions flew out on Friday nights and returned on Sunday after an exciting weekend of entertainment at the illegal casinos in Colonial Beach. The flights were almost as thrilling as the gambling. The age and general decrepitude of the poorly maintained Boeing produced constant problems including a spark-spraying wheels-up landing in May 1957. When Virginia authorities finally got wind of the illicit activity, they closed the casinos and grounded the Champagne Cruiser.[47]

The last commercial operator of the Boeing 247 was Island Airlines of Port Clinton, Ohio, which flew a regular service to the Bass Islands in Lake Erie. A 247-D was acquired in 1954 and flew until the early 1960s when maintenance and parts supply problems forced the airline to suspend operations. The aircraft was sold to an English buyer in 1968.[48]

So ended the Boeing 247's distinguished airline career. Its contributions to air travel were manifest: it had ushered in the modern age of commercial aviation. Even so, this remarkable aircraft also in no small way advanced aviation through the exploits of specially modified or specially employed 247s.

*Constructor's number

ZigZag Airways was another obscure 247-D operator in the United States. (Museum of Flight) *Courtesy Smithsonian Institution.* (*SI 87–11944*)

The *Reno Champagne Cruiser* flew gamblers from Washington, D.C., to Colonial Beach, Virginia, for weekend trips. *Courtesy Smithsonian Institution.* (*SI 83–16426*)

8
Special 247s

Several Boeing 247s served admirably as executive transports and research aircraft. Though not as numerous or as well publicized as the 247s in airline service, these Boeings proved as reliable and effective as their commercial brethren.

Of the first sixty Boeing 247s built, fifty-nine were allocated to United Air Lines's operating divisions while one, a specially modified aircraft, was delivered to United Aircraft and designated the 247-A. Built as an executive aircraft, the 247-A was also used as a flying test bed for several United Aircraft projects, once the design was approved in May 1932.

The primary difference between the 247-A and the standard Boeing was the installation of Pratt & Whitney's latest small diameter radial engine, the Twin Wasp Junior. This new powerplant featured two rows of seven cylinders which produced 625 horsepower and was noticeably smoother in operation than the Wasp. Displacement grew from 1340 to 1535 cubic inches. The extra 70 horsepower enabled the 247-D to reach a maximum speed of 198 miles per hour, some twenty miles per hour faster than the standard Boeing.

Other differences included a lengthened cowling to accommodate the longer engine, along with different air intakes. Passenger capacity was restricted to six but fuel capacity was increased from 273 to 357 gallons. In the course of its career, the 247-A was modified with different antennae, improved Twin Wasp Junior engines, different cowlings and was eventually equipped with a 247-D rudder and tail. Experimental cowlings and other structural items were also tested, particularly successive versions of the Hamilton-Standard variable pitch propellers.[1]

Apparently some thought was given by certain United Aircraft officials to the production of a 247-A version for United Air Lines but plans were never actively pursued.[2] The 247-A was completing its final tests in the late summer of 1933 when reports of the DC-1's remarkable flight tests at Albuquerque were received. The Boeing matched the Douglas' performance (if not its capacity) and offered a solution to the dilemma of the

The Boeing 247-A served UATC well as an executive aircraft and a flying testbed. *Courtesy United Technologies Archive. (Boeing 6831-B)*

The 247-A differed from its stablemates as it was equipped with the more powerful and smoother-running Pratt & Whitney Twin Wasp Junior. These views show both sides of the right engine. *Courtesy United Technologies Archive. (Boeing 6643-B)*

147

new competition. The subsequent decision to produce the less extensively modified—and therefore cheaper—247-D, plus the breakup of the United Aircraft combine, forestalled any further consideration.

The Boeing 247-A served United Aircraft admirably for a decade and was called upon to perform myriad functions. The primary role was as an executive transport. Logging 4438 hours over 700,000 miles, the aircraft flew company officials and distinguished guests, such as Charles Lindbergh, Secretary of the Treasury Henry Morgenthau, and famed Norwegian aviator Bernt Balchen, throughout the country. During the notorious 1936 New England floods, the 247-A ferried company executives between Hartford and isolated East Hartford. The aircraft performed extra duty as a cargo aircraft, rushing deliveries of freight and engine parts.

The 247-A was also called upon for emergency mercy flights and even saved the lives of two young women. In 1938, pilot Ben Whelan flew from Hartford to Baltimore to pick up a desperately needed sulfa drug prescription from Johns Hopkins University Hospital, the only place in the country with a supply of this latest wonder drug. Flying at top speed, Whelan delivered the medicine, with the help of a police escort from the airport, in time to save the life of a 15-year-old girl. Later, in 1943, Ralph Bourdon flew an ailing young woman to Temple University Hospital in Philadelphia for a delicate lung operation. The patient was under an oxygen tent throughout the flight, which was flown solely on instruments. She too was saved.

After the 247-A had been delivered on 4 November 1933, the aircraft subsequently encountered commercial airliners from time to time. United Aircraft company pilots derived particular pleasure when observed by Douglas DC-2 crews in early 1934. Accustomed to overtaking the slower 247s, the Douglas pilots were often shocked by the performance of the lone 247-A. On one occasion, pilot Ralph Bourdon and a Douglas pilot were assigned the same altitude and takeoff times for a flight from Hoover Field across the Potomac River from Washington, D.C. Miffed that he would be forced to fly behind the supposedly slower Boeing, the Douglas pilot complained vociferously to the control tower. "Don't worry son," came the reply from the tower, "you'll never catch him."

The 247-A was a favorite with its pilots and crews. Maintenance was relatively easy, requiring little work to keep the aircraft flying. Affectionately nicknamed "stumblebum," the 247-A was nevertheless called upon to perform the most difficult of tasks under conditions which grounded other aircraft. With pride, Ralph Bourdon stated "that airplane had no bad flying characteristics at all. You could land her on a dime—and get out of

The two 247s bought by Lufthansa for tests were transitional aircraft incorporating the small cowl and direct-drive Wasp of the original aircraft with the rearward sloping windshield of the 247-D under development at that time. (*DLH 3085–1-2*)

fields not much larger. We always asked for the Boeing when we had a tough job to do. This winter (1947) Charlie Cowan had a night hop to Montreal. It was snowing, visibility was low, and he had to land on a short, icy runway. He called for the Boeing and from then on it was just routine." After fourteen years of faithful service, NC13300 was retired and ignominiously consigned to the scrap heap later in 1947.[3]

In February 1934, two 247s were delivered to Germany for evaluation by Deutsches Lufthansa (DLH) and the German aircraft industry. These aircraft were unique. Although they were the first aircraft built from the order for fifteen additional transports, these Boeings were not fully D models, retaining as they did the direct drive S1D1 Wasp engines, two-bladed, variable-pitch propellers, and different cowlings, while incorporating the aft sloped windshield and other modifications of the later series.[4] Ostensibly sold to Deutsches Lufthansa (German Air Lines), the two Boeings were thoroughly examined by airline and industry specialists to learn more about American technology. They were not disappointed.

The Germans were particularly impressed by the superb workmanship of the aircraft. Boeing's reputation for quality was apparently well founded. Favorable comments were made concerning the low fuel consumption of the Wasps, the low pressure warning indicator, the acoustical gear-down indicator, and the excellent throttle response and the lockable control system. The investigators praised the innovative heated pitot tube, adjustable rudder pedals, and the placement of the brake controls on the rudder pedals. This clever design, typical of American aircraft, freed the hands of the pilot to manipulate the controls freely during landings. The investigators were also intrigued by the 247's anodized aluminum exterior finish which protected the metal from corrosion on the outside, as well as the lacquer covering on the interior metal surfaces.

There were, however, some criticisms. While suitable for operations over land, DLH, which operated a fleet of seaplanes as well as landplanes, did not believe that this coating could protect aluminum alloy from salty sea air. It was critical, as was the U.S. Army Air Corps, of the 247's inordinately high rudder forces. The aircraft exhibited a nose-down tendency, especially during right turns. The rudder was ineffective in bringing the aircraft out of the turn, requiring considerable use of the aileron. Furthermore, the aircraft could not be sideslipped because of its inherent stability.[5] Boeing was aware of this problem, though not of this report, and later introduced a modified straight rudder and additional tab on the 247-D to alleviate the rudder problem.

The acquisition of the two 247s by Germany was reported with some nationalistic satisfaction by the American press. The San Francisco Call-Bulletin was bursting with pride: "This editorial is for people who think that Europe makes better airplanes than we do. The Luft Hansa, leading airline of Germany, has just taken delivery of . . . Boeing 3-mile a minute monoplanes like those used in this country on the United Air Lines. And you may be sure that before the officials of the Luft Hansa decided to order these airplanes . . . they tested all European airplanes. . . . The Luft Hansa people could apparently buy no finer airplane in Europe—and are acting on the principle that if this is good enough for the American people, it is probably good enough for the Germans."[6] The Seattle Post-Intelligencer was particularly pleased: "Luft Hansa . . . is adopting Seattle-made transports for its sky routes. . . . This action is a striking answer to the question of whether Europe makes better aircraft that we do right here in Seattle."[7] Although heavily subjective, these editorials emphasized the emerging leadership of the United States in international aeronautics. With the Boeing 247, America had taken the lead in commercial aircraft design.

After the tests were completed, the second German 247, c/n 1945 and registered as D-AGAR, actually entered service with DLH. This aircraft flew until 24 May 1935 when it was damaged beyond repair by an errant Air France transport taxiing at Nürnberg. The other 247 was used as a test bed for an experimental autopilot and crashed on takeoff from Hanover on 13 August 1937.[8]

Originally ordered by Germany but never delivered, *Woolaroc III* flew as a luxury executive transport for Phillips Petroleum from 1935 until 1940. *Courtesy United Technologies Archive.* (*UTC A-315*)

A great deal was learned from the 247 concerning the state of the art of American aeronautics. A significant possibility exists, although unproven, that the 247 influenced subsequent German bomber designs. The aft fuselage and tail section of the formidable Junkers Ju 88 certainly bears a striking resemblance to that of the Boeing 247.

A third Boeing was ordered but never shipped to Germany. Political considerations concerning Adolf Hitler's expanding dictatorial power forestalled the delivery. The aircraft in question, one of the first of the D models, languished in storage at Boeing until it was sold to the Phillips Petroleum Company as an executive aircraft and delivered on 16 September 1935.[9] Given the registration of NC2666, a reflection on the company's Phillips 66 product line, the aircraft was christened *Woolaroc III*, in honor of the famed Travel Air 5000 of the same name which won the 1927 Dole Race, and an airliner then in service.

As delivered, *Woolaroc III* contained additional soundproofing and was given luxurious appointments. Included among these were a refrigerator, a writing desk, a telephone, a radio for receiving entertainment broadcasts, overstuffed easy chairs and berths, walnut cabinets, and cabin flight instruments. On each engine nacelle was painted the name "Wah-shah-ahe-hlu-ah-ki-he-kah," meaning "Osage Eagle Chief." Mr. Phillips had been awarded that title by Osage Indians and proudly wrote it on his aircraft. *Woolaroc III* served with Phillips until 1940 and eventually finished its career with Empire Air Lines.[10]

Two other 247s were actively involved in the turbulent politics of East Asia. In the 1930s, China was a nation in chaos. With the Nationalist government of Chiang Kai-shek locked in mortal battle with the Communist forces of Mao Zedong, and the Japanese expanding first into Manchuria and then into central China, the nation was divided into numerous warring camps. Much of China was controlled by independent administrations—a survival of the era of local war lords who carved out their own territories. One of the most powerful and influential war lords was the youthful Chang Hsüeh-liang, originally from Manchuria. Known as the "Young Marshal," and the "Red Suppression Chief," Chang was a friendly looking man in his late twenties with a well-deserved reputation for ruthlessly crushing Communist activities in his regions of Honan, Hupeh, and Anhwei.[11]

Chang, like other war lords, built a large private army to protect his interests. Furthermore, he purchased an odd assortment of transports from Europe and the United States to improve communications throughout his territories. Impressed by the Boeing 247, Chang managed to purchase a new D model, c/n 1955, through his personal pilot, American Julius Barr. As ordered, the aircraft was delivered with a modified interior to suit the marshal's needs. The cabin was divided into two compartments. The forward area was equipped with a bolstered bunk in place of the two left seats, while the rear compartment contained six standard airline seats. Thus modified, the aircraft was shipped to China on 9 November 1934, arrived in Shanghai in December, flew on the 16th and was delivered soon thereafter.[12]

The distinctive appearance of the Boeing 247 attracted much attention throughout Chang's provinces. The aircraft was generally known as the *White Eagle* (*Bai Ying*) because the Mandarin transliteration of "Boeing" sounded like "bai ying," which meant "white eagle." So named, the aircraft set several speed records over the course of Chang's travels and was a frequent item in the Chinese press. In addition to normal transport duties, Chang's Boeing dropped supplies to his beleaguered troops during action against the Communists and was frequently punctured by enemy bullets.[13]

By the late autumn of 1936, Chang was becoming disenchanted with the unwillingness of Chiang Kai-shek and the Nationalist government in Nanking to fight the Japanese. The Young Marshal was anxious to end the bloody civil war that was paralyzing China and to unify forces against the

"Young Marshal" Chang Hsüeh-liang stands before his 247-D, *Bai Ying* (the White Eagle). *Courtesy United Technologies Archive.* (*UTC A-313*)

Japanese. Seeking a way to persuade Chiang to change his mind, he arranged the kidnapping and arrest of the Nationalist leader at Sian on 12 December 1936. When word spread of the event, Chang Hsüeh-liang received wide support from the troops in the northwest. Communist forces also lent encouragement.

Chang quickly called a meeting of all interested parties. Three of the delegates, including Red Army Vice-Chairman of the military council Zhou En lai, were flown by Chang in his Boeing 247-D to Sian to decide Chiang's fate and the fate of China. After lengthy discussion, Chiang agreed to refocus the Nationalists' efforts against the Japanese and halt, for a time, the civil strife, thus earning his release. Shamed by his extraordinary actions in kidnapping his superior, Chang Hsüeh-liang flew to Nanking in his Boeing and surrendered himself to Chiang Kai-shek. He was subsequently placed under house arrest and has spent the rest of his life under guard, even on Taiwan, until as late as the 1990s.[14] His 247-D was seized and flown by the Nationalists until it was destroyed in a bombing raid at I-ch'ang later in 1937.[15]

Before Chang Hsüeh-liang's arrest and imprisonment, he had ordered a second, highly modified 247-D as his personal transport. This unique

The 247-Y was modified with two fixed 50-caliber machine guns in the nose. (*Boeing 9382-B*)

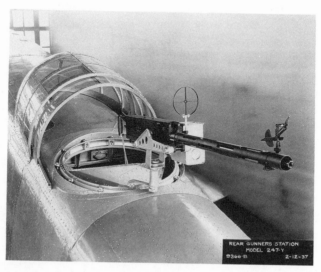

A flexible 50-caliber machine gun was mounted in the cabin in place of the lavatory. (*Boeing 9366-B*)

aircraft was converted from a United Air Lines transport, which was returned to Seattle for modifications. Reflecting the deteriorating political situation of China, this 247-D, unlike the *White Eagle*, was armed. In place of the forward baggage compartment, Boeing installed two Colt Model-53 50-caliber, fixed machine guns. A flexible, 50-caliber machine gun was mounted dorsally, two-thirds of the way down the fuselage, just behind the main cabin door where the lavatory would normally have been. The gunner was protected from the airstream by a sliding glass "greenhouse." The six rear seats remained unchanged but, in the area forward of the rear spar, the four front seats were replaced by four extra fuel tanks that had originally been fitted to Roscoe Turner's MacRobertson Racer. This increased the fuel load to 699 gallons and gave the 247-Y, as the transport was redesignated, a range of 1800 miles. Larger oil tanks were also added. In consequence, the gross weight of the aircraft rose from 13,650 pounds to 15,684 pounds with a slight reduction in its top speed to 190 miles per hour and its service ceiling to 20,700 feet.[16]

By the time the 247-Y was delivered in March 1937, the Young Marshal was in prison. The aircraft was taken by Julius Barr and turned over to the Nationalist government. Little else is known, except that the 247-Y was reportedly destroyed when it flew into a mountain not long afterwards.[17]

Less intriguing but of more lasting significance was the work conducted by United Air Lines' research laboratories with its Boeing 247-D, NC13365. Known as the "flying lab," this aircraft pioneered the development of innumerable advances in aircraft safety. As mentioned earlier, most of the crashes of the 247 had been caused by a combination of bad weather, static discharges, and poor visibility. Beginning in 1937, United's radio laboratory (the United Communications Laboratory), based on the second floor of Hangar 2 at Chicago's Midway Airport, began to explore the solution to these problems with a modified 247-D. During that year, NC13365 was removed from the line and turned over to the laboratory for experimental work and therefore, reregistered as NX13365. The seats were replaced by benches below the windows upon which were located test equipment. In the overhead nets originally designed to hold hats and light clothes was a nest of wires.[18]

The problem of static was the first to be tackled by the flying lab. The buildup of static electricity around aircraft, particularly during inclement weather, often caused sufficient interference to cripple the communications and radio navigation equipment. This static was the direct cause of several 247 accidents and was an ever present danger in air travel. Working with the Bendix Radio Corporation, the United Communications

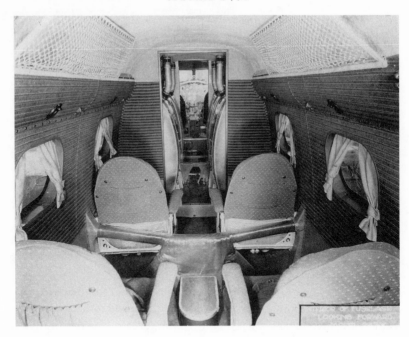

Four fuel tanks, originally used in Roscoe Turner's MacRobertson racer, were installed in place of the four forward seats. *Courtesy Smithsonian Institution.* (*SI 76–3080*)

United Air Lines kept one 247-D, NX-13365, the "Flying Lab," for research. *Courtesy Smithsonian Institution.* (*SI 86–6184*)

The Flying Lab demonstrates the terrain clearance indicator publicly in a flight over New York City. *Courtesy Smithsonian Institution.* (*SI 86–10651*)

Laboratory, piloted by Captain Albert Ball and Ben O. Howard, flew over 25,000 miles conducting many experiments with NX13365, during which a practical static suppressor was eventually developed. During static conditions in flight, a long wire extended from the tail of the aircraft drew the static away from the airframe and discharged it harmlessly into the atmosphere. The wire, whose diameter was smaller than the sharpest point on the aircraft, was equipped with a resistor. A small waxed paper cup was ideal for deploying the five-foot wire. After thorough testing of a variety of devices on the flying lab, practical static suppressors were installed on every aircraft in the United fleet, thus significantly increasing flight safety.[19]

Another important breakthrough developed through tests with NX13365 was the terrain-clearance indicator. Working in conjunction with Bell Telephone and Western Electric, the United Communications Laboratory, under the supervision of P. C. Sandretto, produced a radio altimeter which constantly informed the pilot of his relative position above the ground. A red indicator would be illuminated if the aircraft descended too close to earth. The first public demonstration of this device was conducted on the flying lab over New York City, up the Hudson River, and above the adjoining Palisades. According to William Patterson, "Our engineers and pilots regard the development of this device as one of the most important technological advancements in the history of air transportation. Following completion of service tests now in progress with the device in United's Flying Laboratory, we will make these devices standard equipment on every airliner in the fleet."[20] Patterson was true to his word.

A new instrument landing system was also developed on this remarkable airplane in 1937, preceding the adoption of similar devices on later generations of commercial and military transports. Other scientific tests were conducted concerning terrain-viewing television in cooperation with the Army Air Corps, radiosonde research for weather forecasting, and numerous different antenna installations.[21] Eventually, the flying lab outlived its usefulness and became one of the five 247-Ds sold to LAMSA. It was destroyed in a takeoff accident in Mexico City on 5 May 1952.[22]

9
Survivors

In 1991, just four of the original seventy-five Boeing 247s remained. In Great Britain, c/n 1722 is preserved in the Air Transport Collection of the Science Museum and is on limited display at its hangar at an airfield near Swindon. The aircraft was originally delivered to N.A.T. as NC13340 on 7 July 1933, converted to D standard in 1935, and continued to fly for United until 1942. Between 1942 and 1947, the aircraft, renumbered NC18, was operated by the CAA. After 1947, a variety of owners operated the aircraft, including Island Airlines, until it was purchased in 1971 by Charles Le Master and Jim Burkdoll of Ottawa, Kansas for barnstorming as the "World's Oldest Boeing Airliner" until 1977. The 247-D was then sold to the Wings and Wheels Museum in Orlando, Florida in 1977. When this museum folded, the Boeing was auctioned to the Science Museum in 1982.

Transporting the 247 to Britain was particularly adventurous. The aircraft, which had not been flown in three years, was refurbished sufficiently to make the ferry flight. Unfortunately, after flying only ten miles, one engine seized. Since the aircraft had been reequipped with smaller 450-horsepower powerplants, single-engine performance was marginal at best. Once repaired, the 247 limped from Florida up the coast to Canada, thence to Greenland, on to Iceland, Ireland, and eventually to its new home in England.[1]

One 247 remains in Canada. The National Aeronautical Collection at Ottawa preserves 247-D, c/n 1699. This aircraft entered service with N.A.T. as NC13318 in 3 May 1933, was modified to 247-D standard in 1935, and in 1937 was leased to Western Air Express. Later it passed to P.C.A., until it was sold to the Canadian government in 1940 and redesignated CF-BQS. In 1942, the R.C.A.F. took control of the machine and promptly turned it over for use by Quebec Airways of Canadian Pacific Airlines in the Yukon and Northwest Territories, as CF-BVX. After it returned to the United States in 1945, this 247-D flew as an executive transport for Maguire Industries Inc. and in 1948 with the obscure Zig Zag

N18 is now part of the collection of the Science Museum in London. *Courtesy Smithsonian Institution. (SI 87–8580)*

Airways. The aircraft flew as a cropduster in Yakima, Washington, for the Central Aircraft Company until 1956.[2]

At that time, the California Standard Company of Calgary, Alberta, had begun a search for a transport aircraft with which to assist the exploration of oil in the Canadian arctic. The company needed a machine which was extremely strong, reasonably fast, and could take off from short, unprepared 1500-foot strips.[3] The twenty-year-old 247-D fit the bill admirably. Reregistered as CF-JRQ, the Boeing 247-D selected by California Standard was completely rebuilt by the Oakland Automotive Company, including new aluminum wing spars and updated avionics, and was quickly placed into service. For ten years, CF-JRQ flew men and equipment into and out of remote drilling sites in the arctic wilderness. In 1962 and 1963, this 247-D completely supplied two Yukon sites by air for eight months. Other difficult missions included rescues and ambulance service when necessary.

After a distinguished career, CF-JRQ was finally retired on 11 February 1967, when California Standard transferred ownership to the National Aviation Museum in Ottawa, Ontario, where the aircraft is now exhibited.[4]

Appropriately, the third existing Boeing 247 is preserved by the Museum of Flight in Seattle, Washington. This aircraft is currently undergoing a detailed, conscientious restoration back to flying status and is planned to be the only airworthy 247. In fact, this aircraft will be returning to its birthplace. Part of the Museum of Flight is the original Boeing factory building, the "Red Barn," where parts of this and every 247 were assembled.

The museum's aircraft is Boeing 247-D, c/n 1729, which first flew with Pacific Air Transport as NC13347 on 26 July 1933. It was converted to D standard on 27 August 1935 and served for two more years until purchased by Pennsylvania Central Airlines on 8 February 1937. P.C.A. flew it for several years until 1940, when NC13347 was sold to the Canadian Department of Munitions and reregistered as CF-BTD. Throughout 1940 and 1941, the aircraft served with the R.C.A.F., carrying the military number of 7839. On 17 December 1941, it was purchased by Maritime Central Airways and flown as CF-BTB, until sold to Columbia Airlines in the United States in 1945.

This 247 remained in the U.S. until June 1951 when it was acquired by Aerovias Occidentales, S.A. of San Jose, Costa Rica, receiving the new civil registration of TI-1011. It flew without incident until a jammed throttle caused the aircraft to nose over on landing on 3 January 1952. It remained grounded for the next two years until retrieved by Jesse Bristow and returned to the U.S. under the registration of N3977C. After its acquisition by Marrs Aircraft of Hollywood, Florida, it was ferried to Phoenix, Arizona, in December 1954 for conversion, in May 1955, to a crop duster. From May 1955 until late 1956, Marsh Aviation flew the machine; on 1 October 1956, it was sent to Precipitation Control of Taft, California for use as a cloud seeder in rain-making experiments. Damaged in another landing accident, the aircraft was retired at the Taft Airport in 1961 and fell into general disrepair.[5]

Salvation came in 1966 through the efforts of two members of the Pacific Northwest Aviation Historical Foundation. A United Air Lines captain and early P.N.A.H.F. member, Jack Leffler, discovered c/n 1729 decaying at that desert airfield. With the financial assistance of Ray Pepka of Renton Aviation and another P.N.A.H.F. member, the old 247-D was purchased from its last owner, D. D. Merrill for $10,000.

Leffler and Pepka had the unique experience of flying their veteran 247-D back home to the Seattle area. After making sufficient repairs to prepare the aircraft for its ferry flight, they flew the aircraft gently to Renton on a leisurely thousand-mile flight at 120 miles per hour in several stages. As the electric landing gear had not been activated for six years, they left the wheels extended. Nevertheless, Leffler was able to get a feel for the aircraft. Though heavy on the controls and slow to respond compared with modern jetliners, the 247-D flew well. Underscoring the 247-D's contributions to subsequent types and reflecting the opinions of many other avia-

N3977C may be seen again in the skies of Seattle after restoration to flying status by the Museum of Flight. *Courtesy Smithsonian Institution.* (*SI 82–13969*)

tors, Leffler, a former U.S. Army Air Forces pilot, found the aircraft "a real stable airplane that flies much like a B-17 bomber.[6]

Upon its return, c/n 1729 was christened the "City of Renton" by Mrs. Claire Egtvedt and was soon flying in several local airshows reregistered in its original number as N13347. A failure of one landing gear on 13 August 1967, temporarily grounded the aircraft. The aircraft was repainted in 1976 to participate in the fiftieth anniversary celebration of the birth of Western Air Lines and made numerous appearances in Western livery.

Not long afterwards, N13347 was grounded for repairs. Today it is undergoing a thorough restoration in nearby Everett, Washington, at the hands of a small team of dedicated volunteers of retired Boeing employees from the Boeing Management Association, under the guidance of Museum of Flight officials. Led by George Juneau, the team is almost completely rebuilding the old 247-D. They have had to replace the fuselage keel and floor beams, as well as to arrest the severe corrosion and to repair the wing spars. When the aircraft is completed, it will once again grace the skies of its native Seattle.

The last remaining 247—the very aircraft flown by Roscoe Turner in the MacRobertson Race—is permanently exhibited in the Air Transportation Gallery of the National Air and Space Museum of the Smithsonian Institution in Washington, D.C. It is the only surviving original 247-D.

In 1939, NC13369 was sold to the Air Safety Board and transferred later to the CAA, reregistered as N11, and nicknamed "Adaptable Annie." *Courtesy Smithsonian Institution.* (*SI 83–16419*)

After its notable achievement in the race, the aircraft, c/n 1953, was returned to United Air Lines and flown as NC13369 from 31 December 1934 until 11 January 1937. During that time, the aircraft flew approximately 9200 passengers along United's routes and also served briefly with Western Air Express on loan. From January 1937 until the summer of 1939, Turner's former racer was an executive aircraft for Union Electric Light and Power Company of St. Louis, Missouri.

In August 1939, NC13369 was sold to the Air Safety Board of the U.S. Department of Commerce, serving briefly until turned over to the Civil Aeronautics Authority and reregistered as NC11. During its CAA career, this aircraft made many valuable contributions to the enhancement of flight safety. Its versatility earned it the nickname of "Adaptable Annie." NC11 was used by the CAA's Technical Development and Evaluation Center in Indianapolis, Indiana in a variety of tests of the latest developments in flight-safety research, similar in many respects to the earlier work of United's Flying Laboratory. Annie was used in many research projects including instrument-approach systems, airway markers, omnidirectional range systems, distance-measuring equipment (D.M.E.), automatic approach and landing systems, airport lighting, aircraft blinking navigational lights, and stall-warning devices.

On a test to determine the effects of ice buildup, a thick mixture of dope and sawdust was applied to the leading edge of the wings to disrupt the airflow. Annie still managed to stagger aloft despite the simulated ice, although the take off run was twice as long as usual. Otherwise the handling characteristics were generally unaffected.[7] CAA Administrator Frederick B. Lee summed up his department's feelings towards Annie as she approached retirement in 1953: "There was never any hesitation about changing her outside or insides when these special jobs turned up. You should have seen her in those days when we were trying to find some way of eliminating precipitation static. She looked like a tramp's clothes line, with tattered streamers trailing from all points."[8]

On 17 July 1953, the CAA retired Adaptable Annie and turned her over to the what was then the National Air Museum. With her famous former pilot Roscoe Turner on board, Annie was flown to Washington, D.C. for her presentation to the Museum. According to Frederick Lee, speaking at the formal ceremony, "She has earned her place in the green pastures."[9]

For over twenty years Annie awaited restoration and the completion of a proper museum building on the National Mall in downtown Washington. When the new building was authorized and under construction, National Air and Space Museum curators slated Annie for inclusion in the new Air Transportation Gallery in recognition of her noted accomplishments and the vital role played by the Boeing 247 in revolutionizing commercial air travel. Under normal, less pressing situations, the aircraft would have been restored by the museum's talented cadre of restoration technicians. With the deadline for the opening of the museum in 1976 rapidly approaching and the museum work force totally involved in other tasks, the job of preparing Annie for display was turned over to CNC Industries of Clinton, Maryland. Appropriately sponsored through the generosity of United Air Lines, the $27,000 project was begun in March 1975 after the aircraft was moved by truck from Building 6 at the Silver Hill restoration and storage facility to Hyde Field in nearby Clinton.

Once in the hands of CNC, the work began. Over the ensuing seven months, the aircraft was repaired where necessary and generally spruced up for exhibit. In the fuselage, damaged skin was replaced, corrosion treated on the bottom, corroded cables repaired, damaged windows replaced, the aft bulkhead repaired, the copilot's sliding window remade, and the interior cleaned. The dented leading edges of the wing were carefully straightened, corrosion arrested, and local damage to the wing skin surface repaired. The tail-wheel assembly was also straightened, cleaned and painted. The engines were cleaned and sealed to protect the powerplant from corrosion and future leaks.

Unfortunately, the aircraft could not be restored completely to its

In 1976, NC 13369 was gently suspended in the Air Transportation Gallery of the National Air and Space Museum, in honor of the many contributions of the 247 to aviation history. *Courtesy Smithsonian Institution.* (*SI 75–13938–10*)

former condition as the original counterweighted three-bladed, two-position propellers had been replaced earlier with more modern constant-speed Hamilton Standard Hydromatics. The older propellers are now virtually impossible to find.

It was at first hoped that the original anodized finish could be preserved, but the numerous coats of paint and various markings had left residual, unsightly blemishes which could not be affordably removed. Consequently, NASM restoration technicians carefully blended paint to match the color of the original finish. This was applied to the fuselage and wings but not to the engine cowlings and the fin and rudder, which were sufficiently presentable in their original condition.

In a bold move never before taken at the museum, the aircraft was painted in two different sets of markings that reflected the machine's diverse and historic career. On the left half, the aircraft is painted as it was received by Roscoe Turner in 1934 at the Boeing factory, resplendent in its race colors. Because the colors of subsequent race markings could not be determined, these additional designs were not painted on the aircraft. On the right side, facing the public, the transport is shown as it looked when it flew as the flagship of United's 247 fleet, carrying the race map on its fuselage.

With the restoration completed two months ahead of schedule, NASM's Boeing 247-D was ready for delivery to the mall in October 1975. During the night of 8 October, the aircraft was gently towed on its main gear from Clinton to the new museum in downtown Washington, D.C. by a specially modified truck. The wings were loaded separately on a flatbed truck. The small convoy, escorted by local police, began the move at 11:45 P.M. Proceeding at only five miles per hour, the strange caravan slowly wound its way across Prince George's County and through the capital city's streets, arriving a few hours later.[10] The aircraft was carefully maneuvered directly into the museum through the two huge sliding glass doors on the west end of the building.

Once positioned on the floor of the Air Transportation Gallery, the 247-D was carefully reassembled. Finally, on 24 October, the Boeing was lifted into place and suspended appropriately just beneath and slightly behind its old rival, the Douglas DC-3. When, on 1 July 1976, the new National Air and Space Museum opened to the public as the United States' bicentennial present to herself, the Boeing 247-D was dramatically displayed in a fitting tribute to those men of vision who created and flew this remarkable aircraft—the first modern airliner.

Appendix A

Size and Performance Specifications for 247 Models

Model:	247[a]	247[b]	247-A[c]	247-D[c]
Length	51'4"	51'4"	51'4"	51'7"
Wing span	74'	74'	74'	74'
Height	16'	16'	16'5"	12'6"
Empty weight (lb)	8,375	8,412	8,975	8,940
Gross weight (lb)	12,650	13,100	12,405	13,650
Payload (lb)	2,372	2,400	1,200	2,582
Top speed	182 mph	182 mph	198 mph	200 mph
Cruise speed[d]	161 mph	171 mph	170 mph[e]	189 mph
Range (miles)	485 with 203 gal	750 with 273 gal	650 with 290 gal	750 with 273 gal
Service ceiling	18,400'	20,750'	22,700'	25,400'
Absolute ceiling	20,500'	22,800'	24,100'	27,200'
One-engine ceiling	2,000'	4,000'	unknown	11,500'
Rate of climb	1,070 ft/min	1,320 ft/min	1,170 ft/min	1,150 ft/min
Wing loading (lb/ft^2)	15.13	15.64	14.88	16.3
Power loading (lb/HP)	11.5	11.91	9.94	12.4
Engines-Pratt & Whitney	Wasp S1D1	Wasp S1D1/	Twin Wasp Jr. SGR-1535	Wasp S1H1-G[f]
Horsepower	550 @ 2200 rpm	550 @ 2200 rpm	625 @ 2400 rpm	550 @ 2200 rpm
Displacement (cu.in.)	1,344	1,344	1,535	1,344

Source: Victor D. Seely, "Boeing's Pacesetting 247," *American Aviation Historical Society Journal*, 9 (Winter 1964), p. 241.

a Three-blade fixed-pitch propeller

b Two-blade controllable-pitch propeller

c Three-blade controllable-pitch propeller

d 75% power at 12,000 feet

e 60% power at 12,000 feet

f Fuel consumption of 87 octane for S1H1-G was 22 gallons per hour at 1750 pm (60 percent power), 31 gallons per hour at 2000 rpm (75 percent power), and 50 gallons per hour at 2200 rpm (full power).

Appendix B

Boeing Model 247 Transport Series Service History

by Victor D. Seely

C/N*	License	Operator, Period of Use, and Remarks
1682	NC13301	Pacific Air Transport 5 April 1933 to an unknown date.
	X13301	Boeing used this airplane to develop various modifications that led to the 247-D version. During the test period plane was given the designation 247-E. (Recorded 247-E as of 21 June 1934.)
	NC13301	United Air Lines 1 August 1934 to 8 July 1942. Before final delivery, NC13301 was brought up to 247-D standard and ATC-558 was modified to include it. The 247-E designation stuck with the plane, however. It was named *City of Oakland* about 1940.
	42–68372	U.S. Army Air Force 17 July 1942 to 30 June 1943. with USAF designation C-73. To Ogden 17 July 1942, to Cheyenne 11 September 1942, to National Airport 31 December 1942, to Bolling 10 Mar 1943, Gravely Point 29 June 1943, to Class 26, instructional airframe, 30 June 1943.
1683	NC13302	Boeing Air Transport 30 March 1933 to 30 April 1934.
	NC13302	United Air Lines 1 May 1934 to 7 June 1934. It crashed 6 miles east of Selleck, Washington on 7 June 1934 in bad weather during a flight from Spokane to Seattle. Four persons were injured.
1684	NC13303	Varney Air Lines 10 April 1933 to 30 September 1933.
	NC13303	Boeing Air Transport 1 October 1933 to 30 April 1934.

Source: Victor D. Seeley, "Boeing's Pacesetting 247," *American Aviation Historical Society Journal* 9 (August 1968), 54–66, 75.

*Constructor's number

NC13303   United Air Lines 1 May 1934 to 1 April 1935.

NC13303   Pennsylvania Air Lines 1 April 1935 to 1937. This was one of four 247s in Veracruz, Mexico, awaiting shipment to Spain in March 1937, when it was confiscated by Mexico and auctioned off to reimburse Mexico for debts owed by the Spanish republican government.

unknown   Capt. Sixto del Rio (Mexican Air Force) 1941.

XA-BEY   Cia. Mexicana de Aviación, S.A. 1941.

XA-CAB   Aeronaves de Mexico, S.A. (may be XA-CDA)

XA-CAB   Líneas Aéreas Guerrero Oaxaca, S.A. 1947–50. It crashed near Los Pajaritos on 7 January 1950.

1685   NC13304   National Air Transport 7 April 1933 to 10 October 1933. It crashed on 10 October 1933 near Chesterton, Indiana due to a cargo explosion, killing the crew and four passengers.

1686   NC13305   Boeing Air Transport 13 April 1933 to 30 April 1934.

NC13305   United Air Lines 1 May 1934 to 8 July 1942. It was converted to 247-D standard on 24 May 1935, retaining the forward-swept windshield, and was named *City of Bethlehem* about 1940.

NC13305   Western Air Express 12 April 1935 (leased from UAL).

42–68363   U.S. Army Air Force (as C-73) 7 August 1942 to 3 June 1944. To Modification Center Cheyenne 5 April 1944 and then to UAL Chicago for LAMSA, to Defense Supply Corporation 3 June 1944.

XA-DON   Líneas Aéreas Mexicanas, S.A. November 1944 to November 1947. Named *Estado de San Luis Potosí* by LAMSA. This aircraft had logged 19,035 hours as of 6 November 1945.

XA-DON   Luis Struck November 1947 to December 1947.

XB-JEC   Efren Ochoa and Manual Ramos Espinoza December 1947 to 1949.

XA-JAA   Líneas Aéreas Piche July 1949 to 1952 (leased from J. L. Loperena).

XA-JAA   Servicios Aéreas Chiapas 1952 to at least 1960. It suffered a few minor accidents, one in Durango in 1946, another in Tapchula in 1954, and a third in Petalcingo in 1955.

1687   NC13306   National Air Transport 14 April 1933 to 30 April 1934.

NC13306   United Air Lines 1 May 1934 to 23 December 1934.

NC13306   General Air Lines 23 December 1934 to 31 December 1934.

NC13306   Western Air Express 1 January 1935 to 15 December 1937.

C-147   SCADTA (thru Interamerican) 15 December 1937 to 1939.

C-147   AVIANCA 1939 to at least 1945. 17,861 airframe hours had been accumulated by 30 September 1945. The plane was named *Pascual de Andagoya* by AVIANCA.

1688   NC13307   Varney Air Lines 15 April 1933 to 30 September 1933.

NC13307   Boeing Air Transport 1 October 1933 to 30 April 1934.

NC13307   United Air Lines 1 May 1934 to 1 May 1935.

NC13307   Wyoming Air Service 1 May 1935 to 1 July 1938. It was named *City of Denver* by Wyoming Air Service.

NC13307   Inland Air Lines 1 July 1938 to 17 July 1942.

42–61094   U.S. Army Air Force (as C-73) 18 June 1942 to June 1944. To G.L. Martin, Omaha, 19 June 1942, to Cheyenne 18 February 1943, to Billings 12 March 1943, to Minneapolis 24 May 1943, to Kansas City 3 June 1943, to Cincinnati 15 June 1943. Restored to airline standard for resale by UAL to Defense Supply Corporation June 1944.

XA-DIZ   Líneas Aéreas Mexicanas, S.A. July 1944 to 1948. LAMSA named the plane *Estado de Coahuila*. As of 6 November 1945, 16,456 hours had been logged.

XA-DIZ   Arturo San Roman 1948.

XA-DIZ   Taxis Aéreos Nacionales 1948 to an unknown date.

XA-DIZ   Aerovias Reformas (leased).

XA-DIZ   Aeronaves de Michoacan, S.A. from an unknown date to 8 October 1956 (registration canceled).

unknown   Jesse Bristow, Florida 1956.

N7777B   Airspray Inc., Orlando, Florida 1958–63.

1689   NC13308   Boeing Air Transport 18 April 1933 to 30 October 1934.

NC13308   United Air Lines 1 May 1934 to 1 April 1935.

NC13308   Pennsylvania Air Lines 1 April 1935 to 1942.

42–57208   U.S. Army Air Force (C-73) 11 June 1942 to 1 June 1944. To Bolling 12 June 1942, to Newcastle 16 June 1942, to Presque Isle 28 June 1943, to commercial use 1 June 1944.

XA-DIJ   Aero Transportes December 1943 to 1948.

XA-DIJ   Aeronaves de Michoacan (Tomás Calderón) 1948.

XA-DIJ   Aeronaves Oaxaca. (Luis and Antonio Melgoza)

N76390(?)   Jesse Bristow, Fla. 1956 (N76390 was Cessna according to the FAA). It was damaged in Acapulco 18 July 1949.

1690 NC13309   National Air Transport 20 April 1933 to 30 April 1934.

NC13309   United Air Lines 1 May 1934 to July 1942. It was converted to 247-D standard 4 August 1935, and was named *City of Spokane* about 1940.

NC13309   General Air Lines 23 December 1934 to 31 December 1934 (leased from UAL).

NC13309   Western Air Express 1 January 1935 to 3 July 1935 (leased from UAL).

42–68371   U.S. Army Air Force (C-73) 17 July 1942 to June 1944. To Ogden 17 July 1942, to Eastern Air Lines 28 October 1942, to Cheyenne 17 April 1943, to Milwaukee 6 November 1943, to Newcastle 1 January 1944, to Chicago 15 June 1944, restored to airline standard by UAL, to Defense Supply Corporation June 1944.

XA-DUX   Líneas Aéreas Mexicanas, S.A. April 1945 to late 1945. It was named *Estado de Sonora*. The aircraft logged 17,431 hours 6 November 1945. Boeing records show XA-DUZ.

XB-JEA   Luis Struck 1945–48.

XB-JEA   Capt. Juan Tilghman 1948.

XA-GUV   Servicios Aéreos Nacionales. The Mexican registration was canceled on 30 July 1957, apparently after a crash which occurred while in the service of Servicios Aéreos Nacionales.

1691 NC13310   National Air Transport 23 April to 30 April 1934. It was displayed at the Chicago Century of Progress exhibition of 1933.

| | NC13310 | United Air Lines 1 May 1934 to 3 May 1938. It was converted to 247-D standard 12 April 1935. |

NC13310   United Air Lines 1 May 1934 to 3 May 1938. It was converted to 247-D standard 12 April 1935.

NC13310   Wyoming Air Service 3 May 1938 to 1 July 1938.

NC13310   Inland Air Lines 1 July 1938 to 10 June 1942.

42–56642   U.S. Army Air Force (C-73) 11 June 1942 to 21 June 1944. To Fairfield AD 12 June 1942, it had a forced landing at Blytheville, Arkansas due to failure of both engines 9 July 1942, to Memphis 20 July 1942, to Cheyenne 5 July 1943, to commercial use 1 June 1944.

NC13310   Woodley Airways, Alaska 1944 to 23 August 1945.

NC13310   Pacific Northern Airlines 23 August 1945 to February 1946.

1692   NC13311   Varney Air Lines 25 April 1933 to 30 September 1933.

NC13311   Boeing Air Transport 1 October 1933 to 30 April 1934.

NC13311   United Air Lines 1 May 1934 to 1 April 1936.

NC13311   Pennsylvania Air Lines 1 April 1936 to an unknown date.

NC13311   Wyoming Air Service (?)

C-145   AVIANCA 1945; 13,340 hours 30 September 1945.

N1060M   Atlas Airways Inc., Chicago, IL., 1953.

1693   NC13312   Boeing Air Transport 26 April 1933 to 30 April 1934.

NC13312   United Air Lines 1 May 1934 to 8 July 1942. The plane was converted to 247-D standard 30 September 1935. It was named *City of Seattle* and later *City of Des Moines*.

NC13312   Western Air Express (leased from UAL).

42–68366   U.S. Army Air Force (C-73) 17 July 1942 to 11 June 1944. To McClellan 19 July 1942, to TWA 22 July 1942, to Defense Supply Corporation June 1944.

XA-DIY   Líneas Aéreas Mexicanas, S.A. July 1944 to December 1947. It was named *Estado de Chihuahua*. The plane logged 17,462 hours as of 6 November 1945.

XA-JEB   Luis Struck December 1947 to April 1948.

XA-GUW   Capt. Juan Tilghman April 1948 to an unknown date. This aircraft was involved in an incident due to power failure after leaving Mexico City on 23 February 1952.

1694	NC13313	National Air Transport 27 April 1933 to 30 April 1934.
	NC13313	United Air Lines 1 May 1934 to 8 July 1942. The plane was converted to 247-D standard 17 May 1935. It was named *City of Allentown*.
	NC13313	Western Air Express (leased from UAL).
	42–68365	U.S. Army Air Force (C-73) 8 July 1942 to 29 July 1944. To Chicago 14 September 1942, to LaGuardia 16 October 1942, to Sperry on an unknown date.
	NC13313	Wien Alaska Airlines 1943–46. Logged 16,255 hours 23 October 1945.
1695	NC13314	Varney Air Lines 28 April 1933 to September 1933.
	NC13314	Boeing Air Transport 1 October 1933 to 30 April 1934.
	NC13314	United Air Lines 1 May 1934 to 12 April 1935.
	NC13314	Western Air Express 12 April 1935 to 1 September 1935 (leased from UAL). It crashed in dense fog near Burbank, California on 1 September 1935, killing three persons.
1696	NC13315	Boeing Air Transport 29 April 1933 to 30 April 1934.
	NC13315	United Air Lines 1 May 1934 to 13 June 1935.
	NC13315	Western Air Express 13 June 1935 to 12 January 1937. Leased on 23 December 1934 from UAL and purchased on 3 July 1935 (according to Western) or 13 June 1935 (according to UAL). It crashed on 12 January 1937 near Newhall, California. Five of thirteen aboard were fatally injured.
1697	NC13316	National Air Transport 2 May 1933 to 30 April 1934.
	NC13316	United Air Lines 1 May 1934 to 29 April 1938. It was converted to 247-D standard on 7 October 1935.
	NC13316	Western Air Express 29 April 1938 to 30 May 1942 (Leased from UAL in 1937).
	42–57209	U.S. Army Air Force (C-73) 11 June 1942 to 14 June 1944. To Newcastle 12 June 1942, to Cheyenne 26 March 1943, to Gore Field, Long Beach 22 April 1943, to Presque Island 29 April 1943, to North Atlantic Wing 1 May 1943, to "Caribb" 15 April 1944, to Defense Supply Corporation 14 June 1944. AVIANCA.

1698   NC13317   Boeing Air Transport 2 May 1933 to 30 April 1934.

       NC13317   United Air Lines 1 May 1934 to 7 October 1935. It crashed on 7 October 1935 near Cheyenne, Wyoming, when the pilot reportedly misjudged altitude and hit the ground in a power glide. The crew of three and seven passengers were killed.

1699   NC13318   National Air Transport 3 May 1933 to 30 April 1934.

       NC13318   United Air Lines 1 May 1934 to 1 October 1937. It was converted to 247-D standard 13 July 1935.

       NC13318   Western Air Express (leased from UAL).

       NC13318   Pennsylvania-Central Air Lines 1 October 1937 to 1940.

       CF-BQS   Canadian Department of Munitions 1940 (temporary license only).

       7638   Royal Canadian Air Force 8 June 1940 to April 1942.

       CF-BVX   Quebec Airways 1 June 1942 to 1943.

       CF-BVX   Canadian Pacific Air Lines 1943–45.

       NC41809   Maguire Industries, Inc., 1945.

       NC41809   Zig Zag Airways, about 1948. The slogan "California or Bust" also appeared on the nose.

       N41809   Babb Company, New York City, 1953.

       N41809   Rex Williams, Phoenix, Arizona, operating as a crop duster.

       N41809   Central Aircraft, Yakima, Wash about 1956. Photos show an enlarged entrance door was used by Central.

       CF-JRQ   California-Standard Oil of Calgary January 1959 to at least 1964. It was rebuilt for Standard Oil and featured new spar caps of 24-ST aluminum alloy in place of the old 17-ST material.

       CF-JRQ   Donated to the National Aviation Museum, Ottawa, Ontario, 11 February 1967

1700   NC13319   Boeing Air Transport 8 May 1933 to 30 April 1934.

       NC13319   United Air Lines 1 May 1934 to 23 November 1936. The aircraft was converted to 247-D standard on 11 August 1936. It crashed near Newark, New Jersey on 23 November 1936.

1701	NC13320	National Air Transport 10 May 1933 to 12 May 1933. It crashed on 12 May 1933 on its delivery flight, near Provo, Utah. Photos indicate the plane hit the side of a mountain in fog, severely damaging the wings but sustaining only a few dents in fuselage. The pilot and co-pilot were both injured.
1702	NC13321	Boeing Air Transport 13 May 1933 to 30 April 1934.
	NC13321	United Air Lines 1 May 1934 to 1 June 1942. The aircraft was converted to 247-D standard 27 May 1935. It was named *City of Lincoln* about 1940.
	NC13321	Western Air Express (leased from UAL).
	42–57153	U.S. Army Air Force (C-73) 25 June 1942 to 3 May 1945. To Boeing 25 June 1942, to Great Falls 4 July 1942, to commercial use 3 March 1945.
	XA-FEO	Aero Transportes July 1945 to an unknown date.
	XA-KAJ	Aeronaves de Michoacan, S.A. an unknown date to about 1958 (T.R. Calderón).
	N5501A	Cecil Coffin, Brookley, New York, 8 January 1959 to an unknown date.
1703	NC13322	National Air Transport 18 May 1933 to 10 December 1933. This aircraft was static-tested to destruction by the U.S.A.A.C. at Dayton, Ohio, January 1934. The fuselage was broken under 160% design load. NC13322 was originally used on the Chicago-New York division routes where it accumulated 1408 airframe hours.
1704	NC13323	Boeing Air Transport 19 May 1933 to 30 April 1934.
	NC13323	United Air Line 1 May 1934 to 30 October 1935. It crashed on a test flight near Cheyenne, Wyoming on 30 October 1935, killing the crew of four. The accident was attributed to a too abrupt maneuver at too low an altitude.
1705	NC13324	National Air Transport 20 May 1933 to 24 November 1933. It crashed near Ottawa, Illinois on 9 November 1933, killing the crew.
1706	NC13325	Boeing Air Transport 23 May 1933 to 30 April 1934.
	NC13325	United Air Lines 1 May 1934 to 30 April 1938. The plane was converted to 247-D standard on 1 September 1935.

	NC13325	Pennsylvania-Central Airlines 30 April 1938 to an unknown date. White Pass Airways, Inc., Skagway, Alaska from an unknown date to late 1941.
	CB-BVF	British Yukon Navigation Co. late 1941 to an unknown date.
	CB-BVF	Yukon Southern Air Transport from an unknown date to 1943. It was named *Yukon Sourdough*.
	CF-BVF	Canadian Pacific Air Lines 1943–45.
	NC33172	Columbia Airlines 1945 to an unknown date. It had logged 17,138 hours in the air by 14 December 1945.
	NC33172	J. H. Wentworth, Long Beach, California, from an unknown date to 1948. Exported to Mexico in 1948.
1707	NC13326	National Air Transport 25 May 1933 to 30 April 1934.
	NC13326	United Air Lines 1 May 1934 to 8 July 1942. It was converted to 247-D standard on 15 September 1935, and named *City of San Diego* about 1940. NC13326 was damaged at Newark, New Jersey, in June 1933; it was repaired and reentered service sporting the new aft-sloping windshield.
	NC13326	Western Air Express (leased from UAL).
	42–68367	U.S. Army Air Force (C-73) 17 July 1942 to November 1942. To McClellan 19 July 1942, to Inland Air Lines to TWA 28 July 1942. It was wrecked in a landing accident at Allegheny City Airport, Pennsylvania on 17 November 1942 and surveyed.
1708	NC13327	Boeing Air Transport 29 May 1933 to 30 April 1934.
	NC13327	United Air Lines 1 May 1934 to 23 May 1935.
	NC13327	Western Air Express 12 June 1935 to at least April 1937 (leased 9 February 1935 from UAL)
	C-146	SCADTA (thru Interamerican) 7 December 1937 to 1939.
	C-146	AVIANCA 1939 to an unknown date.
1709	NC13328	Boeing Air Transport 31 May 1933 to 30 April 1934.
	NC13328	United Air Lines 1 May 1934 to 11 June 1942. It crashed near Western Springs, Illinois on 20 December 1934, injuring one passenger and the crew of three. One engine lost

power and the other stopped due to carburetor icing. The plane was repaired and later converted to 247-D standard on 8 July 1935, but retained the forward-slopping windshield. NC13328 was named *Province of B.C.* about 1940.

42–57210   U.S. Army Air Force (C-73) 11 June 1942 to August 1942. To Hensley Field 12 June 1942, to SAAD 2 July 1942, recommended Class 26, instructional airframe, 31 July 1942. It was damaged in a wind storm on 30 August 1942 while moored at Duncan Field, Texas and surveyed.

1710 NC13329   Varney Air Lines 2 June 1933 to 30 September 1933.

NC13329   Boeing Air Transport 1 October 1933 to 30 April 1934.

NC13329   United Air Lines 1 May 1934 to 1 June 1942. It was converted to 247-D standard on 31 August 1935 and named *Iowa City* about 1940.

NC13329   Western Air Express (leased from UAL).

42–68368   U.S. Army Air Force (C-73) 8 July 1942 to June 1945. To San Francisco 14 September 1942.

NC13329   Charles H. Babb 1945.

1711 NC13300   United Aircraft Corporation 4 November 1933 to 1947. The solitary 247-A Executive Transport, it was marked with the "United Airports of Connecticut" emblem. It was also used by Pratt & Whitney for test purposes and had logged 4,086 hours as of 11 December 1945. Scrapped in early 1947.

1712 NC13330   National Air Transport 10 June 1933 to 30 April 1934.

NC13330   United Air Lines 1 May 1934 to 30 July 1938. It was converted to 247-D standard on 24 August 1935.

NC13330   Western Air Express (leased from UAL).

NC13330   Wilmington-Catalina Airlines 30 July 1938 to an unknown date. AVIANCA.

1713 NC13331   National Air Transport 16 June 1933 to 30 April 1934.

NC13331   United Air Lines 1 May 1934 to 1 April 1935.

NC13331   Pennsylvania Air Lines 1 April 1935 to an unknown date. Seized by the Mexican government in Veracruz, March 1937.

	unknown	Capt. Sixto del Rio of the Mexican Air Force.
	XA-BEZ	Cia. Mexicana de Aviación, S.A. Aeronaves de Mexico, S.A., unknown dates.
	XA-KAD	Servicios Aéreos Panini, unknown dates.
1714	NC13332	National Air Transport 21 June 1933 to 30 April 1934.
	NC13332	United Air Lines 1 May 1934 to 30 July 1938. It was converted to 247-D standard on 5 June 1935.
	NC13332	Wilmington-Catalina Airlines 30 July 1938 to an unknown date.
	unknown	AVIANCA.
	N75291	Robertson Aviation about 1962. Modifications included spray rig, extra windows, and BT-13 cowl. Color: White top, red stripe, tan undersides.
1715	NC13333	National Air Transport 20 June 1933 to 30 April 1934.
	NC13333	United Air Lines 1 May 1934 to 8 July 1942. It was converted to 247-D standard on 19 September 1935 and named *City of Santa Barbara*.
	NC13333	Western Air Express 1 July 1935 (leased from UAL).
	42–68370	U.S. Army Air Force (C-73) 17 July 1942 to June 1945. To Ogden 17 July 1942, to Defense Supply Corporation June 1945.
	XA-FEP	Aero Transportes, S.A. July 1945 to 1948. Tomás Calderón.
	XA-FEP	Aeronaves Michoacan 1948 to an unknown date. Tomás Calderón.
1716	NC13334	National Air Transport June 23 to 30 April 1934.
	NC13334	United Air Lines 1 May 1934 to 22 February 1937. It was converted to 247-D standard on 23 April 1935.
	unknown	Inter-American Aero Travel & Supply 22 February 1937 to an unknown date.
	C-143	AVIANCA 1945. As of 30 September 1945, 15,740 hours had been logged.

1717   NC13335   Boeing Air Transport 24 June 1933 to 30 April 1934.

         NC13335   United Air Lines 1 May 1934 to 8 July 1935. It was named *City of Vancouver* about 1940.

         NC13335   Western Air Express (leased from UAL).

         42–68369   U.S. Army Air Force (C-73) 8 July 1942 to 14 September 1942. To Northwest Airlines 14 September 1942. It was a complete wreck at St. Paul on 14 September 1942.

1718   NC13336   Boeing Air Transport 26 June 1933 to 30 April 1934.

         NC13336   United Air Lines 1 May 1934 to 29 April 1939. To 247-D standard 21 September 1935.

         NR13336   This plane carried a restricted license about 1937 or 1938, possibly involving radio systems experiments.

         NC13336   Western Air Express 30 April 1938 to 31 May 1942.

         42–57211   U.S. Army Air Force (C-73) 11 June 1942 to 11 March 1944. To Berry Field 28 June 1942, to Nashville 18 March 1943, surveyed 11 March 1944.

1719   NC13337   Boeing Air Transport 28 June 1933 to 30 April 1934.

         NC13337   United Air Lines 1 May 1934 to 28 December 1935.

         NC13337   National Parks Airways 28 December 1935 to 1 August 1937.

         NC13337   Western Air Express 1 August 1937 to 22 July 1942.

         42–78017   U.S. Army Air Force (C-73) 3 August 1942 to April 1945. To Lockheed 3 August 1942, to Miami 29 December 1942, to Love Field 31 January 1943, to 36th St. Airport (Miami) 26 July 1943, to "Caribb" 12 August 1944, to Defense Supply Corporation April 1945.

         XA-DUA   Servicios Aéreos Panini 1945 to 9 September 1947. It crashed on 9 September 1947 near Obregón, Mexico and was destroyed.

1720   NC13338   Boeing Air Transport 29 June 1933 to 30 April 1934.

         NC13338   United Air Lines 1 May 1934 to 5 December 1936.

         C-141   SCADTA 5 December 1936 to 1939.

         C-141   AVIANCA 1939 to at least 1945. 1720 had logged 16,934 hours as of 30 September 1945.

PP-BHC   Viacao Aérea Bahiana, Brazil, 1945–48.

PP-BHC   C.R. Holck, 1948–53.

PP-BHC   Sold to Raymundo Duarte Muniz, 14 May 1953.

PT-APO   Muniz, 14 May 1953 to Oct. 30, 1958.

PT-APO   SAVA (Servicios Aereos de Abasterimento do Vale Amazonico) Oct. 30, 1958. It was named *Bernardo Saiap* in 1960 and crashed in a swamp 24 April 1963. The aircraft was scrapped in 1971.

1721   NC13339   Boeing Air Transport 6 July 1933 to 30 April 1934.

NC13339   United Air Lines 1 May 1934 to 12 January 1941. It was converted to 247-D standard on 27 September 1935. The aircraft was destroyed in a hangar fire at Salt Lake City on 12 January 1941.

NC13339   Western Air Express (leased from UAL).

1722   NC13340   National Air Transport 7 July 1933 to 30 April 1934.

NC13340   United Air Lines 1 May 1934 to December 1939. It was converted to 247-D standard on 27 July 1935.

NC13340   Pennsylvania-Central Airlines December 1939 to an unknown date.

unknown   Celanese Corporation 1940–41

NC18   U.S. Department of Commerce, Civil Aeronautics Administration, 1942–47. Adolph Krause, Emsworth, PA, 1947; Mrs. M.W. Smith, Chambersburg, PA, 1947; Albert A. de Francesco, Hazelton, PA, 1947–48; Monticello-Sullivan, Monticello, NY, 1948–52.

unknown   Jesse Bristow, Miami, Florida 1952–53. (Installed Pratt & Whitney R-985 450 hp.)

N18E   Robert Uricho Jr., Miami, Florida, 1953.

N18E   Joe Marra, Hollywood, Florida, 1953–54

N18E   Sky Tour, Inc. (Island Airlines) 1954–68.

N18E   Fulkerson Aviation Inc., Gillete, WY, 1968–71.

N18E   Chuck LeMaster and Jim Burkdoll, Ottawa, KS, 1971–77

N18E   Wings and Wheels Museum, Orlando, FL, 1977-October 1982.

N18E   The Science Museum, London, England, 1982 to the present. The aircraft is now part of the Air Transport Collection of the Science Museum.

1723 NC13341   National Air Transport 10 July 1933 to 30 April 1934.

NC13341   United Air Lines 1 May 1934 to December 1939. It was converted to 247-D standard on 6 September 1935.

NC13341   Pennsylvania-Central Airlines December 1938 to 31 January 1941.

NC13341   Western Air Lines 31 January 1941 to 19 July 1942 (also leased from UAL in 1936).

42–68853   U.S. Army Air Force (C-73) 19 July 1942 to June 1944. To Lockheed (Central Dist.) 19 July 1942, to TWA 30 December 1942, to Defense Supply Corporation June 1944.

XA-DUY   Líneas Aéreas Mineras July 1945 to 1 August 1945. It crashed into mountains near San Luis Potosí, Mexico on 1 August 1945. There were no survivors.

1724 NC13342   National Air Transport 17 July 1933 to 30 April 1934.

NC13342   United Air Lines 1 May 1934 to December 1939. It was converted to 247-D standard on 7 July 1935 and named *City of Walla Walla*.

NC13342   Western Air Express (leased from UAL).

NC13342   Pennsylvania-Central Airlines December 1939 to 1942.

42–68373   U.S. Army Air Force (C-73) 11 July 1942 to August 1944. To Dallas 3 August 1942, to Pan American Airways, 12 September 1942, Cincinnati unknown date to 15 August 1944, to Defense Supply Corp, to Varig Airlines, Brazil 1944.

XA-DEZ   Aero Transportes, S.A. August 1944 to 1945.

XA-DEZ   Servicios Aereos Panini 1945–48.

XA-DEZ   Aeronaves Oaxaca (owners: L. & A. Melgoza)

XA-DEZ   Servicios Aéros Nacionales from an unknown date to 26 August 1950. It crashed and burned at Veracruz on 26 August 1950.

1725	NC13343	National Air Transport 18 July 1933 to 30 April 1934.
	NC13343	United Air Lines 1 May 1934 to 22 February 1937. It was converted to 247-D standard on 29 September 1935.
	NC13343	Pennsylvania-Central Airlines 22 February 1937 to an unknown date.
	CF-BQT	Canadian Department of Munitions 1940 (temporary license).
	7637	Royal Canadian Air Force 8 June 1940 to March 1942.
	CF-BVV	Yukon Southern Air Transport 3 March 1942 to 1943.
	CF-BVV	Canadian Pacific Air Lines 1944–45.
	NC41813	Zimmerly Air Lines July 1945 to 27 September 1946. The aircraft was modified to incorporate a large square window in the entrance door. The log showed 15,297 hours as of 30 October 1945.
	NC41813	Empire Air Lines 28 September 1946 to 10 March 1948.
	N41813	Líneas Aéreas del Pacifico (leased from Scott Aero, Long Beach, California 1950). It crashed in 1952 returning to Long Beach from San Clemente Island.
1726	NC13344	National Air Transport 19 July 1933 to 30 April 1934.
	NC13344	United Air Lines 1 May 1934 to 14 May 1935.
	NC13344	Pennsylvania Air Lines 14 May 1935 to an unknown date.
	NC13344	Inland Air Lines.
	CF-BTA	Canadian Department of Munitions 1940 (temporary license).
	7655	Royal Canadian Air Force 1940.
	DZ203	Royal Air Force (Research, communications) 1941–48. In service with the RAF, this aircraft recorded its 10,000th hour of flight in 1944. It is believed to have been scrapped in 1948.
1727	NC13345	Pacific Air Transport 20 July 1933 to 9 November 1933. It crashed and burned near Portland, Oregon on 9 November 1933, in dense fog at night. The pilot and three passengers were killed; six were injured.

1728   NC13346   Pacific Air Transport 25 July 1933 to 30 April 1934.

          NC13346   United Air Lines 1 May 1934 to 8 February 1937. It was converted to 247-D standard 15 August 1935.

          NC13346   Pennsylvania-Central Airlines 8 February 1937 to an unknown date.

          CF-BQU   Canadian Department of Munitions 1940 (temporary license).

          7636   Royal Canadian Air Force 1940 to 25 April 1942 (scrapped).

1729   NC13347   Pacific Air Transport 26 July 1933 to 30 April 1934.

          NC13347   United Air Lines 1 May 1934 to 8 February 1937. It was converted to 247-D standard 27 August 1935.

          NC13347   Pennsylvania-Central Airlines 8 February 1937 to an unknown date.

          CF-BTD   Canadian Department of Munitions 1940 (temporary license).

          7839   Royal Canadian Air Force 1940–41.

          CF-BTB   Maritime Central Airways 17 November 1941 to 1945.

          NC13347   Columbia Airlines 1945. It had logged 16,211 hours by 14 December 1945.

          TI-1012   Aerovias Occidentales, Costa Rica, 1951–54.

          N3977C   Jesse Bristow, Miami, FL, March 1954.

          N3977C   Marsh Aviation, Phoenix, Arizona, operating as a sprayer, 14 May 1955 to 1 October 1956.

          N3977C   Precipitation Control Co. Taft, California, 1 October 1956 to 26 February 1966.

          N3977C   Pacific Northwest Aviation Historical Foundation 26 February 1966 to the present.

          N13347   Registration changed 15 July 1966.

          N13347   Last flight 19 September 1976. (Museum of Flight as of 1981) N13347 is being restored to flying status by the Museum of Flight, Seattle, Washington.

1730 NC13348 Pacific Air Transport 27 July 1933 to 30 April 1934.

NC13348 United Air Lines 1 May 1934 to 30 January 1937.

NC13348 Pennsylvania-Central Airlines 30 January 1937 to an unknown date.

42–38274 U.S. Army Air Force (C-73) 14 March 1942 to October 1944. To Bolling 14 March 1942, to Ferry Command 22 April 1942, blown backwards on incline at Hensley Field, 3 May 1942, to Ellington, 17 July 1942, to Hensley Field, 9 October 1942, to Love Field, 14 October 1942, and to Class 26, instructional airframe, October 1944.

1731 NC13349 Pacific Air Transport 29 July 1933 to 30 April 1934. It was returned to the factory on 4 October 1933 after a minor accident and redelivered to PAT on 5 February 1934.

NC13349 United Air Lines 1 May 1934 to 13 January 1937. Converted to 247-D standard 20 July 1935, NC13349 had the D-version cockpit enclosure installed at an earlier date.

NC13349 National Park Airways 1935 (leased?).

unknown Inter-American Aero Travel 13 January 1937 to an unknown date.

unknown AVIANCA.

1732 NC13350 Pacific Air Transport 8 August 1933 to 30 April 1934.

NC13350 United Air Lines 1 May 1934 to 30 January 1937. It was converted to 247-D standard on 8 August 1935.

NC13350 Pennsylvania-Central Airlines 30 January 1937 to an unknown date.

CF-BQV Canadian Department of Munitions 1940 (temporary license).

7639 Royal Canadian Air Force 8 June 1940 to 1941.

CF-BVT Yukon Southern Air Transport 23 December 1941 to 1943.

CF-BVT Canadian Pacific Air Lines 1944–45.

NC41812 Dan B. Southard, New York City 1945–48. The registration was canceled 23 September 1948.

184

1733	NC13351	Pacific Air Transport 9 August 1933 to 30 April 1934.
	NC13351	United Air Lines 1 May 1934 to 22 March 1937. It was converted to 247-D standard on 9 September 1935.
	NC13351	Pennsylvania-Central Airlines 22 March 1937 to an unknown date.
	42–38275	U.S. Army Air Force (C-73) 14 March 1942 to 6 September 1942. To Bolling 14 March 1942, to Ellington 4 April 1942, to Ferry Command 22 April 1942, to Ogden 28 July 1942, to Class 26, instructional airframe, at Ogden, 6 September 1942.
1734	NC13352	Pacific Air Transport 10 August 1933 to 30 April 1934.
	NC13352	United Air Lines 1 May 1934 to 29 January 1937. It was converted to 247-D standard on 20 June 1935.
	NC13352	Western Air Lines (leased from UAL).
	NC13352	Pennsylvania-Central Airlines 29 January 1937 to June 1942.
	42–57508	U.S. Army Air Force (C-73) 14 June 1942 to 22 July 1944.
	NC13352	Woodley Airways 22 July 1944 to 23 August 1945.
	NC13352	Pacific Northern Airlines 23 August 1945 to February 1946.
	NC13352	Empire Air Lines approximately 1946–48.
	NR13352	Crop duster. It crashed on 27 June 1950, at Walla Walla, Washington. While flying over mountainous terrain, the aircraft struck trees and burned.
1735	NC13353	Boeing Air Transport 11 August 1933 to 30 April 1934.
	NC13353	United Air Lines 1 May 1934 to 26 January 1937. It was converted to 247-D standard 5 October 1935.
	NC13353	Western Air Express (leased from UAL).
	NC13353	Pennsylvania-Central Airlines 26 January 1937 to an unknown date.
	CF-BTC	Canadian Department of Munitions 1940 (temporary license).
	7840	Royal Canadian Air Force 9 October 1940 to February 1942.

CF-BVW   Quebec Airways 28 February 1942 to 1943.

CF-BVW   Canadian Pacific Air Lines 1944–45.

NC41814   Zimmerly Air Lines July 1945 to 27 September 1946.

NC41814   Empire Air Lines 28 September 1946 to 10 March 1948.

N41814   Vest Aircraft and Finance Co., 1951.

XA-KAN   Aero Transportes, S.A. June 1951 (de la Pena).

XA-KAN   Servicios Aéreos de Chiapas, S.A. 1951 to at least 1959. The aircraft had logged 16,922 hours by 30 October 1945.

1736   NC13354   Boeing Air Transport 15 August 1933 to 30 April 1934.

NC13354   United Air Lines 1 May 1934 to 31 December 1935.

NC13354   National Park Airways 31 December 1935 to 1 August 1937.

NC13354   Western Air Express 1 August 1937 to 20 July 1942.

42–68854   U.S. Army Air Force (C-73) 20 July 1942 to June 1944. To Lockheed (Central Dist.) 20 July 1942, to Burbank 14 May 1943, to Wien Alaska.

NC13354   Wien Alaska Airlines June 1944. It had logged 20,164 hours as of 23 October 1945, and 22,000 hours by February 1946.

1737   NC13355   Boeing Air Transport 18 August 1933 to 30 April 1934.

NC13355   United Air Lines 1 May 1934 to 27 December 1936. Converted to 247-D standard 12 September 1935, it crashed about two miles southwest of Newhall, California on 27 December 1936, killing all twelve aboard. The aircraft hit mountains on its approach.

1738   NC13356   Varney Air Lines 18 August 1933 to 30 September 1933.

NC13356   Boeing Air Transport 1 October 1933 to 30 April 1934.

NC13356   United Air Lines 1 May 1934 to 16 May 1935.

NC13356   Pennsylvania Air Lines 16 May 1935 to an unknown date. This plane was involved in an incident near Harpers Ferry, West Virginia, while in the service of PAL. Three passengers were injured due to extremely rough air, although the aircraft was not damaged.

unknown		Peter S. Beasley, Detroit 1937
XA-BFK		Capt. Sixto del Rio 1937. Intended for Spain, it was seized by Mexico and sold at auction.
XA-BFK		Cia. Mexicana de Aviación, S.A. 1937–41.
XA-BFK		Aeronaves de Mexico, S.A. 1941–46.
XA-BFK		Líneas Aéreas Guerrer Oaxaca 1946 to about 1950. When the aircraft arrived in Mexico, it was still in the original 247 configuration. It crashed in 1950.
1739	NC13357	Varney Air Lines 29 August 1933 to 30 September 1933.
	NC13357	Boeing Air Transport 1 October 1933 to 23 February 1934. On 23 February 1934, NC13357 disappeared on a flight outbound from Salt Lake City. Three days passed before the wreckage was found, due to a raging blizzard that hindered the search parties. The plane had hit the ground at a steep angle, killing all eight aboard.
1740	NC13358	National Air Transport 22 August 1933 to 30 April 1934.
	NC13358	United Air Lines 1 May 1934 to 25 March 1937. It was converted to 247-D standard on 21 April 1935.
	NC13358	Pennsylvania-Central Airlines 25 March 1937 to 14 June 1942.
	45–57509	U.S. Army Air Force (C-73) 14 June 1942 to 31 August 1943. It was wrecked at the Army Air Base in Romulus, Michigan on 23 October 1942, from the propwash of other aircraft. To Class 26, instructional airframe, 31 August 1943.
1741	NC13359	National Air Transport 25 August 1933 through 30 April 1934.
	NC13359	United Air Lines 1 May 1934 to 31 March 1937.
	NC13359	Western Air Express (leased from UAL).
	NC13359	Pennsylvania-Central Airlines 31 March 1937 to 16 April 1941. It crashed near Charleston, West Virginia on 16 April 1941, injuring two crew members and six passengers. One crew member was unhurt. The right-hand engine lost power five seconds after takeoff and the aircraft crash-landed in a wooded area.

1944   NC90Y   United Aircraft Export, 16 February 1934.

      D-AKIN   Lufthansa, 1934 to 13 August 1937. C/n 1944 and 1945 differed from other 247s in having the aft-sloping windshield of the 247-D. This aircraft was destroyed on 13 August 1937 when it crashed at Hannover while testing an experimental autopilot.

1945   NC91Y   United Aircraft Export, 23 February 1934.

      D-AGAR   Lufthansa, 1934 to 24 May 1935. The aircraft was destroyed by an Air France airliner in a taxi accident at Nürnburg on 24 May 1935.

1946   X12772   The aircraft was flight tested for Lufthansa in September 1934 but never delivered. It was stored in the factory for about one year.

      NC92Y   Believed intended for Lufthansa export via U.A.E., this license was apparently not used.

      NC2666   Phillips Petroleum, 16 September 1935 to an unknown date. It was named *Woolaroc III*.

      CF-BRM   Canadian Department of Munitions & Supply, 1940 (temporary license).

      7635   Royal Canadian Air Force, 11 July 1940 to May 1942.

      CF-BVZ   Canadian Pacific Air Lines 16 May 1942 to 1945.

      NC41819   Zimmerly Air Lines, July 1945 to 27 September 1946.

      NC41819   Empire Airlines, 28 September 1946 to 10 March 1948.

      N41819   Vest Aircraft Company, Denver, Colorado. Numerically this was the first 247-D though it was not the first 247-D to fly. See C/N 1953. This aircraft had 4,868 airframe hours as of 30 October 1945.

1947   NC13361   United Air Lines 21 September 1934 to July 1942. It was named *City of Pendleton* about 1940.

      42–68364   U.S. Army Air Force (C-73) 7 August 1942 to March 1945. To Eastern Airlines 9 August 1942, to Patterson 1 August 1943, to Defense Supply Corporation March 1945.

      XA-FEL   Servicios Aéreos Panini, June 1945 to July 1949.

      XA-DOZ   Servicios Afeos Panini, June 1945 to July 1949. Boeing records show XA-DOX.

XA-DOZ — Aerovías Reformas, S.A. July 1949 until September 1955, when registration was canceled. It was reportedly shipped to Florida in 1960.

1948 NC13362 — United Air Lines 2 October 1934 to 30 July 1938.

NX13362 — Paramount Pictures for *Men With Wings* 1935.

NC13362 — Western Air Express (leased from UAL).

C-148 — SCADTA 30 July 1938 to 1939.

C-148 — AVIANCA, 1939 to at least 1945. It logged 15,145 hours as of 30 September 1945.

1949 NC13363 — United Air Lines 5 October 1934 to 24 February 1937.

NC13363 — Wyoming Air Service 24 February 1937 to an unknown date.

42–68859 — U.S. Army Air Force (C-73) 20 July 1942 to 21 April 1944. To Cheyenne 20 July 1942, to Defense Supply Corporation 21 April 1944.

C-144 — AVIANCA, 1945. It was named *Rodrigo de Bastidas* by AVIANCA. 16,791 hours logged as of 30 September 1945.

1950 NC13364 — United Air Lines 10 October 1934 to 4 September 1937.

NC13364 — Western Air Express (leased from UAL).

unknown — Inter-American Aero Travel & Supply 1937.

unknown — SCADTA 4 September 1937 to 1939.

unknown — AVIANCA 1939 to an unknown date.

1951 NC13360 — United Air Lines 28 April 1934 to 1 May 1936. This aircraft was displayed at "A Century of Progress" exposition in Chicago during mid-1934 after which it was brought up to 247-D configuration. For its April delivery, it was qualified under ATC 500.

NC13360 — Wyoming Air Service 1 May 1936 to 1 July 1938.

NC13360 — Inland Air Lines 1 July 1938 to an unknown date.

42–68336 — U.S. Army Air Force (C-73) 30 June 1942 to October 1944.

XA-DOM — Servicios Aéreos Panini November 1944 to an unknown date.

189

XA-DOM   Aerovías Reformas S.A., leased for an unknown period.

N2547B   Jesse Bristow, Florida 9 July 1956 to an unknown date.

N7836B   International Air Service (clipped wings) about 1956–57. Latana, Florida.

HP-231   Victor Inchausti, Panama 1957 to an unknown date. A photo of HP-231 appeared in the April 1957 *Air Pictorial*. FAA records show that N7836B was not actually sold in Panama until 1958.

1952   NC13366   United Air Lines 28 October 1934 to 30 September 1936.

NC13366   J. C. Elder, New York City 30 September 1936 to an unknown date.

unknown   Modified about January or February 1937 and designated model 247-Y. Fitted with two 50-caliber machine guns fixed in the nose and one flexible 50-caliber in the dorsal position plus four auxiliary fuel tanks in the fuselage. Reportedly flown into a mountain soon after delivery to China.

1953   unknown   United Air Lines September 1934.

NR257Y   Roscoe Turner (leased) October 1934 to December 1934.

NC13369   United Air Lines 31 December 1934 to 11 January 1937.

NC13369   Western Air Express (leased from UAL).

unknown   Union Electric Light & Power Co. (executive aircraft) 11 January 1937 to 1939, St. Louis, Missouri.

NC11   Department of Commerce, Air Safety Board, then the CAA (A209) 30 August 1939 to 1953.

N11   National Air Museum (Smithsonian) 17 July 1953 and on. The aircraft was restored in 1975 and has been on display in the Air Transportation Gallery of the National Air and Space Museum since 1 July 1976 in the markings of United Air Lines and the MacRobertson Race. This aircraft was known as "Adaptable Annie" during its use with the CAA.

1954   NC13367   United Air Lines 1 November 1934 to 30 July 1938.

NC13367   Western Air Express (leased from UAL).

C-unknown   SCADTA 30 July 1938 to 1939.

C-unknown   AVIANCA 1939 to an unknown date.

1955   unknown   J. A. Barr, Shanghai, 9 November 1934 (shipping date).

       unknown   Marshall Chang Hsüeh-liang, December 1934 to December 1936.

       unknown   Government of China January 1937 to late 1937. Informally named *Bai Ying* (White Eagle), this was a 247-D with the cabin specially fitted with a bunk and six seats. This airplane was bombed to destruction at I-ch'ang, China by the Japanese a few months after full-scale war broke out in July 1937.

1956   NC13368   United Air Lines 22 November 1934 to 31 October 1936.

       unknown   Inter-American Aero Travel Co. 31 October 1936 to an unknown date.

       unknown   George Beidermann, 1945.

1957   NX13370   Used by Boeing for flight testing 1934–35.

       NC13370   Western Air Express 6 September 1935 to 15 December 1936. This airplane crashed on 15 December 1936 into Hardy Peak near Alpine, Utah, killing the crew of three and seven passengers. The crash was attributed to the inability of the pilot to identify the south leg of the Salt Lake City range due to local static conditions that rendered both receivers in the aircraft inoperative. It is believed that this aircraft was intended for United with license NC13369. Photos show NC13370 painted over the earlier number which was then used on C/N 1953.

1958   NC13365   United Air Lines 23 October 1934 to 1937.

       NC13365   Western Air Express (leased from UAL).

       NX13365   United Air Lines (Flight Research) 1937 to 26 October 1945.

       XA-FIH   Líneas Aéreas Mexicanas, S.A. 26 October 1945 to December 1947. Airframe hours totaled 8,162 as of 6 November 1945. It was named *Estado de Sinaloa* by LAMSA.

       XB-LID   Struck December 1947 to July 1949.

       XB-LID   Claudio Robles Ochoa 11 July 1949 to 1951.

       XA-JUV   Taxis Aereos Nacionales, S.A. 1951–52. This aircraft was wrecked at takeoff at Mexico City on 5 May 1952 near a lake. There were no serious injuries.

Appendix C

*247 Models Built and Proposed**

247	The original 247 built. A total of fifty-nine were produced, all for United Air Lines. The design was approved 15 August 1932.
247-A	A special 247 modified for use by UATC as an executive and research aircraft. It featured two Pratt & Whitney SGR-1535 Wasp Jr. 625 hp engines. The design was approved 22 April 1932. One was built.
247-B	A 1932 proposal for a mailplane version of the standard 247. The aircraft was to have been equipped with letter boxes for in-flight sorting and would have carried one or two clerks and a payload of 2310 pounds. It was designed on 24 May 1932. None were built.
247-C	(No C designation was assigned.)
247-D	The first major production modification of 247. It featured geared Wasp engines, NACA cowls, and a rearward-swept cockpit windshield. The design was approved 14 December 1933. Fifteen were built.
247-E	The designation of the standard 247, constructor's number 1692, when it was converted to 247-D configuration. The design was approved 9 June 1934. One was built.
247-F	A twelve-passenger version also designed as an eight-passenger sleeper equipped with Pratt & Whitney Hornet engines. The estimated maximum speed was 213 mph and the cruising speed was 189 mph. Wing span was stretched to 77' and gross weight increased to 16,876 pounds. The design was approved 6 March 1935. None were built. (Performance improvement and the advent of DC-2 and DC-3 did not justify production).
247-S	A proposal by the Boeing School of Aeronautics to fit Besler steam engines to the 247. None were built.

*Source: Boeing Aircraft Co. Model # Description List, Boeing Files, Seattle

247-X   A proposed bomber version of 247-D. It was designed to carry the standard USAAC 2200-pound bombload externally and was armed with two 30-caliber machine guns, one mounted in a nose turret. The design was approved October 27, 1934. None were built.

247-Y   A special conversion of 247-D C/N 1952 for Marshal Chang Hsüeh-liang. It was equipped with two forward-firing, 150 round 50-caliber machine guns in the nose and one flexible 30-caliber machine gun in dorsal gun ring. It could carry six passengers and a crew of two. The design was approved February 1937. One was built.

247 (seaplane)   A proposed seaplane version of the standard 247 equipped with Edo floats. It would have carried up to nine passengers, 483 pounds of cargo, and 203 gallons of fuel. The estimated maximum speed was 168 mph. The design was approved 12 January 1933. None were built.

247 (skis)   A proposed version of the standard 247 with retractable skis. It would have carried up to ten passengers, 892 pounds of cargo, and 203 gallons of fuel. The estimated maximum speed was 180 mph. The design was approved 12 January 1933. None were built.

Other versions included a twin-tailed, a swept-wing, and a trimotor. None were built.

Appendix D

Detailed Technical Description*

Strength

1. The weight of the principal structural members is calculated at a gross weight of 13,650 pounds (6197 kg.).

2. The landing design factor is 4.99.

3. The design diving speed is 230 mph (370 km/h).

4. The airplane is designed for a low angle of attack acceleration of 3.5 at 230 mph.

5. The airplane is designed for a high angle of attack acceleration of 3.5 at maximum lift.

6. The following gust conditions were used in the design calculations: A 30 ft/sec. gust is applied at all speeds within 230 mph. The maximum positive acceleration is 3.7 at 230 mph. The maximum negative acceleration is -1.8 at 230 mph.

7. A factor of safety of 1.5 is added to all of the above flight accelerations to give the design load factors.

8. In all strength calculations, the value used for the allowable ultimate stress intensity is that given in the material specifications.

9. When the strength of parts was in doubt, their strength was determined by static test.

Wing Group

1. The principle members of the wing truss are designed for the conditions noted above.

2. The wing is an all-metal cantilevered structure. It is tapered in plan form and thickness. The connection between the wing and wing stub is a bolted joint, such that the wing may be readily detached from the stub. Four taper bolts and seven shear bolts per spare are used in the connections. The bolt holes are jig drilled and jig reamed for interchangeability.

3. The wing tips outboard of the ailerons are removable for replacement in case of damage. Two straight bolts per spar are used in the joints. The bolt holes are jig drilled and jig reamed for interchangeability.

*Abridged From Official Boeing 247-D Specifications, May 3, 1934

194

4. The spars are trusses constructed of square and rectangular aluminum alloy tubes (17ST). The members are assembled with gusset plates and rivets. The spar terminal fittings are steel except the removable wing tip terminals, which are aluminum alloy.

5. The ribs are Warren truss structures. The chord members are aluminum alloy channel sections and the web members are aluminum alloy tubes. The ribs are assembled with rivets and are jointed to the spars with extruded "Tee" sections and formed aluminum alloy fittings.

6. The wing covering together with the spars and compression struts between the spars are designed to carry the drag loads in the wing. The wing covering is smooth aluminum alloy sheet.

7. The trailing edges of the wings are removable for repair or shipment.

8. Hinged doors are provided in the wing stub leading edges for access to the fuel lines, engine controls, etc. The doors are secured with latches of ample strength.

9. The ailerons are constructed of aluminum alloy. They consist of front and rear spars, and ribs, all of channel sections, assembled in a Warren truss and covered with smooth sheet.

10. The ailerons are provide with a "Friese"-type balance equal to 20 percent of the mean chord.

11. The aileron hinges are equipped with ball bearings.

12. The design of the ailerons permits a movement of 21½ degrees either side of the neutral position.

13. A hinged flap is provided in the trailing edge of the left aileron similar to the those in the elevator and rudder, to correct for "wing-heaviness." The flap is controlled from the cockpit so that adjustments may be made in flight.

Tail Group

1. The tail surfaces are cantilevered structures of aluminum alloy construction, consisting of front and rear spars braced with ribs, all of which are Warren trusses with channel section chords, and covered with smooth sheet. The rudder and elevators are constructed of aluminum alloy ribs and braces covered with doped fabric.

2. The stabilizer leading edge is not removable.

3. The tail-surface hinges are equipped with ball bearings.

4. The stabilizer is not adjustable but is fixed in the position which gives correct balance at cruising speed with full load. The airplane is trimmed for various speed and loading conditions by means of the flaps provided in the trailing edge of the elevators. The flaps are controlled from the cockpit.

5. The elevator is balanced.

6. The movement of the elevator is 27 degrees either side of neutral.

7. The fin is not adjustable. Correction for engine torque or single-engine operation is made by means of a hinged flap in the trailing edge of the rudder. The flap is controllable from the cockpit.

8. The rudder has an overhung leading-edge balance.

9. The rudder is so located that it is protected from damage in case of failure of the tail wheel.

10. The movement of the rudder is 27 degrees either side of neutral.

Body Group

1. The fuselage is an all-metal semi-monocoque structure consisting of longerons, bulkheads, and covering. The longerons and all other brace members are aluminum alloy channel sections.

2. Brazier head rivets are used in the fuselage. Aluminum alloy bolts and nuts are also used and are locked by staking or spinning.

3. The body is designed to accommodate two pilots, ten passengers and a total of 125 cubic feet (3.54 cubic meters) of additional space for cargo, namely mail, express, and passenger baggage.

4. Space for the installation of radio sets is provided in the upper rear portion of the nose mail compartment. Access to this space is through the nose door.

5. A compartment for the battery is provided in the leading edge of the left wing stub. This compartment is drained so that spilled acid will be discharged clear of all portions of the airplane structure, and is forcibly ventilated.

6. The body is constructed in four sections, so that it may be disassembled for repair and shipment, as follows: nose section-front wing stub spar forward; center section-wing stubs and fuselage between front and rear spars; tail section-rear wing stub spar to tail wheel bulkhead; tail-fairing cone. The nose and tail sections are joined to the center section by two circumferential rows of special steel streamline head screws staked after insertion. Special 1/4" and 5/16" dural bolts in shear are employed to tie the four longerons together. The tail-fairing cone is connected to the tail section with bolts, nuts, and cotter keys.

7. The joints in the fuselage skin are filled with a sealing compound to make them raintight.

8. The engine nacelles are equipped with firewalls constructed of .040 aluminum alloy.

9. The engine mounts are constructed of electrically welded chrome-molybdenum steel tubing. They are attached to the wing stubs with taper and straight bolts so that they are readily detachable. Rubber-cup-type shock absorber units are incorporated in the engine mounting ring.

Landing Gear

1. Wheel landing gear of the divided-axle type is provided, equipped with brakes and Boeing oleo shock absorbers.

2. Towing eyes are provided at the lower end of each axle.

3. The landing gear is retractable into the wing stub.

4. A position indicator and signal lights are provided on the instrument board to indicate the position of the landing gear.

5. No fairing is provided in the landing gear nor are mudguards installed.

6. The telescoping part of the shock absorber is protected with a leather boot.

7. The brake system consists of wheel brakes actuated hydraulically from the rudder pedals. The brakes may be operated individually or simultaneously. The brakes are operable only from the pilot's rudder pedals. For locking either or both brakes in the "on" position, a hand-operated spring ratchet is provided in the cockpit.

8. The landing gear is so designed that the angle between the thrust line and the ground is eight degrees.

9. The wheels are equipped with 42×15.00l-16 Goodrich non-skid tires inflated to 24 pounds per square inch.

Tail Wheel

1. The tail wheel is not steerable but will swivel through 360 degrees. It is provided with a spring which restrains it in a trailing position.

2. The tail wheel is equipped with a Boeing oleo shock absorber of the same type used on the landing gear.

3. The tail wheel is equipped with a 7.00–3×16 airwheel inflated to 25 pounds per square inch.

Power Plant

1. The engines are Pratt & Whitney geared Wasps. These engines are supercharged to deliver 550 horsepower at 2200 rpm under conditions corresponding to air under standard conditions at 8000 feet (2440 meters) altitude. With the propellers set to absorb 550 horsepower at 2200 rpm at 8000 feet, the engines will deliver not less than 550 horsepower at sea level at a manifold pressure of 33 inches of mercury.

2. An operator's manual, tool kit, and engine, plane, and pilot's log as furnished by Pratt & Whitney Aircraft Co., are furnished with each airplane.

3. All parts, such as magnetos, generators, distributors, carburetors, etc., which require frequent inspection of adjustment are readily removable from the engine when it is installed in the airplane.

4. Each engine is provided with a radio shielded ignition harness.

5. A special twin-motor ignition switch unit is installed. This consists of individual switches for each motor, having the conventional positions, and a master switch consisting of a knob which, when pulled out, will cut off both ignition systems.

6. The carburetor air intake system consists of warm air intakes, cold air intakes, mixing valves, and controls. The warm air intakes consist of a housing around the exhaust tail stack. The cold air intake is a scoop on the inboard side of the nacelle between the engine cylinders. From both intakes the air is carried through pipes to the mixing valve and hence to the carburetor. The mixing valve is

controlled from the cockpit. Surplus warm air is discharged from the valve outside the cowling.

7. Each exhaust system consists of a collector ring (manifold) and a single discharge stack under the wing.

8. One five-pound "Lux" fire extinguisher is installed in the fuselage, with the discharging pipes to each nacelle.

9. Spark controls are not provided. The spark controls on the magnetos are secured in the fully advanced position.

10. The engine controls are mounted on a pedestal between the two control columns. Individual locks are provided to secure the controls against creeping in any position. A scale graduated from 0 to 100 is installed between the two mixture control handles to indicate the setting of the handles. The engine controls are operated by push-pull rods and cranks. Ball bearings are used throughout.

11. Three-bladed controllable pitch propellers are used, having aluminum alloy blades and steel hubs. The propeller normally operates at a "high" pitch, which is adjustable, and may be changed to a "low" pitch for take-off or climbing by simply operating a control handle in the cockpit. The engine oil pressure is utilized to change the pitch. When the control is returned to the "high" position the propeller is shifted and held in that position by centrifugal forces on counterweights. The high and low position stops are adjustable on the ground. When the airplane is operating under conditions where ice may form, the propeller should be provided with a spinner to protect the pitch control mechanism.

12. The starting system consists of Eclipse Hand Inertia starters (Series XI), battery, booster coils, and a double-throw hand crank. Starter engaging controls are provided in the nacelles only. An integral booster switch is incorporated in the engaging control. Self-priming carburetors are used by which the engines may be primed. The priming is accomplished by placing the mixture control in the full lean position and pumping the throttle lever. The starter crank is provided with a universal joint so that the starters may be cranked from the ground. Electrically operated starters may be substituted by special arrangement. The starters are cranked from the outboard side of the nacelles and the starter engaging control is located below the crank extension.

13. Pressure-type intercylinder baffles are installed to aid in cooling the engine. A nose shutter is not installed.

Lubrication

1. A single oil tank is located on the forward side of the firewall in each nacelle. The capacity of each tank, exclusive of expansion space, is ten gallons. The expansion space in each tank is equal to two gallons.

2. All oil piping is 4 SO aluminum adequately supported and protected with a short length of split rubber hose at all supports.

3. Oil coolers are installed to regulate the oil temperatures.

4. Valves are placed in the oil tank outlet lines at such a point that the oil system can be completely drained.

Fuel System

1. Two fuel tanks are installed, one in each wing stub on either side of the fuselage. The tanks are built of aluminum to Boeing specifications, and have an elliptical cross section with convex ends. They are built to withstand an internal pressure of four pounds per square inch. The total capacity of the tanks is 273 gallons (1033 liters). The right hand tank contains a reserve compartment of seventy gallons. The fuel tanks are supported by cork-padded metal straps. Each tank is installed in a well drained and ventilated compartment which eliminates the possibility of the wings becoming filled with explosive vapor.

Instruments

1. The following instruments are installed:

Left Hand Panel

Ice warning thermometer

Landing gear position indicator

Center Panel

Directional Gyroscope

Artificial horizon

Airspeed indicator

Turn and bank indicator

Rate of climb indicator

Altimeter #1

Clock

Supercharger pressure gauge

Thermocouple indicator

Fuel gauge-left tank

Fuel gauge-right tank

Oil thermometers (two), right and left engines

Tachometers (two), right and left engines

Right Hand Panel

Fuel pressure gauges (two), right and left engine

Oil pressure gauges (two), right and left engine

Ammeter

2. All instruments are so installed as to be readily visible to the pilot without artificial illumination during the daylight hours. The three panels of the instrument board are connected through shock absorbers and the assembly mounted in the airplane on shock absorbers.

3. All instruments have luminous markings and are illuminated for night flying. The lights consist of hooded flood lights with clarostat control. There is an "on" and "off" switch for the instrument lights. In addition, there is a push-button switch in the inboard end of each control wheel rim, by which the

instrument lights may be turned on regardless of the position of the main switch.

4. All instruments are plainly labeled to indicate their use.

Cockpit Furnishings

1. The following cockpit furnishings are provided:

Pilot's and copilot's seats

Seat cushions

Safety belts

Floor

Windshield and enclosures

Log book pocket

2. The left hand seat is adjustable vertically in flight by the pilot, three inches up and three inches down from the normal position.

3. A cushion is provided in the bottom of both pilot's seats. A cushion is also provided on the back of each seat.

4. A quick-release safety belt is installed on each seat. The belt is fastened to the seat and hooks are provided to hold them off the floor when not in use.

5. The windshield and side windows are safety glass.

6. The cockpit roof is arranged as follows: A hatch of clear Plasticine is provided in the center rear. It is covered by a curtain which is quickly detachable by pulling backward from the front. The rest of the roof is metal.

7. The cockpit is equipped with a smooth surface floor. All openings in the floor for moving controls are made draft-proof with leather boots.

8. A container is provided in the cockpit for the necessary log books and maps.

9. The sides and floor of the cockpit are covered with a heat insulating material.

10 The cockpit entrance is in the cabin. Two peep holes are provided in the door, with swinging covers on the cockpit side.

Electrical Equipment

1. The electrical equipment consists of the battery, generator, switches, lights, and wiring.

2. The battery cut-out switch is provided with a push-pull control in the cockpit.

3. The Eclipse 25 ampere engine-driven generator is installed on the left engine.

4. The electrical wiring is installed in conduit with junction boxes at the proper locations to permit replacements of the wiring. Connector panels are provided to permit removal of the electrical units and disassembly of the airplane. The

conduits are so installed that wiring for hand-generated inertia starters may be installed without the necessity of changing any of the conduits or boxes.

5. All lamps are the double-contact type.

6. The following switches are provided:

Navigation lights

Landing lights

Courtesy lights

Master switches for the cabin and mail compartment lights

Instrument board lights

Cabin Furnishings

1. The cabin entrance is on the right rear side. The door swings outward and forward and is provided with handles on both sides. The door latch can be operated from either side of the door. A key-operated lock is also provided on the outside of the door. A latch is provided to hold the door in the open position. This latch also serves as a safety latch to hold the door closed during flight.

2. An emergency exit is installed in the left rear side of the cabin. This consists of a rectangular door, in which is mounted the rear window. The door is secured by a toggle-type latch operable from inside the cabin only. If necessary in an emergency, the toggle is accessible from the outside after breaking the window.

3. All cabin windows are safety glass and cannot be opened.

4. A smooth surface wood floor, covered with linoleum, is installed in the cabin. The under side of the floor is coated with a fire-resistant paint.

5. Ten passenger seats are installed. The seats are anchored by the legs to the floor with the fittings which allow the seats to be removed quickly.

6. The seats are constructed of metal and are well upholstered. They are of adequate size, the two rear being 18 inches between the arms and the remaining are 20 inches between the arms. The seats are spaced 40 inches between the backs, with a nine inch minimum aisle. The seat backs can be lowered to a reclining position and locked where desired. The headrest pad is hollowed to keep a sleeping passenger's head in place. A pocket is provided on the back of each of the forward eight seats.

7. Quick-release safety belts are installed on each passenger seat. The belts are anchored to the seats and are readily adjustable to fit passengers of various sizes.

8. The cabin is provided with a wall-type reading light at each seat, two dome-type ceiling lights and one light in the lavatory. The ceiling lights are installed so that they do not shine to the rear.

9. A switch for the ceiling lights is installed near the cabin entrance. The lavatory and reading lights have individual switches. Master switches for all cabin lights are placed in the cockpit.

10. An ash receiver is mounted on the wall at each seat. The receivers are quickly detachable for cleaning.

11. The cabin is equipped with heat- and sound-proofing lining, the floor also being insulated. The cabin lining permits conversation in a voice only slightly louder than normal.

12. A hot-air system is used for heating the pilot's cockpit and passenger cabin. This system consists of "stoves" installed in the exhaust manifold tail stack of each engine. By means of ducts, the hot air is led from the stoves to grills located in the cockpit floor and on the cabin floors beside the spar. Valves are provided for controlling the amount of heat required to keep the cockpit and cabin at comfortable temperatures.

13. The cockpit, cabin, and lavatory ventilating systems are each independent of the other. A fresh-air inlet and foul-air outlet is provided in the cockpit. The fresh air is taken in through a scoop on the bottom of the fuselage nose section and discharged through an opening on the left side. The foul air is drawn out through an opening located above the aft of the copilot's seat on the right side.

14. Fresh air for the passenger cabin is taken in through scoops on the lower surface of the wing stubs. It is discharged into the cabin through four outlets, two each located on either side of the cabin above the windows. The foul air is removed through two openings, one each located on either side of the cabin near the floor.

15. Two control levers are provided in the rear of the cabin, one for controlling the amount of fresh air entering the cabin, and the other for controlling the foul air exhausted therefrom.

16. The lavatory is equipped with a separate scoop and duct which draws air from the lavatory at all times in flight.

17. A lavatory is provided at the left rear end of the cabin. It is equipped with a water tank and wash bowl, soap dispenser, towel rack, mirror, toilet paper holder, and a dry-type chemical toilet. A water tank is removable for filling. The lavatory has a window on the roof.

18. A one-quart hand Pyrene fire extinguisher is installed in the forward end of the cabin.

19. A first-aid kit is installed in the cabin.

20. Hat clips are mounted on the wall at each passenger seat.

21. Above the seats is a rack constructed of netting for carrying light parcels and clothing.

22. On the forward wall of the cabin is mounted an electric warning sign with a combination switch in the cockpit. This sign may be lighted to display the words "No Smoking" or "Fasten Seat Belts" or both.

Cargo and Baggage Compartments

1. Two cargo and baggage compartments are provided. The forward compartment occupies the space forward of the cockpit and is loaded through a door in the nose of the airplane. The door is secured with a toggle latch and also with a key-operated lock. The same key is used for the cabin door lock. A latch is provided to hold the door open while loading.

2. A rear compartment is located immediately aft of the cabin and is entered through a door on the left side of the fuselage. The door swings outward and forward, and is secured by both a latch and lock. The lock key is the same as used for the nose compartment and cabin doors. A latch is provided to hold the door open.

3. Both cargo compartments are illuminated by wall lights with integral switches.

Night Flying Equipment

1. Navigation lights are installed in the wing tips and tail fairing.

2. Fixed landing lights are installed in the leading edge of each wing just outboard of the propeller circle. The lights are covered with a glass plate shaped to the leading-edge contour. The lights are adjustable both vertically and horizontally on the ground.

3. Each landing light is equipped with a "courtesy" light, which consists of a colored lamp, corresponding to the navigation light, mounted in front of the reflector. A switch in the cockpit permits turning these "courtesy" lights on to augment the navigation lights when passing other airplanes on or in the vicinity of landing fields.

4. Two three-minute parachute-type landing flares are installed. Controls are provided in the cockpit so that each flare can be released individually.

Radio Equipment

1. The airplane is completely bonded and shielded for a radio installation.

2. Space for the installation of radio equipment is provided in the upper rear end of the nose cargo compartment.

Appendix E

Boeing 247-D Cockpit Check List

Pre-Starting

1. Adjust seat and rudder pedals
2. Set parking brake, unlock controls
3. Trim tab set
4. Oil shutters as desired
5. Carburetor heat—cold
6. Check cabin air
7. Landing gear neutral
8. Propellers forward
9. Throttles set
10. Mixture emergency—rich
11. Master battery switch ON
12. Master ignition switch ON
13. Gas ON
    a. Left engine on left tank
    b. Right engine on right tank
14. Generators ON
15. Remote compass ON
16. Windshield wipers and propeller de-icers OFF
17. Check instruments left to right
18. Start engines:
    Wobble 2 pounds fuel pressure
    Prime 3 to 6 full strokes with throttles
19. Idle 700–800 RPM until oil pressure drops to normal

Before Taxiing

1. Check radio, altimeter, time and taxi instructions
2. Controls free
3. Chock removed, both
4. Seat Belt, No Smoking signs ON

Run Up

1. 1000 RPM check pressures and temperature
2. 1500 RPM check:
    a. Propellers (exercise)
    b. Carburetor heat (ON and OFF)
    c. Check feather buttons
    d. Generators (volts and amps)
3. Check magnetos at 28 inches of mercury.
    a. Pressure, temperature, and suction

Pre-Take Off

1. Tabs set
2. Oil shutters as desired
3. Carburetor heat cold
4. Gear handle neutral
5. Props forward and locked
6. Mixture emergency rich
7. Seat Belt and No Smoking sign ON
8. Magnetos ON BOTH
9. Gas:
    a. Left engine on left tank
    b. Right engine on right tank
10. Generators ON
11. Check remote compass on
12. Windshield and Propeller de-icers as desired
13. Pitot tubes both on static
14. Check instruments Left to Right
15. Set gyros
16. Manual gear control—raise position
17. Control free

After Take-Off

1. Gear up
2. Reduce power—31 inches, 2100 RPM
3. Carburetor heat 100 degrees F
4. Carburetor mixture—climb position
    DO NOT APPLY BRAKES AFTER TAKE-OFF

Cruising

1. Reduce power 27 1/2 inches, 2000 RPM
2. Carburetor heat 100 degrees

Pre-Landing

1. Oil shutters as desired
2. Carburetor heat cold
3. Gear down and checked
4. Mixture emergency rich
5. Seat Belt and No Smoking signs ON
6. Gas ON
   a. Left engine on left tank
   b. Right engine on right tank
7. Check instruments Left to Right
8. Propellers in low pitch

Single Engine Procedure

1. Wobble pump
2. Gear up
3. Maintain heading and airspeed 90–100 MPH
4. Adjust power 34 inches of mercury, 2000 RPM on good engine
5. Bad engine:
   a. Throttle back
   b. Propeller back
   c. Mixture full lean
   d. Feather propeller—Ignition OFF
   e. Gas OFF, generator OFF
6. Set fire extinguisher on bad engine
7. Trim and decrease power if possible
8. Get out check list

NOTE

IN CASE OF ENGINE FIRE OR ENGINE FAILURE ON TAKE-OFF, FEATHER PROPELLER FIRST THEN PROCEED WITH NORMAL PROCEDURE ABOVE

Single Engine Emergency Operations—Maximum (91 Octane Fuel)

	Altitude	RPM	Manifold Pressure
One Minute Emergency:	0–3000	2250	36"
	3000-Above	2250	35"
Continuous Emergency:	0–4000	2200	35"
	4000–7600	2200	34"
	7600-Above	2000	33"

General Information

1. Best gliding rate at 98 MPH indicated airspeed
2. Keep carburetor temperature 100 degrees F.
3. CAUTION: DO NOT PUT BRAKES ON AFTER TAKE-OFF. This can do damage to landing gear retraction mechanism.
4. LOADING: Two pounds in nose for one pound in rear until maximum load of 1000 pounds is reached in rear baggage compartment
   a. Rear compartment 1000 pounds
   b. Front compartment 1400 pounds

Appendix F

*Illustrations by Victor D. Seely**

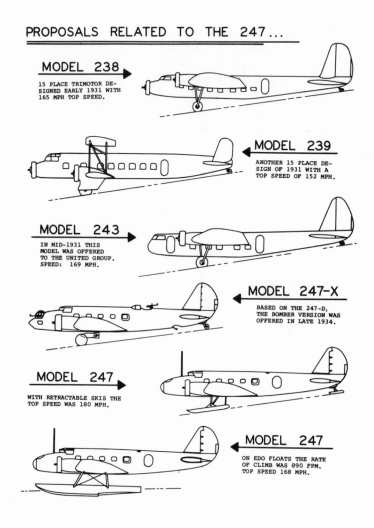

PROPOSALS RELATED TO THE 247...

MODEL 238
15 PLACE TRIMOTOR DE-
SIGNED EARLY 1931 WITH
165 MPH TOP SPEED.

MODEL 239
ANOTHER 15 PLACE DE-
SIGN OF 1931 WITH A
TOP SPEED OF 152 MPH.

MODEL 243
IN MID-1931 THIS
MODEL WAS OFFERED
TO THE UNITED GROUP.
SPEED: 169 MPH.

MODEL 247-X
BASED ON THE 247-D,
THE BOMBER VERSION WAS
OFFERED IN LATE 1934.

MODEL 247
WITH RETRACTABLE SKIS THE
TOP SPEED WAS 180 MPH.

MODEL 247
ON EDO FLOATS THE RATE
OF CLIMB WAS 890 FPM.
TOP SPEED 168 MPH.

*Source: "Boeing's Pacesetting 247," *American Aviation Historical Society Journal* 9 (August 1968), 54–66, 75.

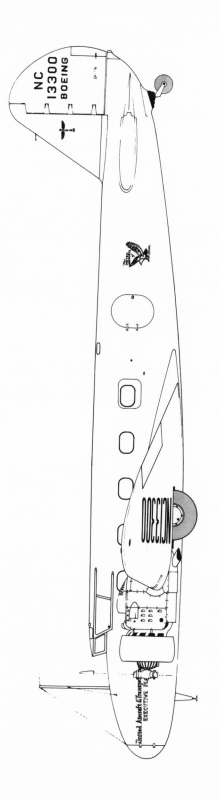

C/N 1711 United Aircraft and Transport Corporation 247-A, November 1933.

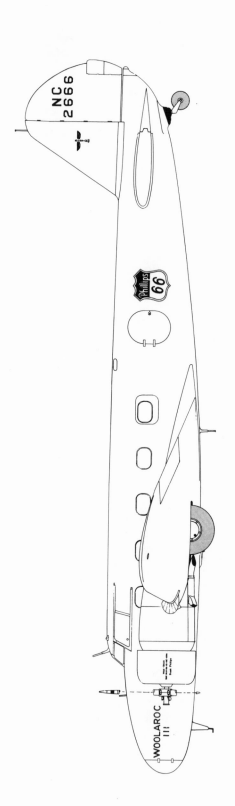

C/N 1946 Phillips Petroleum 247-D, "Woolaroc III," September 1935. The emblem is orange and black. (Note: The registration number on the lower wing is not shown.)

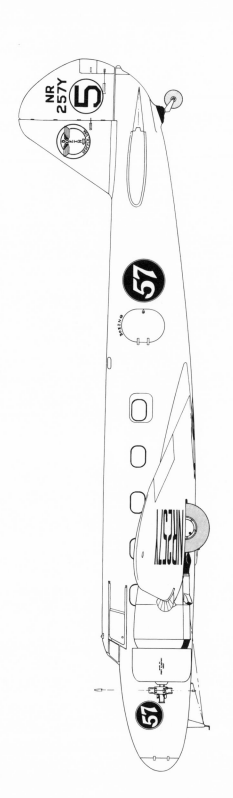

C/N 1953 The 247-D flown by Roscoe Turner in the MacRobertson Race, shown in its original factory markings at time of delivery, September 1935. The white "57" is on a red background, the black "5" is on a white background. A large black "5" on a six-foot white circle is on the underside.

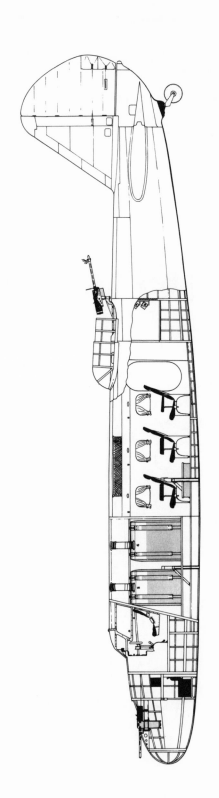

C/N 1952 Partial cutaway of the 247-Y, the special armed executive version ordered by Marshal Chang Hsüeh-liang.

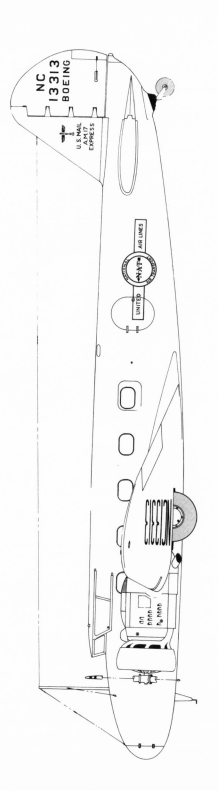

C/N 1694 National Air Transport 247, 1933, shown with the original antenna mast.

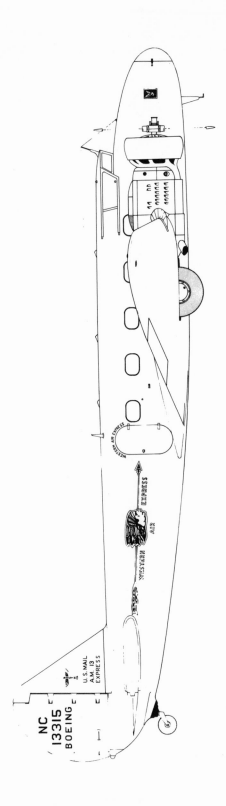

C/N 1696 Western Air Express 247, 1936.

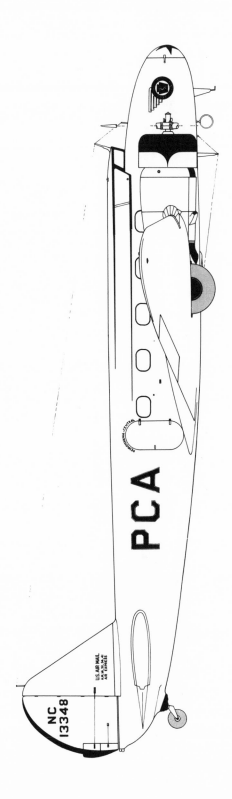

C/N 1730 Pennsylvania-Central Airlines 247-D, 1937. The trim colors are red and silver.

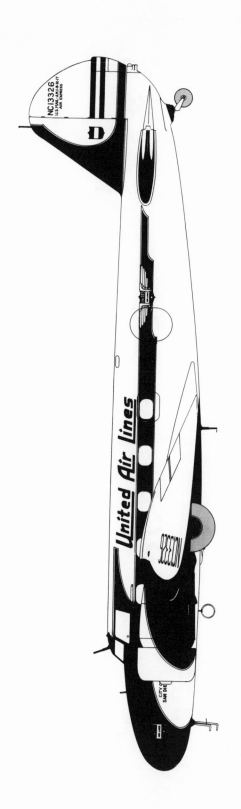

C/N 1707 United Air Lines 247-D, *City of San Diego*, 1941. The trim color is blue; name, top third of shield, upper rudder stripe and inboard aileron stripe, red; trim around shield, yellow-gold.

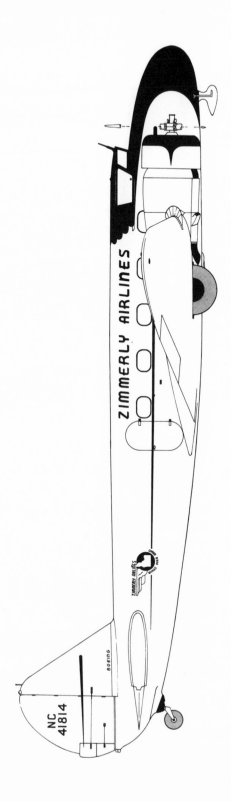

C/N 1735 Zimmerly Airlines 247-D, 1945. Trim Color is believed to be green.

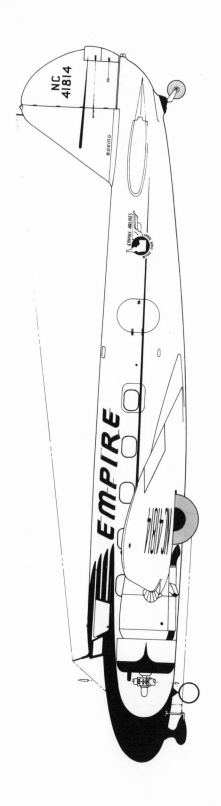

C/N 1735 Empire Airlines 247-D, 1946. The trim color is thought to be green, while the company name was painted in red and green.

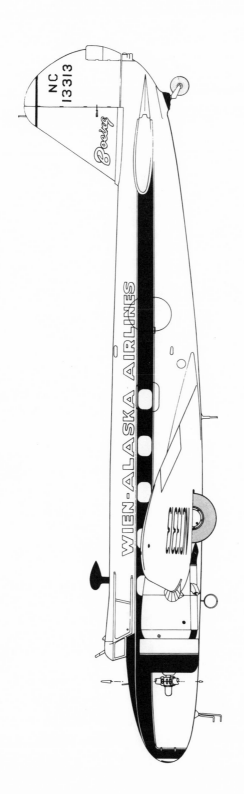

C/N 1694 Wien-Alaska Airlines 247-D, February 1946. The trim colors are yellow and black.

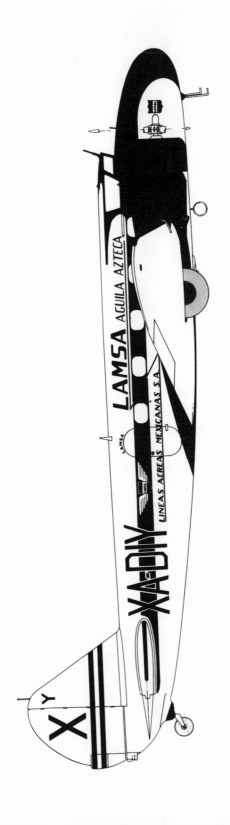

C/N 1693 Líneas Aéreas Mexicana (LAMSA) 247-D, 1945. LAMSA's colors were red, white, and green, in the same style as United Air Lines. The registration numbers are in black.

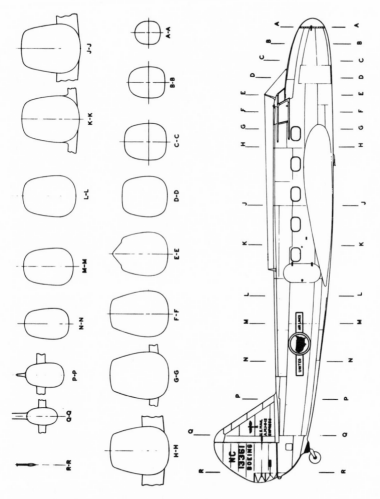

View 1 of 5-view detailed drawing of United Air Lines Boeing 247-D NC13361.

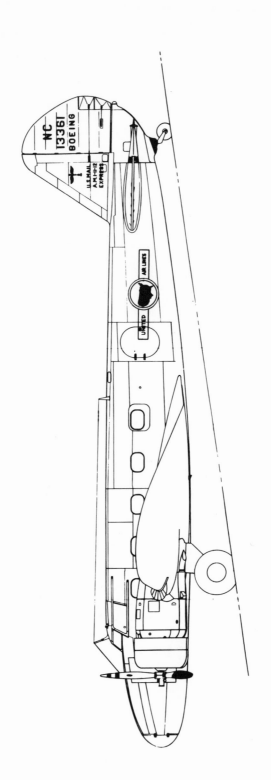

View 2 of 5-view detailed drawing of United Air Lines Boeing 247-D NC13361.

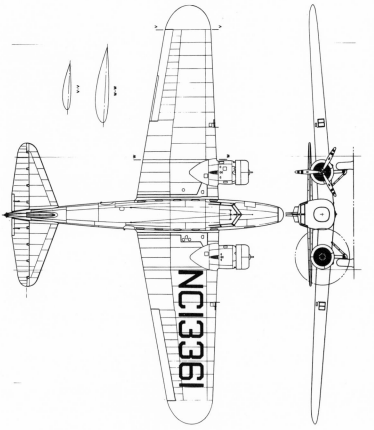

Views 3 & 4 of 5-view detailed drawing of United Air Lines Boeing 247-D NC13361.

View 5 of 5-view detailed drawing of United Air Lines Boeing 247-D NCf13361.

Notes

Chapter 1. Boeing and the Aircraft Industry

1. *Seattle Times*, 31 March, 1 April, 2 April, 3 April 1933.

2. Peter W. Bowers, *Boeing Aircraft Since 1916* (New York: Funk and Wagnalls, 1968), 7.

3. R. E. G. Davies, *Airlines of the United States Since 1914* (Washington, D.C.: Smithsonian Institution Press, 1982), 10–12.

4. Bowers, 57.

5. Ibid., 65–67.

6. Davies, 17–18.

7. Ibid., 19.

8. Ibid., 33.

9. Ibid., 35.

10. Ibid., 42.

11. Frank J. Taylor, *High Horizons: Daredevil Flying Postmen to Modern Magic Carpet—The United Air Lines Story* (New York: McGraw Hill, 1951), 16.

12. Davies, 47.

13. Taylor, 21–22.

14. Ibid., 27.

15. Davies, 58.

16. Taylor, 29.

17. Bowers, 108.

18. Ibid., 108–17.

19. "Mr. Rentschler," *The Bee-Hive*, Summer 1956, 2–5.

20. Robert Schlaifer and S. D. Heron, *Development of Aircraft Engines and Fuels* (Boston: Harvard University, 1950), 162–70.

21. Ibid., 185.

22. Ibid., 189–90.

23. Bowers, 100.

24. Davies, 70.

25. Taylor, 30–32.

26. Davies., 71.

27. Bowers, 122.

28. Schlaifer and Heron, 190–91.

29. Bowers, 112, 124–25.

30. Taylor, 70–71.

31. Ibid., 49–50.

32. Davies, 71.

33. Ibid., 50–51.

34. Ibid., 62.

35. Ibid., 61.

36. Taylor, 51.

37. United Air Lines, *Corporate and Legal History of United Air Lines and Its Predecessor and Subsidiaries, 1925–1945* (Chicago: Twentieth Century Press, 1953), 112.

38. Davies, 114, Taylor, 74.

39. Davies, 93.

40. Ibid., 115.

41. Ibid., 116.

Chapter 2. New Technology and New Aircraft

1. Ronald E. Miller and Davis Sawers, *The Technical Development of Modern Aviation* (London: Routledge and Kegan Paul, 1968), 56.

2. Ibid., 65–66.

3. Miller and Sawers, 62.

4. James R. Hansen, "The Cowling Story at Langley Laboratory, 1926–1936," *Aerospace Historian*, 32 (Fall, September 1985): 162.

5. "Northrop Past: An Interview with John K. Northrop, Founder of the Company," *Technical Digest*, (February 1979): 3–6.

6. Minutes of the Second, Third, and Fourth Technical Advisory Committee Meetings, United Aircraft and Transport Corporation, Archive and Historical Resource Center, United Technologies Corporation.

7. Bowers, 175.

8. Ibid., 175–76.

9. Hansen, 165.

10. Bowers, 176–78.

11. Miller and Sawers, 18.

12. Cary Hoge Mead, *Wings Over the World: The Life of George Jackson Mead* (Wauwatosa, Wisconsin: The Swannet Press, 1971), 1–15, 60–85.

13. Minutes of the Second Meeting of the Technical Advisory Committee Meetings, December 1929, United Aircraft and Transport Corporation, Archive and Historical Resource Center, United Technologies Corporation, 290.

14. Mansfield, 39, 67.

15. Minutes of Second Meeting, 277–78.

16. Minutes of the Third Meeting of the Technical Advisory Committee Meetings, May 1930, United Aircraft and Transport Corporation, Archive and Historical Resource Center, United Technologies Corporation, 390.

17. Ibid., 392.

18. Minutes of Second Meeting, 278.

19. Ibid., 301.

20. Minutes of Third Meeting, 682a.

21. Ibid.

22. Model 238 Specifications, 7238–7238.2. The Boeing Company Historical Services and Archives, Seattle, Washington.

23. Model 239 Specifications, 7239–7239.3. Boeing Archives.

24. Model 243 Specifications, 7243–7243.2. Boeing Archives.

25. Harold Mansfield, *Vision: A Saga of the Sky* (New York: Duell, Sloan and Pierce, 1956), 99.

26. Frederick B. Collins, memorandum to Philip G. Johnson, "Twin Engine Plane for Commercial Production," 12 February 1931, M 247 File, Boeing Archives.

27. Mansfield, 99.

28. "Portrait of 'P. G.'," *Boeing Magazine*, (October 1944): 3–4, 18, "Phil Johnson," *Western Flying*, (September 1940): 21.

29. P. G. Johnson, memorandum to Frederick B. Rentschler, "Replacement Equipment—United Air Lines—Single Motor Equipment," 30 September 1931, Section VIII A-1, Box 5, Boeing Archives.

30. Ibid.

31. Ibid.

32. Taylor, 75.

33. P. G. Johnson, memorandum to F. B. Rentschler, "Replacement Equipment—United Air Lines—Single Motor Equipment," 30 September 1931, Section VIII A-1, Box 5, Boeing Archives.

34. Erik H. Nelson to Claire L. Egtvedt, 20 October 1931, Section VIII B-2, Box 5, Boeing Archives.

35. Ibid.

36. P. G. Johnson, memorandum to C. L. Egtvedt, 20 October 1931, Section VIII B-2, Box 5, Boeing Archives.

37. C. L. Egtvedt, memorandum to P. G. Johnson, "Proposed Twin Engine Transport Plane," 2 November 1931, Section VIII B-2, Box 5, Boeing Archives.

38. Ibid.

39. P. G. Johnson, memorandum to C. L. Egtvedt, "New Transport Ships," 11 November 1931, Section VIII B-2, Box 5, Boeing Archives.

40. Gardner W. Carr, memorandum to C. N. Montieth and Frederick P. Laudan, "Mockup, Work Order 9045," 14 November 1931, Model 247 File, Boeing Archives.

41. G. W. Carr, memorandum to C. L. Egtvedt, 19 November 1931, Boeing Archives.

42. C. L. Egtvedt to P. G. Johnson, "New Transport Plane," 9 December 1931, VIII B-2, Boeing Archives.

43. C. L. Egtvedt, memorandum to Boeing Airplane Company, attention E. H. Nelson, "247 Specifications," Model 247 File, Boeing Archives.

44. Duard B. Colyer, memorandum to Boeing Airplane Company—Seattle, attention E. H. Nelson, "Subject: Airplane #247," 24 December 1931, Program Management—Model 247, Box 37, Folder 2, Boeing Archives.

45. E. P. Lott, memorandum to P. G. Johnson, "BAC Comments on Model 247 Airplane," 23 December 1931, Program Management—Model 247, Box 37, Folder 2, Boeing Archives.

46. E. H. Nelson, memorandum to P. G. Johnson, "Model 247 Transport," 28 December 1931, Program Management—Model 247, Box 37, Folder 2, Boeing Archives.

47. BAC Work Order Supplement #3, "Revamp Model 247," 5 January 1932, Program Management—Model 247, Box 37, Folder 3, Boeing Archives.

48. E. H. Nelson to William A. Patterson, 21 January 1932, Program Management—Model 247, Box 37, Folder 3, Boeing Archives.

49. D. B. Colyer, memorandum to P. G. Johnson, 3 February 1932, Program Management—Model 247, Box 37, Boeing Archives.

50. Telegram, E. H. Nelson to BAC, 6 February 1932, Program Management—Model 247, Box 37, Folder 3, Boeing Archives.

51. Telegram, BAC to E. H. Nelson, 8 February 1932, Program Management—Model 247, Box 37, Folder 3, Boeing Archives.

52. George J. Mead, memorandum to P. G. Johnson, 9 February 1932, Program Management—Model 247, Box 37, Folder 3, Boeing Archives.

53. Telegram, C. L. Egtvedt to G.J. Mead, 9 February 1932, Program Management—Model 247, Box 37, Folder 3, Boeing Archives.

54. Note on Telegram, C. L. Egtvedt to G.J. Mead, 9 February 1932, Program Management—Model 247, Box 37, Folder 3, Boeing Archives.

55. E. H. Nelson to C. L. Egtvedt, 11 February 1932, Program Management—Model 247, Box 37, Folder 3, Boeing Archives.

56. Telegram, P. G. Johnson to BAC, 14 February 1932, Program Management—Model 247, Box 37, Folder 3, Boeing Archives.

57. Work Order 9052, 16 February 1932, Program Management—Model 247, Box 37, Folder 3, Boeing Archives.

58. Telegram, C. L. Egtvedt to P. G. Johnson, 15 February 1932, Program Management—Model 247, Box 37, Folder 3, Boeing Archives.

59. P. G. Johnson to F. B. Rentschler, 29 February 1932, Program Management—Model 247, Box 37, Boeing Archives.

60. P. G. Johnson to D. L. Brown, 10 March 1932, Program Management—Model 247, Box 37, Folder 4, Boeing Archives.

61. Miller and Sawers, 73.

62. C. N. Montieth, memorandum to C. L. Egtvedt, "Ref.: Mr. Rentschler's Memo of October 16, 1931," 22 October 1931, Program Management—Model 247, Box 37, Folder 2, Boeing Archives.

63. D. B. Colyer, memorandum to BAC, Attention E. H. Nelson, 23 December 1931 Program Management—Model 247, Box 37, Folder 2, Boeing Archives.

64. E. P. Lott, memorandum to E. H. Nelson, 11 February 1932, Program Management—Model 247, Box 37, Folder 3, Boeing Archives.

65. E. H. Nelson, memorandum to G. W. Carr, 15 January 1932, Program Management—Model 247, Box 37, Folder 3, Boeing Archives.

66. John Harding Jr., Liaison Engineer, memorandum to Thorp Hiscock, 20 November 1931, Program Management—Model 247, Box 37, Boeing Archives.

67. D. B. Colyer, memorandum to BAC, 4 January 1932, Program Management—Model 247, Box 37, Folder 3, Boeing Archives.

68. G. W. Carr, confidential memorandum to C. L. Egtvedt, "Model 247 Transport," 29 January 1932, Program Management—Model 247, Box 37, Folder 3, Boeing Archives.

69. Ibid.

70. P. G. Johnson, memorandum to C. L. Egtvedt, "Subject: Model 247 Transport, reference: Your Letter to January 30, 1932," 8 February 1932, Program Management—Model 247, Box 37, Folder 3, Boeing Archives.

71. Ibid.

72. C. L. Egtvedt, memorandum to P. G. Johnson, "Model 247 Transport, ref: Your Letter of February 8, 1932," Program Management—Model 247, Box 37, Folder 3, Boeing Archives.

73. Ibid.

74. E. H. Nelson to P. G. Johnson, 26 February 1932, Program Management—Model 247, Box 37, Folder 3, Boeing Archives.

75. C. L. Egtvedt to P. G. Johnson, "Mock-up Conference Model 247," 20 February 1932, Program Management—Model 247, Box 37, Folder 3, Boeing Archives.

76. E. H. Nelson, memorandum to P. G. Johnson, "Report—Model 247 Transport and Mock-up Board," 26 February 1932, Program Management—Model 247, Box 37, Folder 3, Boeing Archives.

77. C. L. Egtvedt to P. G. Johnson, "Mock-up Conference Model 247," 20 February 1932, Program Management—Model 247, Box 37, Folder 3, Boeing Archives.

78. "Boeing Control Flap and Balance, Leslie R. Tower, Serial Number 557,830," 1933, Engineering—General Box 1, Folder 26, Boeing Archives.

79. E. H. Nelson, letter to P. G. Johnson, "Model 247," 26 February 1932, Program Management—Model 247, Box 37, Folder 3, Boeing Archives.

Chapter 3. The 247 in Production

1. Telegram, C. L. Egtvedt to P. G. Johnson, 29 February 1932, Program Management—Model 247, Box 37, Folder 3, Boeing Archives.

2. Work Order Supplement #2, #9052, 28 March 1932, Program Management—Model 247, Box 37, Folder 4, Boeing Archives.

3. Work Order Supplement #3, #9052, 29 March 1932, Program Management—Model 247, Box 37, Folder 4, Boeing Archives.

4. C. L. Egtvedt, letter to P. G. Johnson, 5 March 1932, Program Management—Model 247, Box 37, Folder 4, Boeing Archives.

5. P. G. Johnson, memorandum to F. B. Rentschler, 2 April 1932, Program Management—Model 247, Box 37, Folder 4, Boeing Archives.

6. G. W. Carr, memorandum to C. L. Egtvedt, 21 March 1932, Program Management—Model 247, Box 37, Folder 4, Boeing Archives.

7. T. Hiscock, memorandum (United Air Lines) to P. G. Johnson, 11 March 1932, Program Management—Model 247, Box 37, Folder 4, Boeing Archives.

8. F. B. Collins, memorandum to T. Hiscock, "Model 247 Transport Design," 8 April 1932, Program Management—Model 247, Box 37, Folder 4, Boeing Archives.

9. Memorandum, BAC to Sales Department, 5 April 1932, Program Management—Model 247, Box 37, Folder 4, Boeing Archives.

10. T. Hiscock, memorandum to P. G. Johnson, "Model 247," 7 April 1932, Program Management—Model 247, Box 37, Folder 4, Boeing Archives.

11. G. W. Carr, memorandum to Phil Marsh (Purchasing Agent, C. N. Montieth, E. H. Nelson, 7 April 1932, Program Management—Model 247, Box 37, Folder 4, Boeing Archives.

12. Minutes of the Fourth Meeting of the Technical Advisory Committee Meetings, 2 May 1932, United Aircraft and Transport Corporation, Archive and Historical Resource Center, United Technologies Corporation, 6–7, 14.

13. Ibid., 9.

14. F. B. Collins (for E. H. Nelson), memorandum to United Air Lines—Chicago, "Mirror for Lavatory," 13 October 1932, Program Management—Model 247, Box 37, Folder 7, Boeing Archives.

15. G. W. Carr, memorandum to C. N. Montieth, F. P. Laudan, John Wilson, Phil Marsh, H. E. Bowman, "Subject: Transport Project," 2 June 1932, Program Management—Model 247, Box 37, Folder 5, Boeing Archives.

16. Supplemental Work Order #4-B/4-C, #9052, 9 June 1932, Program Management—Model 247, Box 37, Folder 5, Boeing Archives.

17. W. A. Patterson, memorandum to BAC-Seattle, 22 July 1932, Program Management—Model 247, Box 37, Folder , Boeing Archives.

18. BAC, memorandum to A. H. Marshall, 22 September 1932, Program Management—Model 247, Box 37, Folder 6, Boeing Archives.

19. F. B. Collins, for E. H. Nelson,, memorandum to E. P. Lott, 10 October 1932, Program Management—Model 247, Box 37, Folder 7, Boeing Archives.

20. F. B. Collins, memorandum to E. H. Nelson, "Miscellaneous Report," 11 October 1932, Program Management—Model 247, Box 37, Folder 7, Boeing Archives.

21. G. W. Carr, memorandum to C. L. Egtvedt, "Subject: Model 247 Transports," 4 November 1932, Program Management—Model 247, Box 38, Folder 1, Boeing Archives.

22. G. W. Carr, memorandum to E. H. Nelson, "Subject: Transport Finishes," 8 November 1932, Program Management—Model 247, Box 38, Folder 1, Boeing Archives.

23. P. G. Johnson, memorandum to E. H. Nelson, "Subject: Transport Finishes," 17 November 1932, Program Management—Model 247, Box 38, Folder 1, Boeing Archives.

24. Brig. Gen. H. Conger Pratt, Chief of the Materiel Division, secret memorandum to BAC, 2 December 1932, Program Management—Model 247, Box 38, Folder 1, Boeing Archives.

25. P. G. Johnson to Brig. Gen. H. Conger Pratt, 21 December 1932, Program Management—Model 247, Box 38, Folder 1, Boeing Archives.

26. G. W. Carr, memorandum to P. G. Johnson, "Report on Model 247 Covering Week Ending December 24, 1932, Program Management—Model 247, Box 38, Folder 1, Boeing Archives.

27. G. W. Carr, memorandum to P. G. Johnson, "Report on Model 247 Covering Week Ending December 31, 1932, Program Management—Model 247, Box 38, Folder 1, Boeing Archives.

28. Telegram, C. L. Egtvedt to P. G. Johnson, 18 January 1933, Program Management—Model 247, Box 38, Folder 3, Boeing Archives.

29. Telegram, C. L. Egtvedt to P. G. Johnson, 27 January 1933, Program Management—Model 247, Box 38, Folder 3, Boeing Archives.

30. *Boeing News*, February 1933, 1.

31. *Boeing News*, February 1933.

32. Victor D. Seely, "Boeing's Pacesetting 247," *American Aviation Historical Society Journal*, Winter 1964, 241.

33. P. G. Johnson, memorandum to F. B. Rentschler, 23 February 1933, Program Management—Model 247, Box 38, Folder 3, Boeing Archives.

34. F. B. Rentschler, memorandum to P. G. Johnson, 23 February 1933, Program Management—Model 247, Box 38, Folder 3, Boeing Archives.

35. G. W. Carr, memorandum to C. L. Egtvedt, "Modification of Model 247," 4 March 1933, Program Management—Model 247, Box 38, Folder 5, Boeing Archives.

36. P. G. Johnson, memorandum to C. L. Egtvedt, "Modification of Model 247—Various Engines," Program Management—Model 247, Box 38, Folder 5, Boeing Archives.

37. F. B. Rentschler to P. G. Johnson, 15 March 1933, Program Management—Model 247, Box 38, Folder 5, Boeing Archives.

38. Approved Type Certificate #500, Program Management—Model 247, Box 38, Folder 4, Boeing Archives.

39. P. G. Johnson, memorandum to C. L. Egtvedt, "Subject: Model 247 Deliveries," Section VIII C-9, Boeing Archives.

40. G. W. Carr to P. G. Johnson, 3 May 1933, Section VIII C-9, Boeing Archives.

41. H. E. Bowman, memorandum (personal) to P. G. Johnson, "Costing Out of Model 247," 11 May 1933, Finance and Accounts—General, Boeing Archives.

42. Seely, 240.

Chapter 4. The 247 Enters Service

1. John McCullough Hodgson, letter to the author, 18 April 1986.

2. *Boeing News*, May 1933, 10.

3. C. L. Egtvedt, memorandum to G. Johnson, "Subject: Gross Weight," 11 April 1933, Program Management—Model 247, Box 38, Folder 3, Boeing Archives.

4. Miller and Sawers, 74.

5. Charles H. Chatfield, "Controllable Pitch Propellers in Transport Service," *Aviation*, 180–81.

6. *The Bee-Hive*, July 1933, 8; *Air Pictorial*, July 1962, 162.

7. Timetable, United Air Lines, 11–12 June 1933, Timetable Collections, Aeronautics Department, National Air and Space Museum, Smithsonian Institution, Washington, D.C.

8. New York *Herald-Tribune*, 13 June 1933.

9. *Aviation*, December 1933; *United Air Lines News*, February 1936, 20, April 1936, 24.

10. Brochure, United Air Lines, "6000 Miles Across America in One Year," 1934; "Announcing the World's Fastest Multi-motored Passenger Plane Service," ca. 1933; United Air Lines Files, National Air and Space Museum Archives, Smithsonian Institution, Washington, D.C.

11. Brochure, United Air Lines, ca. 1933; United Air Lines File, National Air and Space Museum Archives, Smithsonian Institution, Washington, D.C.

12. Brochure, United Air Lines, "So You've Never Traveled by Air Before?," ca. 1933, R. E. G. Davies Collection, National Air and Space Museum Archives, Smithsonian Institution, Washington, D.C.

13. Brochure, United Air Lines, "The Why What and Where of 'A Century of Progress International Exposition, Chicago, 1933,' " United Air Lines File, National Air and Space Museum Archives; *Boeing News*, May 1933, 1.

14. Brochure, United Air Lines, ca. 1933, United Air Lines File, National Air and Space Museum Archives, Smithsonian Institution, Washington, D.C.

15. "Building the Popular Aviation Contest Model," *Popular Aviation*, October 1933, 255.

16. E. C. Gordon England, "The American Way," *Popular Flying*, March 1934, 624–26, 660.

17. Dick Rummel, memorandum to G. W. Carr, E. H. Nelson, Donald R. Drew, C. N. Montieth, H. E. Bowman, 11 October 1933, General Management—Administration File—Accidents, Box 9, Folder 1, Boeing Archives.

18. C. L. Egtvedt, telegram to C. N. Montieth, 25 October 1933, General Management—Administration File—Accidents, Box 9, Folder 1, Boeing Archives.

19. Seattle *Post-Intelligencer*, 13 October 1933.

20. Dick Rummel, memorandum (BAC) to C. L. Egtvedt, G. W. Carr, E. H. Nelson, C. N. Montieth, "Subject: Accident at Chesterton, Indiana," 13 October 1933, General Management—Administration File—Accidents, Box 9, Folder 1, Boeing Archives.

21. Secret Memoranda, War Department, Air Corps Materiel Division, Engineering Section, "Airplane, Department of Commerce No. 13322," 11 December 1933; Vibration Characteristics of Airplane No. NC-13322, 18 December 1933; "Static Test of NC No. 13322 Fuselage," 21 December 1933; "Aluminum Alloy Sheet Taken From Airplane NC 13322," 26 December 1933; "Natural Frequency of Vibration Tests Conducted on Airplane No. NC 13334," 26 December 1933; "Aluminum Alloy Sheet From Airplane NC-13322," 27 December 1933; "Flying Characteristics of Transport Airplane, Department of Commerce No. NC-13334, 29 December 1933; "Comparative Data Obtained from Airplanes NC No. 13322 and NC No. 13334," 2 January 1934; "Aluminum Alloy Sheet Taken from Airplane N.C. 13322," 2 January 1934; "Pilot's Comments—Airplane, Department of Commerce Airplane, 3 January 1934; Model 247—Static Test, Boeing Archives.

22. *New York Times*, 11 February 1934.

23. E. H. Nelson, memorandum to L. Marsh, "Model 247—Failures, Structural," 20 November 1933, Program Management—Model 247—Failures, Box 39, Folder 1, Boeing Archives.

24. Telegram, Mentzer, Cheyenne to BAC, 27 November 1933, Program Management—Model 247—Failures, Box 39, Folder 1, Boeing Archives, Telegram, C. N. Montieth to BAC, 28 November 1933, Program Management—Model 247—Failures, Box 39, Folder 1, Boeing Archives.

Chapter 5. Improving the Breed

1. Rene J. Francillon, *McDonnell-Douglas Aircraft Since 1920* (London: Putnam and Company, 1979), 165–73. Davies, 93.

2. Francillon, 166.

3. Ibid., 167.

4. Northrop Past: "An Interview with John K. Northrop, Founder of the Company," *Technical Digest*, February 1979, 3–6.

5. E. H. Nelson, memorandum to C. L. Egtvedt and P. G. Johnson, "Subject: March Field Visit," 26 November 1932, General Management—Administration—General, Box 7, Folder 3, Boeing Archives.

6. Confidential Report on the Navy Cruise, C. N. Montieth to P. G. Johnson, February 1933, p. 15, General Management—Administration—General, Box 7, Folder 4, Boeing Archives.

7. C. N. Montieth, memorandum to P. G. Johnson, 1 May 1933, General Management—Administration—General, Box 7, Folder 4, Boeing Archives.

8. Alfred H. Marshall, letter to C. N. Montieth, 18 September 1933, United Technologies Archives.

9. P. G. Johnson, memorandum to C. N. Montieth, "Modification of Model 247—Various Engines," 6 March 1933, Program Management—Model 247, Box 38, Folder 5, Boeing Archives.

10. Seely, 240, 242.

11. C. L. Egtvedt, memorandum to P. G. Johnson, "Subject: Model 247 Changes, Balances and Weights," 25 October 1933, Program Management—Model 247, Box 38, Folder 5, Boeing Archives.

12. E. H. Nelson, memorandum to T. Hiscock, "Model 247—New Type Windshield," 27 October 1933, Program Management—Model 247, Box 38, Folder 5, Boeing Archives.

13. C. L. Egtvedt, memorandum to P. G. Johnson, "Model 247 Changes—Balances and Weights," 25 October 1933, Program Management—Model 247, Box 38, Folder 5, Boeing Archives.

14. Richard P. Hallion, *Legacy of Flight: The Guggenheim Contribution to American Aviation* (Seattle: University of Washington, 1977), 109–13.

15. Minutes of the Fourth Meeting of the Technical Advisory Committee Meetings, May 1932, United Aircraft and Transport Corporation, Archive and Historical Resource Center, United Technologies Corporation, 3.

16. T. Hiscock, memorandum to C.H. Hatfield, "Design and Development of De-Icers," 31 August 1933, Program Management—Model 247, Box 38, Folder 3, Boeing Archives.

17. E. H. Nelson, memorandum to BAC, 29 November 1933, Program Management—Model 247, Box 38, Folder 3, Boeing Archives.

18. William E. Leuchtenburg, *Franklin D. Roosevelt and the New Deal: 1932–1940* (New York: Harper Colophon Books, 1963,), 91, 162.

19. Davies, 167.

20. Ibid., 163.

21. United Air Lines, 128–29.

22. Davies, 163.

23. Ibid., 130.

24. "Specification—Boeing 247-D Transport Airplane, Issue #158," 3 May 1934, National Air and Space Museum Collection, Archival Support Center, Paul E. Garber Preservation, Restoration and Support Facility.

25. Seely, 241.

Chapter 6. The MacRobertson Race

1. Arthur Swinson, *The Great Air Race: England-Australia 1934* (London: Cassell, 1968), 4–6.

2. *The Aeroplane*, 31 January 1934, 164.

3. *United Air Lines News*, October 1934, 1.

4. Roscoe Turner to editor, undisclosed periodical and date, Museum of Flight Files, Seattle, Washington.

5. P. G. Johnson, memorandum to BAC, 1 July 1934, General Management—Flights, Box 11, Folder 2, Boeing Archives.

6. Seely, 248.

7. C. M. Daniels, "Roscoe Turner: Throttle Bendin' Devil," *Air Classics*, August 1969, 66.

8. Race Log Book of Boeing 247-D, NR-257Y, Boeing 247-D Curatorial File, Aeronautics Department, National Air and Space Museum.

9. Henry Heinz to Richard K. Smith, 2 November 1984, Curatorial File, Aeronautics Department, National Air and Space Museum.

10. Daniels, 66.

11. Race Log Book of Boeing 247-D, NR-257Y.

12. Swinson, 88–89.

13. *The Aeroplane*, 24 November 1934, 475.

14. Ibid., 476.

15. Race Log Book of Boeing 247-D, NR-257Y.

16. MacRobertson Race Rules and Regulations, Curatorial File, Aeronautics Department, National Air and Space Museum.

17. "Official Program—MacRobertson International Air Race: England to Australia," 1934—London/Melbourne, File #J1019900, National Air and Space Museum Archives.

18. Radio Log of Boeing 257Y and Radio Station KHASH, Curatorial File, Aeronautics Department, National Air and Space Museum.

19. Ibid.

20. Ibid.

21. Ibid.

22. Ibid.

23. Daniels, 68; Swinson, 146.

24. Radio log.

25. Ibid.

26. Swinson, 150.

27. Race Log Book of Boeing 247-D, NR-257Y.

28. Radio Log.

29. Swinson, 157.

30. Sir Phillip Sassoon, "On Belittling An Achievement," *Flight*, 15 November 1934, 1192–93.

31. London *Morning Post*, 24 October 1934.

32. *Flight*, 25 October 1934.

33. Roscoe Turner, telegram to BAC, 23 October 1934, General Management—Flights, Box 11, Folder 2, Boeing Archives.

34. BAC, telegram to Roscoe Turner, 23 October 1934, General Management—Flights, Box 11, Folder 2, Boeing Archives.

35. (Crary), memorandum to BAC, "Suggestions for Exploiting the London—Melbourne Race," no date, General Management—Flights, Box 11, Folder 2, Boeing Archives.

36. C. N. Montieth, letter to C. L. Egtvedt, 28 November 1934, General Management—Flights, Box 11, Folder 2, Boeing Archives.

37. Ibid.

38. C. L. Egtvedt, telegram to BAC, 4 December 1934, General Management—Flights, Box 11, Folder 2, Boeing Archives.

39. Seely, 248.

40. Brochure, United Air Lines' Boeing 247-D, Curatorial File, Aeronautics Department, National Air and Space Museum.

41. United Air Lines, 359.

42. Timetable, United Air Lines, 1 June 1936, Timetable Collections, Aeronautics Department, National Air and Space Museum, Smithsonian Institution, Washington, D.C.

43. Brochure, United Air Lines, "Now Overnight Coast-to-Coast," Curatorial File, Aeronautics Department, National Air and Space Museum.

44. Helen Huntley Brumley letter to the author, 18 April 1986.

45. Dick Wood letter to the author, 22 March 1986.

46. United Air Lines, 359.

47. Brochure, United Air Lines, "Nation's Greatest Playgrounds," Curatorial File, Aeronautics Department, National Air and Space Museum.

48. Brochure, United Air Lines, "The Modern World is Growing Smaller—United Air Lines and Imperial Airways," Curatorial File, Aeronautics Department, National Air and Space Museum.

49. James H. Farmer, *Celluloid Wings* (Summit, Pennsylvania: Tab Books, 1984), 94–96.

50. Davies, 336.

Chapter 7. Secondary Airline Service

1. United Air Lines, 364–65.

2. Seely, 244.

3. United Air Lines, 370–71.

4. Ibid., 372.

5. Seely, 246.

6. Robert J. Serling, *The Only Way to Fly: The Story of Western Airlines, America's Senior Air Carrier* (Garden City, New York: Doubleday and Company, 1976), 148.

7. Ibid., 152.

8. Ibid., 155.

9. Ibid.

10. Ibid., 246.

11. Edward P. O'Donnell, interview with author, 20 March 1986.

12. William C. "Tex" Guthrie, interview with author, 20 March 1986.

13. Marian O'Donnell, interview with author, 20 March 1986.

14. William C. "Tex" Guthrie, interview with author, 20 March 1986.

15. Ralph Read, interview with author, 20 March 1986.

16. Edward P. O'Donnell, interview with author, 20 March 1986.

17. Seely, 246.

18. Charles Baptie, interview with author, 9 March 1986.

19. United Air Lines, 372.

20. Seely, 246.

21. Gordon Swanborough and Peter M. Bowers, *United States Military Aircraft Since 1908* (London: Putnam and Company, 1971), 539.

22. Seely, 251.

23. *Boeing Magazine*, December 1944, 16.

24. Peter W. Moss, letter to the editor, *Air Pictorial*, October 1962, 331.

25. John A. McDonald, letter to the editor, *Flight International*, 30 April 1944, 737.

26. Seely, 251.

27. Ibid., 246.

28. "Empire Expands with 417s," *Boeing Magazine*, September 1946, 10–11.

29. Seely, 248.

30. Press Release, BAC, 22 February 1946, Museum of Flight Files.

31. *Boeing News*, 21 February 1946, 1–2.

32. Seely, 250.

33. Ibid.

34. Ibid., 252.

35. R. E. G. Davies, *Airlines of Latin America Since 1919* (London, Putnam and Company, 1984), 235–36.

36. Ibid., 240.

37. Seely, 252.

38. Carlos Dufriche, letter to R. E. G. Davies, 4 June 1987.

39. Jose Villela Gomez, *The Boeing 247*, 23 January 1958, article from unknown publication translated from Spanish, Museum of Flight Files.

40. Seely, 251.

41. Davies, *Latin America*, 32.

42. Ibid., 53.

43. Seely, 251.

44. Davies, *Latin America*, 102.

45. Ibid., 160.

46. Seely, 252.

47. Neil November, letter to Kenn Rust, 26 January 1965, Victor Seely Collection, Museum of Flight.

48. H. A. Taylor, "Boeing's Trend-Setting 247," *Air Enthusiast*, February-May 1979, 52.

Chapter 8. Special 247s

1. Seely, 248.

2. Furlong Flynn letter to "Alf," 13 September 1933, Model 247-A file, United Technologies Archives.

3. "A Requiem for Old 247," *The Bee-Hive*, Spring 1947, 16–17.

4. Seely, 252.

5. Report, in German, no attribution, Museum of Flight Files.

6. *San Francisco Call-Bulletin*, 6 March 1934.

7. *Seattle Post-Intelligencer*, 22 March 1934.

8. Seely, 252.

9. Photograph and caption, Model 247 file, United Technologies Archives.

10. W. J. Robb, Aviation Sales—Phillips Petroleum Company, letter to Victor Seely, April 24, 1964, Victor Seely Collection, Museum of Flight.

11. Edgar Snow, *Red Star Over China* (New York: Grove Press, 1973), 380–91.

12. Seely, 250.

13. Ibid.

14. Snow, 382, 390.

15. Seely, 250.

16. Ibid., 251.

17. Ibid.

18. George L. Lantz, letter to author, 24 March 1986.

19. William Blair, "United Perfects New Static Suppressor," *Airlines*, February 1939, 14.

20. P. C. Sandretto, "Terrain Clearance Indicator," *Airlines*, November 1938, 14–15, 18.

21. Alfred C. Kubitz, letter to author, 4 April 1986.

22. Seely, 246.

Chapter 9. Survivors

1. John A. Bagley, curator, National Aeronautical Collection, Science Museum, letter to J. V. Mann, Museum of Flight, 3 January 1985.

2. Tom Weissman, "Born 1933 . . . Retired 1967," *Canadian Aviation*, August 1970, 24–26.

3. Lesley Forden, "From CPA Flagship to Exploration Workhorse," *Canadian Aviation*, August 1970, 35–36.

4. Weissman, 26.

5. Boeing 247-D N3977C Curatorial File, Museum of Flight.

6. Gordon Holt, "Old 1729 Flies Home to Rest," [Renton] *Record-Chronicle*, 9 March 1966, 1.

7. J. C. Hromada, Engineer in Charge—Technical Development Service, Civil Aeronautics Administration, letter to Jim Douglas, managing editor, BAC, 18 April 1947, Boeing 247 File, Museum of Flight.

8. Kenneth Calkins, "New Name in the Hall of Fame," *Boeing Magazine*, August 1953, 13.

9. "Adaptable Annie Enters Hall of Fame," *U.S. Air Services*, November 1953, 22.

10. Edward D. Williams, "MacRobertson 247 to be Restored by United," *Vintage Airplane*, April 1975, 4–6; "Roscoe Turner and 247D," *Vintage Airplane*, March 1976, 3–6.

Bibliography

Primary Sources

Archives

The Boeing Company Historical Services, Seattle, Washington. Company records, files, correspondence, and photographs concerning the design, construction, and dispositions of the Boeing 247 and its predecessors.

Museum of Flight, Seattle, Washington. The museum's Boeing 247 file and the Victor Seely collection of documentary and photographic material compiled for his 1964 article on the 247 as well as additional correspondence.

National Air and Space Museum Archives, Washington, D.C. Contains a general aircraft file on the 247 and a curatorial file on the museum's 247-D in addition to files on the MacRobertson Race. Also preserved in the Archival Support Center are detailed maintenance and operating manuals.

United Technologies Archival and Historical Resource Center, East Hartford, Connecticut. The records of the former United Aircraft and Transport Corporation including transcripts and notes of the Technical Advisory Committee Meetings and details on the Wasp engine and Hamilton Standard propeller as well as material on the 247-A and supplementary correspondence and photographs.

Interviews

Charles Baptie, Edward O'Donnell, Marion O'Donnell, Mary Jane Read, Ralph Read, William C. "Tex" Guthrie.

Correspondence

E. L. Anderson, Helen Huntley Brumley, Theodore J. Cochran, Henry Dreyer, Carlos Dufriche, Ralph J. Gibbons, Ernest Heiss, John McCullough Hodgson, J. D. Hutchinson, Alfred C. Kubitz, Alvar H. Lunn, Angie Riddell MacKenzie, C. L. "Jim" Newman, O. H. Schaller, Zay Smith, Dick Wood.

Secondary Sources

Books

Bowers, Peter M. *Boeing Aircraft Since 1916.* New York: Funk and Wagnalls, 1968.

Brooks, Peter W. *The Modern Airliner: Its Origins and Development.* Manhattan, Kansas: Sunflower University Press, 1982.

Davies, R. E. G. *Airlines of Latin America Since 1919*. London: Putnam and Company; Washington, D.C.: Smithsonian Institution Press, 1984.

————. *Airlines of the United States Since 1914*. London: Putnam and Company, 1972; Washington, D.C.: Smithsonian Institution Press, 1983.

Farmer, James H. *Celluloid Wings*. Summit, Pennsylvania: Tab Books, 1984.

Francillon, Rene J. *McDonnell Douglas Aircraft Since 1920*. London: Putnam and Company, 1979.

Hallion, Richard P. *Legacy of Flight: The Guggenheim Contribution to American Aviation*. Seattle: University of Washington Press, 1977.

Hawley, Ellis W. *The New Deal and the Problem of Monopoly*. Princeton: Princeton University Press, 1974.

Komons, Nick A. *Bonfires to Beacons: Federal Civil Aviation Policy Under the Air Commerce Act, 1926–1938*. Washington, D.C.: U.S. Government Printing Office, 1978.

Leonard, Royal. *I Flew for China*. Garden City, New York: Doubleday, Doran and Company, 1942.

Leuchtenburg, William E. *Franklin D. Roosevelt and the New Deal: 1932–1940*. New York: Harper Colophon Books, 1963.

Mansfield, Harold. *Vision: A Saga of the Sky*. New York: Duell, Sloan and Pierce, 1956.

Mead, Cary Hoge. *Wings Over the World: The Life of George Jackson Mead*, Wauwatosa, Wisconsin: The Swannet Press, 1971.

Miller, Ronald E. and Sawers, David. *The Technical Development of Modern Aviation*. London: Routledge and Kegan Paul, 1968.

Munson, Kenneth and Swanborough, Gordon. *Boeing: An Aircraft Album No. 4*. New York: Arco, 1972.

Rae, John B. *Climb to Greatness: The American Aircraft Industry, 1920–1960*. Cambridge, Massachusetts: The MIT Press, 1968.

Rentschler, Frederick B. *An Account of Pratt and Whitney Aircraft Company: 1920–1950*. United Technologies, 1950.

Schlaifer, Robert and Heron, S. D. *Development of Aircraft Engines and Fuels*. Boston: Harvard University, 1950.

Serling, Robert J. *The Only Way to Fly: The Story of Western Airlines, America's Senior Air Carrier*. Garden City, New York: Doubleday and Company, 1976.

Simonson, G. R., ed. *The History of the American Aircraft Industry: An Anthology*. Cambridge, Massachusetts: The MIT Press, 1968.

Snow, Edgar. *Red Star Over China*. New York: Grove Press, 1973.

Sorrell, Lewis C. and Wheeler, Harry A. *Passenger Transport in the United States, 1920–1950*. Chicago: Railway Business Association, 1944.

Swanborough, Gordon and Bowers, Peter M. *United States Military Aircraft Since 1908*. London: Putnam and Company, 1971.

Swinson, Arthur. *The Great Air Race: England-Australia 1934*. London: Cassell, 1968.

Taylor, Frank J. *High Horizons: Daredevil Flying Postmen to Modern Magic Carpet—The United Air Lines Story.* New York: McGraw-Hill, 1951.

Time Incorporated. *Time Capsule/1933: A History of the Year Condensed from the Pages of Time.* New York: Time Incorporated, 1967.

United Air Lines. *Corporate and Legal History of United Air Lines and Its Predecessors and Subsidiaries, 1925–1945.* Chicago: Twentieth Century Press, 1953.

Articles

"Adaptable Annie Enters Hall of Fame." *U.S. Air Services* 38 (November 1953): 22.

"After the Winners." *Flight* 26 (1 November 1934): 1144–61.

"Air Transport: A New Boeing Transport Plane." *Flight* 24 (August 12, 1932): 756.

Allen, Edmund T. "Breath-Taking Stunts Test New Transport Planes." *Popular Science* 124 (March 1934): 26–28, 112–113.

"American Transport Airplanes Win Universal Praise for Performance in England-Australia Race." *U.S. Air Services* 19 (December 1934): 15–17.

"ATC Tests Now Being Conducted on first 247-Ds." *United Air Lines News* 4 (September 1934): 1.

"Aztec Eagles in LAMSA Service." *United Air Lines News* 13 (September 1944): 7.

"Baco Completes Delivery of our 247-D Transports." *United Air Lines News* 4 (December 1934): 2.

Blair, William. "United Perfects New Static Suppressor." *Airlines* 4 (February 1939): 14–15.

"Boeing Pioneer." *RAF Flying Review* 17 (February 1962): 45.

"Boeing Transport." *Aero Digest* 22 (April 1933): 50–51.

"Boeing Transport." *Aviation* 34 (June 1935): 19–21.

"Boeing 247D Comes Home After 33 Years of Service." *Boeing News* 25 (10 March 1966): 1, 3.

Boeson, Victor. "UAL—Line of the Flying Lab." *Skyways* 3 (December 1944): 32, 78, 80, 82.

Brooks, Peter W. "The First Transport Aeroplanes." *Aeronautics* 37 (October 1959): 28–35.

"Building the Popular Aviation Contest Model." *Popular Aviation* (October 1933): 255–58, 269.

Bushnell, Sue J. "Boeing 247: Beginning of a Dynasty." *Aircraft Illustrated,* 20 (March 1987): 126–29.

Bye, Roger. "Adaptable Annie." *Boeing Magazine* 17 (1947): 12.

Cain, Charles W. "Belligerent Boeing." *Air Pictorial* 22 (January 1960): 30.

Calkins, Kenneth. "New Name in the Hall of Fame." *Boeing Magazine* 23 (August 1953): 12–13.

Campbell, Chester D. "Bill Boeing's Medal-Winning '247'." *Air Progress* (Summer 1961): 66–69.

Chatfield, Charles Hugh. "Controllable Pitch Propellers in Transport Service." *Aviation* 32 (June 1933): 180–81.

"Commercial Aviation: Third in the Speed Race." *Flight* 26 (8 November 1934): 1180–81.

"Controllable Pitch Propellers Step Up Performance of New Wasp-Powered Boeing." *The Bee-Hive* 7 (June 1933): 7–8.

"Current Practice in Instrument Panel Layout." *Aero Digest* 27 (December 1935): 40.

Daniels, C.M. "Roscoe Turner: Throttle Bendin' Devil." *Air Classics* 5 (August 1969): 8–19, 66, 68, 70, 72.

"Delivery of New 247-D Planes to Commence Soon." *United Air Lines News* 4 (August 1934): 1.

"Douglas Planes Being Built for Our Routes." *United Air Lines News* 5 (April 1936): 12.

Ellis, J.R. "Canadian Boeing 247s." *Air Pictorial* 25 (April 1963): 112.

"Empire Expands with 417's." *Boeing Magazine* 16 (September 1946): 10–11.

England, E.C. Gordon. "The American Way." *Popular Flying* 2 (March 1934): 624–26, 660.

"The Eve of the Race." *Flight* 26 (25 October 1934): 1125–29.

"Famous Boeing 247s of United Air Lines 'Are in the Army' Now." *United Air Lines News* 11 (August 1942): 6.

"Flying Equipment: Boeing's New Model 247 Transport." *Aviation* 32 (April 1933): 124–26.

Forden, Lesley. "From CPA Flagship to Exploration Workhorse." *Canadian Aviation* 31 (October 1958): 35–36.

"The Great Race." *Flight* 26 (18 October 1934): 1071–98, 1123.

Hansen, James R. "The Cowling Story at Langley Laboratory, 1926–1936." *Aerospace Historian* 32 (Fall, September 1985): 161–70.

Hart, Edward J. "Organizing the MacRobertson Race." *Flight* 26 (30 August 1934): 890–94, 910.

"Here Come the British—Bang! Bang!." *U.S. Air Services* 19 (November 1934): 16–21.

Gordon Holt. "Old 1729 Flies Home to Rest." [Renton] *Record-Chronicle* (9 March 1966): 1.

"The Latest Boeing: A Few Notes on the Improved Version of the Boeing 247 Commercial Type." *Aircraft Engineering* 7 (February 1935): 44.

Macdougall, Neil A. "RCAF Boeings." *Air Pictorial* 24 (December 1962): 390.

"Makers of History: C. W. A. Scott and T. Campbell Black—Winners of the World's Greatest Race." *Flight* 26 (25 October 1934): 1109–18.

McCarthy, Dan B. "Prairie Queen." *Air Classics* 10 (January 1974): 42–51, 64.

McDonald, John A. "The First Automatic Landing." *Flight International* 85 (30 April 1964): 737.

Miller, F. M. S. "From England to Australia." *Western Flying* 26 (November 1934): 9–13, 25–26.

Moss, Peter W. "R.A.F. Boeing 247D." *Air Pictorial* 10 (October 1962): 331.

"Mr. Rentschler." *The Bee-Hive* (Summer 1956): 2–5.

"New Boeing Commercial Transport Surpasses Expectations in Test Flight." *U.S. Air Services* 18 (April 1933): 13–15.

"The New Boeing 247-D." *U.S. Air Services* 19 (November 1934): 27.

"News of the Month: Speed by Boeing." *Aviation* 32 (June 1933): 189.

"Northrop Past: An Interview with John K. Northrop, Founder of the Company." *Technical Digest* (February 1979): 3–6.

"Old Plane Plays New Role." *Boeing Magazine* 29 (April 1959): 3.

"Paramount Production Filming '13 Hours By Air' Praise United." *United Air Lines News* 5 (February 1936): 9.

"Phil Johnson." *Western Flying* 20 (September 1940): 21.

"Portrait of 'P.G.' " *Boeing Magazine,* 14 (October 1944): 13–14, 18.

Powell, Dennis M. "Boeing 247 Postscript." *Air Pictorial* 24 (November 1962): 348.

———. "Chinese Boeing." *Air Pictorial* 22 (July 1960): 255.

———. "Pioneering an Airliner Formula: The Boeing 247." *Air Pictorial* 24 (July 1962): 194–97.

"A Requiem for Old 247." *The Bee Hive* 22 (Spring 1947): 16–17.

Robertson, Bruce. "U.S. Aircraft in the British Services 1914–55." *Air Pictorial and Air Reserve Gazette* 19 (November 1957): 381.

Rose, Bert. "Plant Modernizes Wien Alaska 247D Transport." *Boeing News* 5 (21 February 1946): 1, 3.

Sandretto, P.C. "Terrain Clearance Indicator." *Airlines* 3 (November 1938): 14–15, 28.

Sassoon, Sir Philip. "On Belittling An Achievement." *Flight* 26 (15 November 1934): 1192–93.

Seely, Victor D. "Boeing's Grand Old Lady." *Air Classics* 4 (August 1968): 54–66, 75.

———. "Boeing's Pacesetting 247." *American Aviation Historical Society Journal* 9 (Winter 1964): 239–71.

Sliprule. "Engineering News: Tremendous Strength of Boeing 247." *U.S. Air Services* 19 (April 1934): 21.

"Speed! Comfort! Economy!: Details of the New Boeing Bi-Motored Low Wing Transport." *Western Flying* 13 (April 1933): 18–19.

"Story of United's Communications Lab." *United Air Lines News* 5 (January 1936): 3.

"The Successful Machines." *Flight* 26 (25 October 1934): 1119–22.

Taylor, H.A. "Boeing's Trend-Setting 247." *Air Enthusiast* 9 (February-May 1979): 43–54.

Technical Staff—Boeing Airplane Company. "The Latest Boeing Low-Wing Transport." *Popular Aviation* 12 (June 1933): 362–64.

"Turner, Pangborn Cut Loose in 247-D To Set Fast Mark." *United Air Lines News* 4 (October 1934): 1, 22.

"247-D Shows Fine Performance; Nine Delivered to U.A.L." *United Air Lines News* 4 (November 1934): 2.

"United Speeds Up Schedules; Adds New D's." *United Air Lines News* 4 (April 1935): 1.

"Wasp Engines to Power New United Air Lines Transports." *The Bee-Hive* 6 (June 1932): 6–7.

"Wasp-Powered Twin Engine Boeing Transport Shows Remarkable Performance in Initial Tests." *The Bee-Hive* 7 (April 1933): 8–10.

Watson, David. "Adaptable Annie." *Flying* 54 (January 1954): 36.

Weissman, Tom. "Born 1933 . . . Retired 1967." *Canadian Aviation* 43 (August 1970): 1–3.

"Who's Who in the MacRobertson Race." *Flight* 26 (11 October 1934): 1048–1055.

"Wien 247 Flies Back to Alaska." *Boeing News* 5 (28 March 1946): 2.

Williams, Edward D. "MacRobertson 247 to be Restored by United." *The Vintage Airplane* 3 (April 1975): 4–6.

———. "Roscoe Turner and 247D." *The Vintage Airplane* 4 (March 1976): 3–6.

Index